Word Processing

with WordPerfect

6.0 for DOS

ISBN 0-03-098591-9

1

WordPerfect 6.0 for DOS

Word Processing Basics:
Creating a Document

OBJECTIVES

After completing this chapter you will be able to:

1 Explain the general capabilities of a word processing program.

2 Describe the procedures to start and exit WordPerfect 6.0 for DOS.

3 Explain the various components of the work screen and the way you can alter their appearance.

4 Explain the use of the Enter key.

5 Describe the difference between the insert and typeover modes.

6 Enter text onto the screen and save it as a document.

7 Clear the screen, open a document, and prepare a printed copy.

WP

OVERVIEW This chapter introduces the concept of word processing by presenting the basic techniques for using WordPerfect, perhaps the most well-known word processing package in the world. First, you will learn how to start WordPerfect 6.0 for DOS, how to interpret its screen, and how to enter text. Then, you will learn how to save and open documents, edit them to correct mistakes or improve content, and print them. You will also learn how to quit the program correctly.

Word Processing

Word processing is the use of computer technology to create, manipulate, save, and print text materials such as letters, memos, manuscripts, and other documents. Most word processing packages on the market offer the same basic capabilities. If you learn one, you will know what to expect from most others, even if the commands are different.

The instructions presented in this section pertain to WordPerfect Version 6.0 for DOS. Many of WordPerfect's capabilities can be invoked by typing command keystrokes or accessed through a menu-driven structure by using arrow keys or a mouse. Function key commands as well as pull-down menus are presented—use whichever you prefer.

Starting Word–Perfect

WordPerfect allows you to create, edit, format, save, revise, and print documents. The exercises in this chapter provide detailed instructions for creating several short documents. Keystroking has been kept to a minimum so that you can concentrate on learning the basic word processing functions. Before you begin, be certain you have all the necessary tools: you will need a hard disk that contains DOS and WordPerfect (or separate floppy diskettes with DOS and the Word-Perfect program) and a formatted diskette on which you will store the documents you create. It is assumed that you will be using WordPerfect on a hard-disk drive, although directions for dual-diskette systems and networks are also included. Your data disk should have a subdirectory named \XWP, which will be used in some of the exercises. If \XWP is not in your disk's directory, create it by typing MD A:\XWP (or B: in a dual-diskette system) and pressing the Enter key at the C:\> prompt.

Using a Hard-Disk Drive.   It is assumed that the WordPerfect program is in a subdirectory called WP60 on your hard disk, which is identified as Drive C. Check with your instructor as to the exact directory name on your system (if it differs, use its name in place of WP60). To start WordPerfect:

1.   Boot the operating system, and get to the C:\> prompt

Note: If your hard disk automatically boots a menu, go on to Step 3 in the next section, on using a network.

2.   Insert your data diskette into Drive A

3.   Type **CD \WP60** and press ⏎

This will access the WordPerfect subdirectory in which WordPerfect is stored. (Type the subdirectory name in your system if it differs from WP60.) You should now be at the WordPerfect subdirectory prompt, which resembles "C:\WP60>." If you are not, check your typing in Step 3 and repeat the procedure.

4.   Type **WP** and press ⏎

Using a Network.   WordPerfect may be available to you through a local network. In this case, WordPerfect is kept on the hard-disk drive of another computer that is shared by many users. To use WordPerfect, you must access the program from your own microcomputer. There are so many network configurations in use today that it is difficult to predict which one you will use. Check with your instructor for exact directions. In general, however, to start WordPerfect:

1.   Boot the network operating system (perhaps with your own disk)
2.   Type any command needed to get the network menu

In many networks, this is done by typing **LAN** and pressing the Enter key.

3. Make sure your data diskette is in Drive A
4. Select (or type) the appropriate command on your screen to begin Word-Perfect

Once you are in WordPerfect, follow the instructions for hard-disk systems.

Using a Dual-Diskette System. If you are using a dual-diskette system to access WordPerfect, you will need both program disks (labeled "1" and "2") for WordPerfect and a formatted data disk. Both disk drives must have a capacity of 720K or larger. To start WordPerfect:

1. Boot the operating system, and get to the A> prompt

2. Insert WordPerfect program disk 1 into Drive A

3. Insert your data disk into Drive B

4. Type **WP** and press ⏎

5. Remove WordPerfect program disk 1 when the screen instructs you to do so, and replace it with WordPerfect program disk 2

6. Press ⏎

Under-standing the Word-Perfect Screen

A WordPerfect copyright screen appears briefly on the screen and is quickly replaced by a blank work screen. However, other messages may sometimes appear. Watch for these messages and take the appropriate action. For example, if you did not properly exit from WordPerfect the last time you used it, a "Backup File Exists" error message may appear. You would then be directed by the screen to either rename the old file, delete it, or open it for use before beginning WordPerfect. Be aware of all error messages and follow their instructions carefully before continuing.

If all goes well, you should now be looking at the screen shown in Figure WP1–1. WordPerfect is known for its clean screen—that is, a screen that is not cluttered with unnecessary information, displaying only the bare essentials. As you invoke various commands, however, menus and other information may appear.

WordPerfect 6.0 offers three display modes that present your work in increasing detail:

- *Text mode* presents text in equally spaced characters (as in normal typing) but does not display any graphics on the screen. This mode is fastest for editing or general typing.
- *Graphics mode* simulates a WYSIWYG ("What you see is what you get") screen by displaying text and graphics as they will appear when printed. Graphics can also be manipulated with a mouse in this mode.
- *Page mode* extends the graphics mode to show the entire page contents, including page numbers, footnotes, and other material that appears near the edges of the page.

You may use whichever mode you prefer, but be aware that the graphics and page modes require additional computer power and speed. You may find them too slow for normal work and may want to use them only when necessary. Text mode is best if you are not using different type styles or graphics. Although the figures in this chapter display the graphics mode, it does not matter which mode you use for now. (You will learn how to change modes in Chapter 2.)

Figure WP1–1

The WordPerfect Work Screen (in Graphics Mode)

The WordPerfect work screen is "clean"—only a menu bar, an insertion point (cursor), and a status line are normally displayed.

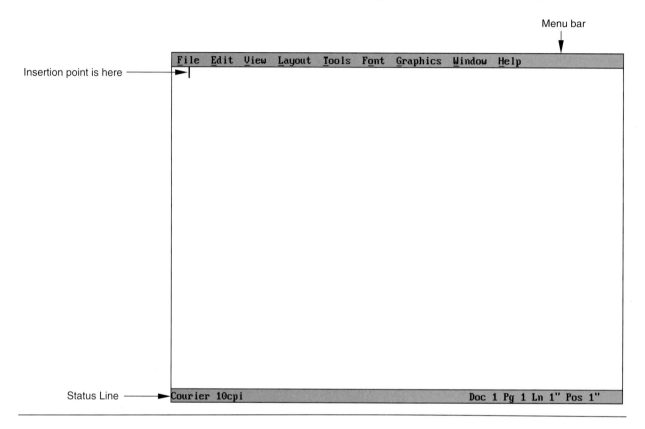

Menu bar

Insertion point is here ——————

File Edit View Layout Tools Font Graphics Window Help

Status Line ————▶ Courier 10cpi   Doc 1 Pg 1 Ln 1" Pos 1"

The Status Line

As in Figure WP1–1, the work screen is mostly blank except for a **menu bar** at the top, an **insertion point** or *cursor* (usually represented by a blinking underline character in text mode or a vertical line in other modes) at the upper left corner, and a line of information—called the **status line**—at the bottom.

The menu bar (located at the top of the screen) allows you to access WordPerfect features through a system of pull-down menus. Your screen may not currently display the menu bar (more on this shortly).

The insertion point (cursor) is simply a placeholder—it shows where the next keystroke you type into your document will appear. The status line provides information about the insertion point's current location and the modes selected for text entry. You will now learn about the various components of the status line more fully. Examine your screen and identify each component as it is discussed.

Courier 10cpi.   The leftmost portion of the status line displays the active type style and size of text. WordPerfect's default type style of Courier is currently displayed. (Your type style may differ.)

Doc 1.   WordPerfect can retain up to nine document files in memory at the same time. The status line displays a **document number** to identify the active document (the one in which you are currently working). For example, the status line will display *Doc 1* if you are working in the first document or *Doc 2* if you are working in the second.

It might happen that you accidentally switch from one document to another. If you suddenly see a blank screen, read the Doc message on the status line to see if you have changed to another document. Change between screens now, as follows:

1. Press **Shift** + **F3**

The status line now reads *Doc 2.*

2. Press **Shift** + **F3** again to switch back

The Shift and F3 keys act as a toggle to switch back and forth between two document screens. (F3 alone can be used to select from among all active document screens.) Leave your screen in Doc 1.

Pg 1.   The **Pg message** shows you the document page on which the cursor is currently located. As you move onto a new page or return to a previous one, the Pg message will change appropriately. It is not always easy to judge page position by looking at the cursor alone. When you start creating multipage documents, you will greatly appreciate the page indicator.

Ln 1''.   The **Ln message** tells you the vertical position of the insertion point within the current page. This position is usually expressed in inches, as in *2"* (which means two inches down from the page top). It can also be expressed as a line number, as in *Ln 10* (which means the tenth line of the page). The Ln message will change each time you begin a new line or move back through your document. Try this:

1. Press **↵** three times

Notice how the Ln message now reads *1.5".*

2. Press **← Backspace** three times

The Ln message has returned to *1".*

Pos 1".   The **Pos message** shows the current horizontal position of the insertion point from the left page edge. As the margins are currently set, each line has space for approximately 65 characters. WordPerfect normally leaves a one-inch left margin, so the insertion point is positioned at the extreme left of the screen—which corresponds to one inch (1") from the edge of the page. As you type, the Pos message will change appropriately. Try this:

1. Type your name

Notice how the Pos message changed to show your current typing position.

2. Press **↵**

Notice that the insertion point returned to the left margin and that the Pos message again displays *1".*

WordPerfect also uses the Pos message to indicate various keyboard toggles that you have set. These include Caps Lock, Num Lock, underline, and boldface. For example, to see the Caps Lock indicator, try this:

3. Press **Caps Lock**

Notice that the letters in "POS" are all capitalized. This indicates that the Caps Lock feature has been turned on.

4. Press **Caps Lock** again

Notice that the letters in the word "Pos" have returned to their normal appearance, indicating that the Caps Lock feature is now off.

Figure WP1–2

The Status Line

This WordPerfect status line indicates that the insertion point is positioned in Document 2, Page 2, 1.67 inches from the top, and 1.8 inches from the left of the page. It also shows that Caps Lock and underlining are on.

Courier 10cpi	Doc 2 Pg 2 Ln 1.67" POS 1.8"

WordPerfect also alters the appearance of the position *number* to indicate various changes in text appearance, such as underline and boldface. Try the following:

5. Press **F8** to turn on the underline toggle

Notice that the number next to "Pos" has been modified—depending on your screen mode, the number may now be underlined or shown in a different color. This indicates that any text you now type will be underlined.

6. Press **F8** again to turn off the underline toggle

The number returns to its normal display appearance.

Other color or text changes are used on the screen to indicate other alterations to text appearance, including boldfaced text, italicized text, or a combination of these.

Examine the screen shown in Figure WP1–2. Notice that it indicates an insertion point position in Document 2, Page 2, 1.67 inches from the top, and 1.8 inches from the left page edge. Notice also that the Caps Lock and underline toggles are on.

Other Status Line Messages. The left side of the status line (currently displaying the type style) is reserved for other messages and toggle displays. Such messages include the filename of the current document as well as indicators for typeover mode, block, and outline. These will be discussed later in detail.

Learning how to read the status line and its subtle messages will significantly enhance the ease with which you use WordPerfect in the future.

The Function Keys

Turn your attention away from the screen for a moment to examine the function keys on your keyboard. They may be located at the extreme left in two vertical rows of five keys each (labeled F1–F10) or, more likely, across the top in one horizontal row (labeled F1–F12). WordPerfect uses the function keys to invoke various commands.

When used alone, these function keys generate 12 different commands. The function keys may also be pressed in combination with the Shift key, the Ctrl key, or the Alt key to produce 36 additional functions, for a total of 48 commands. When pressing any one of these keys in combination with a function key, you hold down the key, briefly press the desired function key, and then quickly release both. For example, Shift + F7 is used to print a document. This means that you depress and hold the Shift key first, tap the F7 key, and then release both keys to invoke the PRINT command.

Figure WP1–3 lists all the function combinations that can be produced with the function keys. You may also want to place a plastic or cardboard template directly on your keyboard as a handy reference to these functions. The WordPerfect template displays four commands listed next to each function key,

Key	Used with Ctrl	Used with Alt	Used with Shift	Used Alone
F1	Shell	Writing Tools	Setup	Help
F2	Speller	Replace	Backward Search	Forward Search
F3	Screen	Reveal Codes	Switch	Switch To
F4	Move	Block	->Indent<-	->Indent
F5	Outline	Mark	Date	File Manager
F6	Decimal Tab	Flush Right	Center	Bold
F7	Notes	Columns/Tables	Print/Fax	Exit
F8	Font	Style	Format	Underline
F9	Merge/Sort	Graphics	Merge Codes	End Field
F10	Record Macro	Play Macro	Open/Retrieve	Save As
F11	Tab Set	Table Edit	WP Characters	Reveal Codes
F12	Save	Envelope	Bookmark	Block

Figure WP1—3
Features Accessed Using Function Keys

WordPerfect can produce 48 different functions by combining Ctrl, Alt, and Shift with the function keys.

imprinted in one of four colors. Red commands indicate that the Ctrl key should be used with the function key; green indicates the Shift key; blue indicates the Alt key; and black commands indicate that you should press the function key alone.

For example, the word "Center" next to the F6 key is green. This indicates that centering can be invoked by holding the Shift key and then pressing the F6 key. You may want to refer to the template as you work in WordPerfect until the commands become second nature to you.

Function keys either invoke commands (like Center) directly or initiate a command menu that appears at the bottom of your screen. Learn to look at your screen's status line for continuing command menus invoked by pressing various function key combinations or responding to previous options.

Invoking the CANCEL Command.   A most useful key is Esc—the CANCEL feature. The **CANCEL command** can be used to exit a command menu (providing you haven't finished the entire sequence of keystrokes) or to restore deleted text. If you press the wrong function key or menu by mistake, press the Esc key to cancel it.

☞ **Tip: If you delete the wrong text, press the Esc key and then press the 1 (or R) key to restore the deletion.**

Using the Help Feature.   WordPerfect also provides a **Help feature**—a built-in reference for every WordPerfect command. The F1 key is used to initiate this Help feature as follows:

1. Press F1

A screen explaining the Help feature will appear. If your hard disk or program diskette contains the Help file, you may now highlight the desired help topic and press the Enter key (or click the mouse) to select it. (If your program disk does not contain the Help file, press ESC to cancel at this point.)

You can also view an electronic image of the function key template while in the Help feature. To see the template,

2. Highlight *Template* (press [↓] three times or point to it with a mouse)

3. Press [↵] (or click the mouse)

To learn more about a particular function, highlight and select it. For example,

4. Press [↵] to select *Shell*

When you are finished using the Help feature, you can press the Esc key to exit.

5. Press [Esc] to exit the Help feature for now.

Pull-Down Menus

Many of WordPerfect's commands are also available through an alternate menu system consisting of an initial menu bar and a series of **pull-down menus,** which can be operated by keystrokes or with a mouse. (See the Appendix for a complete list of menus.)

Activating the Menu Bar.   One way to use WordPerfect's menu system is to activate the menu bar. If you have a mouse, you can press ("click") its *right* button. If you prefer to use the keyboard, you can press the Alt key and the equal symbol (=) key to activate the menu bar.

☞ **Tip: If the menu bar does not appear on the screen, press Alt + = (equals key), then type VP to install it.**

1. Press [Alt] + [=] (or click the right mouse button)

The first choice in the menu bar, "File," shown in Figure WP1–4a, will appear highlighted at the top of the screen. To deactivate the menu bar,

2. Press [Esc] (or click the right mouse button). The menu bar is deactivated

Selecting a Menu Item.   You can select an item on the active menu in one of three ways:

*   Point to the desired item with the mouse and then click the *left* mouse button.
*   Press the arrow keys to move the highlight to the desired item and then press the Enter key.
*   Type the mnemonic letter that is highlighted (or underlined) on the screen (e.g., "F" for "File" or "T" for "Tools").

For example.

1. Activate the menu bar ([Alt] + [=] or right mouse button)

2. Select *File* ([↵] or [F] or click "File" and press the mouse button

As shown in Figure WP1–4b, selecting an item in the menu bar causes a pull-down menu to appear below the item, offering a new active menu with additional choices. If an item can also be invoked with function keys, the appropriate keys will be listed to the right (as a reminder). A triangle (▶) symbol appearing to the right of a choice (such as in "Setup") indicates that another menu will follow if the item is selected. Items that appear in light gray text (or in square brackets) are not available in the current menu.

Figure WP1—4
The Pull-Down Menus

(a) The menu bar. (b) A pull-down menu appears when an item is selected.

File	Edit	View	Layout	Tools	Font	Graphics	Window	Help

Courier 10cpi   Doc 1 Pg 1 Ln 1" Pos 1"

(a)

File	Edit	View	Layout	Tools	Font	Graphics	Window	Help

New	
Open...	Shft+F10
Retrieve...	
Close	
Save	Ctrl+F12
Save As...	F10
File Manager...	F5
Master Document	Alt+F5 ▶
Compare Documents	Alt+F5 ▶
Summary...	
Setup	Shft+F1 ▶
Print/Fax...	Shft+F7
Print Preview...	Shft+F7
Go to Shell...	Ctrl+F1
Exit...	F7
Exit WP...	Home,F7

Courier 10cpi   Doc 1 Pg 1 Ln 1" Pos 1"

(b)

WP

3. For now, press `Esc` twice (or click the right mouse button) to deactivate the menu

☞ **Tip: To move one menu back, press the Esc key or hold the left mouse button down and then click the right button. (Clicking the right mouse button alone will deactivate the entire menu.)**

A faster way to access the initial menu bar items (if the menu bar is displayed on the screen) is to hold the Alt key and then tap the mnemonic letter that corresponds to the desired item. Try this:

4. Press `Alt` + `F` (that is, depress the Alt key, tap the F key once, and then release both)

Note that the "File" menu has been invoked. You can then select items in the succeeding menus by simply typing their mnemonic letter alone. For example,

5. Press `F` to select *File Manager*

6. Press `Esc` to cancel the menu entirely

If you have a mouse, it is even simpler to just point to and click each desired item on the menu bar and all succeeding menus. With a keyboard, try the high-lighting and mnemonic techniques and then decide which one you prefer. (Of course, you can switch among all the methods at any time.)

Using Function Keys or Menus.   You may use the function key commands or the pull-down menus as you prefer. This manual shows both. The WordPerfect menu is listed after each numbered tutorial step, followed by the equivalent function key shown at the right in square brackets. (If no equivalent menu appears, the function key command will be shown.)

Note for pull-down menu users: The initial word "Select" in a menu series means "activate the menu bar if needed, and select the sequence of menu choices that follow separated by commas, with their mnemonic letters underlined. Of course, you may also press Alt and the mnemonic letter of the first menu choice. As you reach each word in turn, examine the choices on the screen menu to help you understand the selection. Then, select the choice by moving to it on the screen and pressing the Enter key (or left mouse button) or pressing the mnemonic letter key directly.

For practice, try this sequence of commands to erase your screen:

1. Select File, Exit   [F7]

Remember, if you use function key commands, simply press the F7 key. If you use the pull-down menus, the words "Select File, Exit" tell you to activate the menu bar and then select the "File" and then "Exit" choice. Note that the un-derlined letters remind you about pressing mnemonic letters directly.

2. Press `N`   `N`

Because there is only one command shown in Step 2, press the N key twice whether you are using menus or function key commands. (More on this in a moment.)

The Arrow Keys

The four keys that display directional arrows can be used to move the insertion point one space (left, right, up, or down) through text material on your screen—anywhere from the beginning to the end of your document. However, they will not move beyond the last character of your document. You will see this in a moment.

Figure WP1—5
The WordPerfect Arrow Key Movements

To Move the Insertion Point . . .	Press These Keys
One character left	←
One character right	→
One word left	Ctrl ←
One word right	Ctrl →
Left side of screen	Home ←
Right side of screen	Home →
One line up	↑
One line down	↓
Top of screen	Home ↑
Bottom of screen	Home ↓
Previous page	Pg Up
Next page	Pg Dn
One paragraph up	Ctrl ↑
One paragraph down	Ctrl ↓
Beginning of document	Home Home ↑
End of document	Home Home ↓

WP

Figure WP1—6
Using Arrow Keys

Type these sentences. Do *not* press the Enter key until the end (as shown).

```
This is an example of moving the insertion point within a document
using the arrow keys by themselves, and in combination with the
Ctrl and Home keys. Two other keys, PgUp and PgDn, also move the
insertion point around the document. (PRESS ENTER).
```

The arrow keys can also be used together with the Ctrl or Home key to produce a variety of larger insertion point movements within a document. Figure WP1–5 lists the possible keystrokes. Try the following to see the effect.

1. Type the sentences shown in Figure WP1–6

Do not press the Enter key until the very end, as indicated.
   Try some insertion point movements as follows:

2. Press **Home** **Home** ↑ to move the insertion point to the beginning of
   the document

3. Press ↓ to move down one line

4. Press → to move one *character* to the right

5. Press **Ctrl** + → to move one *word* to the right

6. Press **Home** **Home** → to move to the end of the line

7. Press **Home** **Home** ↓ to move to the end of the document

8. Press →

Note that nothing happens. Remember that you cannot move beyond the end of the document.

Get the idea? Try a few insertion point movements on your own. Although you do not need them all now, these movements will become more useful to you as your documents grow longer.

Checkpoint

☐ Start WordPerfect and get to the WordPerfect screen.

☐ What is the meaning of the status line message *Doc 2 Pg 3 Ln 1″ POS 1″*?

☐ What key do you press to cancel? To access the Help feature?

The Basics:
Saving, Opening, and Exiting

Before you begin to type and edit, you should understand how to save and retrieve your work and how to exit from WordPerfect. Once you know these procedures, whenever you want to stop, you can first save your work on disk and then exit from the program. (You may also want to mark the spot where you stopped in this text.) Then, when you return, you can boot your computer, start WordPerfect, open your document, find your place in the text, and continue from where you left off.

Now, add this brief sentence to your screen:

1. Type **This is a sample of typing.**

2. Press ↵

Although this is just a small amount of typing, it is nonetheless a document and can be used to practice the basic techniques of saving, opening, and quitting.

Saving a Document to Disk

Because your documents always should be saved to your data diskette, it is wise to change the default drive to A or B (in a dual-diskette system) before saving or opening.

Setting the Default Drive.   To set the default drive, do the following:

1. Select File, File Manager   [F5]

A "Specify File Manager List" dialog box will appear as in Figure WP1–7a. The Directory line may show "C:\WPDOCS*.*" (or "A:*.*"). Note that subdirectories can be included in the default directory path.

2. Press = to change the default directory

```
┌─────────────────────────────────────────────────┐
│              Specify File Manager List            │
│                                                   │
│  Directory: C:\WPDOCS\*.*                         │
│                                                   │
│    [QuickList... F6]  [Use QuickFinder... F4]     │
│                                                   │
│    [Directory Tree... F8]   [Redo F5] [OK] [Cancel]│
└─────────────────────────────────────────────────┘
```
(a)

```
┌─────────────────────────────────────────────────┐
│                  Save Document 1                   │
│                                                   │
│   Filename: _                                     │
│                                                   │
│   Format:  WordPerfect 6.0                    [▼] │
│                                                   │
│  [Setup... Shft+F1]  [Code Page... F9]            │
│                                                   │
│  [File List... F5] [QuickList... F6] [Password... F8] [OK] [Cancel]│
└─────────────────────────────────────────────────┘
```
(b)

Figure WP1–7
Opening and Saving a Document

a) The Specify File Manager list lets you set a default directory.
b) The Save Document dialog box lets you name a file for saving. (partial screens)

A "Change Default Directory" dialog box appears.

3. Type **A:** (or **B:** in a dual-diskette system)

4. Press ↵ (or click the "OK" button)

The new default directory prompt now appears in the dialog box on your screen ("A:*.*" or "B:*.*" for dual-diskette). For now,

5. Press **Esc** to return to your document

Your default drive for saving and opening documents is now set. You will not need to reset the default drive again as long as you stay in WordPerfect. When you save (or open) a document now, it will be stored on (or fetched from) your data diskette.

☞ **Tip: You should check the default drive whenever you start the WordPerfect program (and change it if needed).**

Even if you do not change the default drive, you can still save and open documents, but you will have to include a disk identifier in front of the document's name (as in A:EXAMPLE) each time you save it, to ensure that the data diskette is used. It is simpler to change the default drive before saving or opening. It is also safer—you will not run the risk of mistakenly saving your documents onto the wrong disk.

Naming and Saving a File. You can now save your document onto your data diskette with the name EXAMPLE. Make sure that you have placed your diskette into the appropriate disk drive (Drive A or Drive B for dual-diskette systems).

1. Select File, Save   [Ctrl + F12]

(Remember that you can press Alt + F to access the File menu quickly, then press S to save.) Because this is the first time you are saving this file, you must first give it a name. A "Save Document 1" dialog box appears as in Figure WP1–7b. Examine this screen for a moment. Note the blinking cursor (horizontal line)

Figure WP1—8
Document Opening

After a document has been opened, its disk identifier and filename usually appear in the lower left corner of the screen.

A:\EXAMPLE	Doc 1 Pg 1 Ln 1.33" Pos 1"

in the "Filename" line; it is prompting you to type a filename. Note, too, as seen in the "Format" line below it, that the file will be saved in "WordPerfect 6.0" format (the default).

☞ **Tip: WordPerfect allows you to save a file in 34 other word processing formats, including Ami Pro, ASCII text, DisplayWrite, MS Word, earlier WordPerfect formats, WordStar, and many others. This is useful if you are planning to use another word processing program to edit or print your document.**

A word about dialog boxes in general: To select an item, you can press its mnemonic letter (if one is displayed) or use the Tab key, or any arrow key, to move the highlight to the desired item and then select it by pressing the Enter key. Of course, you can also point and click with a mouse. For example.

2. Press ⭤ once

Note that the dotted (or colored) rectangular highlight (depending on the current screen mode) has moved to the "Format" line, making it the active choice at the moment.

3. Press ↓ three more times to move to the "OK" button

4. Press ↓ twice more to return to the Filename line

5. Type **EXAMPLE** (the name of your document)

6. Press ↵

The drive light will flash briefly as the document is being saved. When the process is finished, the document name may appear in the lower left corner of the screen, as in Figure WP1—8 (or the word "Typeover" will be shown—more on this later). You can now continue working on your document.

The SAVE command—which copies (or "backs up") the current version of your document from primary memory to disk—should be used frequently as you work. In this way, if power is lost for any reason, a recent copy of your document will be available on your disk.

"Save As" versus "Save."   Once you have saved your document, you can easily save it again as you work by selecting the File-Save command. The document will immediately be saved to disk with the same name, automatically replacing the old file. For example,

1. Select File, Save   [Ctrl + F12]

The file has been saved. Any changes you have made in your document have been safely copied to your disk.

At times, however, you may want to save a document with a different name than its current one so you don't erase the old file. To accomplish this, you must use *Save As* when you save the file to disk instead of just *Save*. Try this:

2. Select <u>F</u>ile, Save <u>A</u>s [F10]

The "Save Document" dialog box appears. Note that the current document name "A:\EXAMPLE" (or "B:\EXAMPLE") automatically appears on the line following the "Document" prompt.

    If you wanted to change the name, you would just type a new one in its place and press the Enter key to save the document under a new filename. In this example, however, you will save it with the same name again:

3. Press ⏎ (or select "OK")

Because WordPerfect finds a file already on your disk with the same name, it asks "Replace A:\EXAMPLE?" It is simply warning you that a file with the name EXAMPLE already exists on the same disk. To save the file again with the same name,

4. Press **Y** (or select "Yes")

As expected, the older version of the document is now replaced with the current one.

☞ **Tip: Use *Save* when you want to save the current document immediately with the same filename. Use *Save As* when you want to change the filename or confirm a file replacement. Both techniques will save—it's your choice.**

Clearing the Screen

There are times when you want to clear your screen of an old document so that you can start a new one. This is especially true when you want to retrieve a document onto the screen. Try this:

1. Select <u>F</u>ile, <u>C</u>lose [F7]

The screen may respond with "Save changes?" If it does, to indicate that you do not want to save the document for now

2. Press **N** (or select the "No" button)

Note that you could have saved the document by pressing Y (or selecting "Yes"). You will try this technique shortly.

    If you began the close process by pressing F7, the screen now asks "Exit WordPerfect?" Because you do not want to exit the program,

3. Press **N** (or select "No")

This will clear the screen.

☞ **Tip: You can also clear the screen by selecting <u>F</u>ile, <u>E</u>xit and then typing NN.**

Opening a Document

You can now open a document for additional editing or printing. The **open** command retrieves a document from disk and places it into a new document window. Because your screen is clear, the new document will appear as "Doc 1." In WordPerfect, there are two ways to open a document—type its name or select it from a list.

Typing a Document's Name. If you know a document's name, the most direct way to open it is to use the File, Open command. (*Note:* If you have just restarted WordPerfect, make sure to set the default drive appropriately before continuing.) Try this:

1. Select <u>F</u>ile, <u>O</u>pen [Shift + F10]

An "Open Document" dialog box appears.

2. Type **EXAMPLE** in the "Filename" box

3. Press ↵

The document is opened for use. If your screen reads "ERROR—File not found" then either you spelled the filename incorrectly (now or when you saved it) or you did not set your default drive correctly. If you were not successful in opening the document, check for these mistakes and try again.

Selecting a Document from a List.   If you do not remember the name of a document, or forget its exact spelling, you may prefer this second opening technique. In this procedure, you display a list of all files on the disk, and then select the one you want. Try this:

1. First, clear your screen (with File, Close)   [F7, N, N]

2. Select File, Open   [Shift + F10]

The "Open Document" box appears as before.

3. Now, press **F5** (or click "File Manager") to select the File Manager

Your screen should display the directory "A:*.*" (or "B:*.*" in a dual-diskette system). This indicates that WordPerfect will list the files on the default disk (currently your data disk, not the program disk). If the proper drive is not shown, change the default drive now—then continue.

4. Press ↵ to access "File Manager" for drive A (or B)

Your screen should resemble Figure WP1–9a, displaying all the files on your diskette (your screen may have more files than shown in the figure).

5. Use your arrow keys to move the highlight onto the filename *EXAMPLE* (as in Figure WP1–9b)

6. Press **O** to open this file (or click the "Open" line)

Because the dotted highlight (or color in text mode) already indicates the "Open" choice, you could also press the Enter key to select "Open."

☞ Tip: If you had not cleared your screen before invoking the open command, the new document would be placed in a Doc 2 (or higher) window. If this occurs, close the file (Alt + F, C) and then follow the procedure in Step 1 above to clear the screen before attempting to open again.

If all went well, your document should now appear on the screen. Practice the save and open routines a few times; then use them as needed when you want to stop and continue later.

Exiting from the Program

Now that you have experienced the basics of WordPerfect, you should also learn how to exit from the program when you are finished. There are actually two decisions you must make when exiting. First, should you save the current document? Second, do you want to exit from WordPerfect entirely, or just clear your screen?

☞ Tip: You could also cancel the exit entirely by pressing the Esc (cancel) key.

Here's one way to exit the WordPerfect program:

1. Select File, Exit WP   [Home, F7]

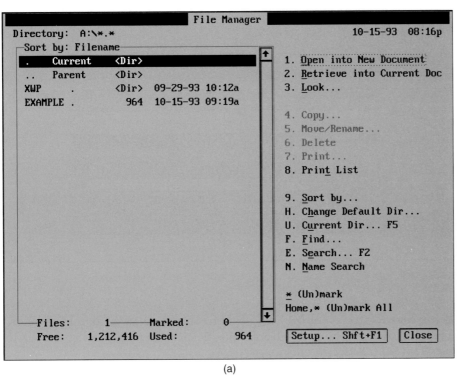

Figure WP1—9
The File Manager Screen

Using File Manager is an effective way to retrieve a document by selecting it from a list of all files on the disk. (a) The initial screen. (b) The desired file (EXAMPLE) has been highlighted. (partial screen)

The screen responds with an "Exit WordPerfect" dialog box, as in Figure WP1–10. The "Exit WordPerfect" dialog box displays all currently open documents so that you may decide what to do with them before exiting the program. (On your screen, as in Figure WP1–10, only one document—EXAMPLE—is open.) To the left of each document is a "Save box" that indicates whether the file will be saved.

At this point, you can mark any documents you want to save or "unmark" them so that they will not be saved. For example,

2. Press **A** to mark Document 1 for saving

Note that an "X" appears in the Save box as in Figure WP1–10b. To "unmark" this document,

3. Press **A** again to cancel the "X"

☞ **Tip: You can mark (or unmark) a document for saving by pressing its corresponding letter (A through I). You can also press M to change the save status of all the documents.**

Figure WP1–10
The "Exit WordPerfect"
Dialog Box

(a) The file is not marked for
saving. (b) Pressing "A" places
an "X" in the Save box. (partial
screens)

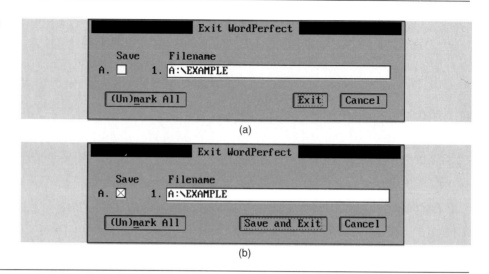

If you were to press A (or M), you would be able to save your document before exiting. Leaving the Save box blank skips the *Save* routine, moving directly to the "Exit WordPerfect?" question.

4. Press ⏎ to exit WordPerfect (or click "Exit")

A DOS prompt (or menu) should now appear on your screen.

In general, F10 (Save) is used for copying a document from time to time as you work on it—a safety precaution. The Home, F7 Exit routine can be used to save your document when you are finished or want to exit WordPerfect entirely.

If you plan to continue, you may have to change the default drive back to the disk that contains DOS. If so, type *C:* (*A:* in a dual-diskette system or network) and press the Enter key. Of course, if you're stopping for now, simply shut off your computer.

Checkpoint

☐ Start WordPerfect; set the default drive appropriately.

☐ Type your name on the first line and your class underneath it. Save this document as EXAMPLE (replace the old file).

☐ Clear the screen and use the File Manager to open the EXAMPLE document to the screen. Then exit WordPerfect.

Creating a Document

As you have seen, entering text into WordPerfect is similar to using a typewriter, with a few notable exceptions. The most important is the use (or, more appropriately, nonuse) of the Enter key. To prepare for these exercises:

1. Start WordPerfect
2. Set the default drive to A: (or B: for dual-diskette)

```
Type today's date here¶
¶
¶
Mr. Phil D. Basket¶
People Against Littering¶
2000 Environment Boulevard, Suite 999¶
Seattle, WA 98101¶
¶
Dear Mr. Basket:¶
¶
Thank you for your letter regarding Shrub-Garb products.  Our
company takes pride in being the first to develop a garbage
disposal product that is not only completely biodegradable, but
environmentally pleasing as well.¶
¶
As you know, our Shrub-Garb brand garbage bags are made to
resemble bushes and shrubs that are native to each geographic
area in the United States.  On garbage day, there are no
unsightly plastic containers to mar your view, but rather a
collection of green "shrubs" growing around your house.  As you
add more garbage, the shrubs just get larger.¶
¶
Our garbage bags come in five sizes, ranging from the tiny
"Azalea" to our very popular "Sequoia" model for large families.
We even have red, gold, and white varieties for those locales
that experience seasonal color changes in the fall and winter
months.¶
¶
Enclosed please find our new Price List.  We look forward to your
order and appreciate your interest in Shrub-Garb.  If I can be of
further assistance, do not hesitate to contact me.¶
¶
Sincerely,¶
¶
¶
¶
Type your name here¶
Regional Sales Manager¶
```

Figure WP1—11
The SAMPLE1 Document

Remember to press the Enter key only where you see a paragraph symbol. Your margins may cause some words to wordwrap differently than shown here.

WP

The Enter Key

On a typewriter, the Enter (or Return) key is pressed at the end of each line. This is known in word processing as a **hard return**. A hard return moves the insertion point to the next line—creating a "line break" at the point where the Enter key was pressed.

Word processing programs, however, do not require hard returns to move to the next line. Instead, when text reaches the right margin, it will wrap automatically to the next line as you continue typing. This action, called **wordwrap**, automatically inserts a **soft return** at the end of each line. If you later add or delete text, or change margins, WordPerfect will be able to reformat your document by shifting these soft returns to new locations. Hard returns, on the other hand, cannot be moved by the WordPerfect program.

Thus, the only time you must press the Enter key is when you want to end a line *before* it reaches the right margin, as in the case of an address line, a salutation, or the end of a paragraph. Until you get used to this, a paragraph symbol (¶) will be used in this chapter (as seen in Figure WP1–11) to remind you when to press the Enter key.

Entering Text

Create a short letter by entering text as follows:

1. Start WordPerfect (or clear the screen)

Remember: do not press the Enter key at the end of each line; press the Enter key *only* when you see the paragraph symbol (¶) in the figure.

2. Type the letter shown in Figure WP1–11

☞ **Tip: If you make a mistake while typing, press the Backspace key to remove the error, and retype the correct text.**

3. Save this document as **SAMPLE1** (with File, Save or F10)
4. Clear the screen

Checkpoint

☐ Create a new document called EXAMPLE1. Type a few sentences of your choice. Save the document.

☐ Press the Enter key in the middle of a sentence in EXAMPLE 1 to create a line break. Use Backspace to fix it. Do not save

☐ Open EXAMPLE1. Skip two lines under your class and type today's date. Save the document again, and then exit WordPerfect.

Editing a Document

Typing in WordPerfect is relatively easy as long as you allow the program to wordwrap for you as you type. Otherwise, text entry is much like that on a typewriter.

The true power of WordPerfect, however, lies in its ability to help you *edit*, or change, the content or appearance of your document. Perhaps you need to correct typing mistakes, or want to modify a first draft. Whatever the reason, WordPerfect (like most word processing programs) allows you total editing flexibility to add, delete, and modify or move words in your document. You can add new text, type over existing text, or delete old text. The following exercises examine all three techniques. If SAMPLE1 is not on your screen,

1. Start up WordPerfect or clear the screen
2. Open the SAMPLE1 document

Adding New Text

There are many ways to add new text to your document. You can retrieve, or copy, text from another document into your screen (as you will see later). You can also type text directly from the keyboard. When typing, you can have the new text combine with existing screen text, or replace it. You do this by selecting either the insert mode or the typeover mode before you begin to add text.

The Insert Mode. Unlike typewriters, word processing programs allow you to add, or insert, text into material that is already in your document. WordPerfect is normally set to insert. As you type, the **insert mode** ensures that existing screen text will move over to make room for the new characters. Before you attempt to insert, you should always check to see that the insert toggle is on. To check, glance at the left side of the status line. If the left side is blank, shows a document name, or displays a type style, then the insert mode is on. However, if the word "Typeover" appears, then the program is in typeover mode and *is not* ready to insert. To see this, try the following:

1. Press **Insert**

Notice that "Typeover" appears, as in Figure WP1–12.

2. Press **Insert** again

Figure WP1—12

The Insert Mode

If "Typeover" appears on the left side of the status line, WordPerfect is not in the insert mode.

Typeover	Doc 1 Pg 1 Ln 1" Pos 1"

Figure WP1—12

The Insert Mode

If "Typeover" appears on the left side of the status line, WordPerfect is not in the insert mode.

Figure WP1—13

Insert Exercise

These two words and one phrase are about to be placed into your document.

```
 File  Edit  View  Layout  Tools  Font  Graphics  Window  Help
 November 1, 199X


 Mr. Phil D. Basket
 People Against Littering
 2000 Environment Boulevard, Suite 999
 Seattle, WA 98101
                                    great
 Dear Mr. Basket:                   recent
 Thank you for your letter regarding Shrub-Garb products.  Our
 company takes pride in being the first to develop a garbage
 disposal product that is not only completely biodegradable, but
 environmentally pleasing as well.
                                     durable and popular
 As you know, our Shrub-Garb brand garbage bags are made to
 resemble bushes and shrubs that are native to each geographic
 area in the United States.  On garbage day, there are no
 unsightly plastic containers to mar your view, but rather a
 collection of green "shrubs" growing around your house.  As you
 add more garbage, the shrubs just get larger.

 Our garbage bags come in five sizes, ranging from the tiny
 "Azalea" to our very popular "Sequoia" model for large families.
 We even have red, gold, and white varieties for those locales
 that experience seasonal color changes in the fall and winter
 months.

 Enclosed please find our new Price List.  We look forward to your
A:\SAMPLE1                              Doc 1 Pg 1 Ln 1" Pos 1"
```

"Typeover" is no longer displayed. Pressing the Insert key "toggles" the insert mode on and off as needed. Make sure that the insert mode is on before continuing.

You will now practice the three inserts shown in Figure WP1–13. Try the first insert carefully as follows:

3. Press the arrow keys to move the insertion point to the first insert position— the "l" in "letter" on the first line of the first paragraph

The insertion point should now be to the immediate left of the "l," as shown in Figure WP1–14a. (If you are using text mode, the cursor will be directly *beneath* the letter "l".)

4. Type **recent**

Your text should now resemble Figure WP1–14b. Notice that the words to the right of the insertion point have moved over to make room for the new word. Words may even move beyond the right margin, depending upon what has been inserted. This will be fixed in a moment.

5. Press   **Space**   to separate "recent" and "letter"

Figure WP1—14

Inserting Text

(a) The insertion point is positioned for insert. (b) The new word has pushed the old text to the right to make room.

November 1, 199X

Mr. Phil D. Basket
People Against Littering
2000 Environment Boulevard, Suite 999
Seattle, WA 98101

                                Insertion point is here
Dear Mr. Basket:

Thank you for your |letter regarding Shrub-Garb products. Our
company takes pride in being the first to develop a garbage
disposal product that is not only completely biodegradable, but
environmentally pleasing as well.

(a)

November 1, 199X

Mr. Phil D. Basket
People Against Littering
2000 Environment Boulevard, Suite 999
Seattle, WA 98101

Dear Mr. Basket:

Thank you for your recentletter regarding Shrub-Garb products. Our
company takes pride in being the first to develop a garbage
disposal product that is not only completely biodegradable, but
environmentally pleasing as well.

(b)

Notice that the wordwrap feature automatically *reformats* the paragraph to fit within the margins again.

A common mistake is to press the Enter key when the insert is completed. This is wrong! It will only break the line in the middle (as in Figure WP1–15a). If you ever do this by mistake, simply press the Backspace key to erase the extra keystroke and return the line to normal (as in Figure WP1–15b).

Now, repeat this procedure for the second and third inserts shown in Figure WP1–13 as follows:

6. Move to the "p" in "pride" on the second line of the first paragraph

7. Type **great** and press   **Space**

8. Move to the "S" in "Shrub-Garb" on the first line of the second paragraph

9. Type **durable and popular** and press   **Space**

Your screen should now resemble Figure WP1–16.

10. Save this document again as **SAMPLE1**

The Typeover Mode.   There are times when you will want to simply replace old text with new. Perhaps you noticed transposed (reversed) letters, or want to replace an old word with a new one. In these situations, it may be easier to switch

A common mistake is to press the Enter key after inserting. (a) Pressing the Enter key will break your line in the wrong place. (b) Pressing the Backspace key will remove the Enter and fix the line.

November 1, 199X

Mr. Phil D. Basket
People Against Littering
2000 Environment Boulevard, Suite 999
Seattle, WA 98101

Dear Mr. Basket: The Enter key was pressed
                                    here by mistake

Thank you for your recent
letter regarding Shrub-Garb products. Our company takes pride in
being the first to develop a garbage disposal product that is not
only completely biodegradable, but environmentally pleasing as
well.

(a)

November 1, 199X

Mr. Phil D. Basket
People Against Littering
2000 Environment Boulevard, Suite 999
Seattle, WA 98101

Dear Mr. Basket:

Thank you for your recent letter regarding Shrub-Garb products.
Our company takes pride in being the first to develop a garbage
disposal product that is not only completely biodegradable, but
environmentally pleasing as well.

(b)

to the typeover mode. In the **typeover mode,** new text replaces old text character for character in the document. When insert is toggled on, typeover is off (and vice versa). As you have seen, the Insert key toggles between the insert and typeover modes. The following exercises provide some practice with the typeover mode. Figure WP1–17 displays the changes you will make.

1. Press   **Insert**   if the word "Typeover" does not appear at the lower left of your screen

2. Move the insertion point to the first "9" in "Suite 999"

3. Type **876**

Notice how the new text *types over* the old, replacing it character for character. As with insert, do not press the Enter key when you are finished. Try one more:

4. Move to the "f" in "five" in the third paragraph

5. Type **four**

Figure WP1—16

*The SAMPLE1
Document with All
Three Inserts*

```
November 1, 199X


Mr. Phil D. Basket
People Against Littering
2000 Environment Boulevard, Suite 999
Seattle, WA  98101

Dear Mr. Basket:

Thank you for your recent letter regarding Shrub-Garb products.
Our company takes great pride in being the first to develop a
garbage disposal product that is not only completely biodegradable,
but environmentally pleasing as well.

As you know, our durable and popular Shrub-Garb brand garbage bags
are made to resemble bushes and shrubs that are native to each
geographic area in the United States.  On garbage day, there are no
unsightly plastic containers to mar your view, but rather a
collection of green "shrubs" growing around your house.  As you add
more garbage, the shrubs just get larger.

Our garbage bags come in five sizes, ranging from the tiny "Azalea"
to our very popular "Sequoia" model for large families.  We even
```
A:\SAMPLE1   Doc 1 Pg 1 Ln 3.5" Pos 4.7"

Figure WP1—17

Typeover Exercise

These two changes are about to
replace text in your document
using the typeover technique.

```
November 1, 199X

                                                        876
Mr. Phil D. Basket
People Against Littering
2000 Environment Boulevard, Suite 999
Seattle, WA  98101

Dear Mr. Basket:

Thank you for your recent letter regarding Shrub-Garb products.
Our company takes great pride in being the first to develop a
garbage disposal product that is not only completely biodegradable,
but environmentally pleasing as well.

As you know, our durable and popular Shrub-Garb brand garbage bags
are made to resemble bushes and shrubs that are native to each
geographic area in the United States.  On garbage day, there are no
unsightly plastic containers to mar your view, but rather a
collection of green "shrubs" growing around your house.  As you add
more garbage, the shrubs just get larger.
                                                    four
Our garbage bags come in five sizes, ranging from the tiny "Azalea"
to our very popular "Sequoia" model for large families.  We even
```
A:\SAMPLE1   Doc 1 Pg 1 Ln 1" Pos 1"

Typeover is a straightforward way to replace text—with the word "Typeover"
appearing at the lower left corner of the screen, simply type the replacement
characters.

6. Resave this document as **SAMPLE1**

7. Press **Insert** to turn off the typeover toggle

Figure WP1—18
WordPerfect Delete Commands

To Delete . . .	Press These Keys:
One character to the left of the cursor	**← Backspace**
One character at the cursor	**Del**
One word at the cursor	**Ctrl** + **← Backspace**
From the cursor to the end of the line	**Ctrl** + **End**
From the cursor to the end of the page	**Ctrl** + **Pg Dn** , then **Y**
Text that has been blocked	**← Backspace** , then **Y** or **Del** , then **Y**
From the cursor to the start of a word	**Home** , then **← Backspace**
From the cursor to the end of a word	**Home** , then **Del**

Figure WP1—19
Delete Exercise

These five areas of text are about to be deleted from your document using various delete commands.

```
Mr. Phil D. Basket
People Against Littering
2000 Environment Boulevard, Suite 876
Seattle, WA  98101

Dear Mr. Basket:

Thank you for your recent letter regarding Shrub-Garb products.
Our company takes great pride in being the first to develop a
garbage disposal product that is not only completely biodegradable,
but environmentally pleasing as well.

As you know, our durable and popular Shrub-Garb brand garbage bags
are made to resemble bushes and shrubs that are native to each
geographic area in the United States.  On garbage day, there are no
unsightly plastic containers to mar your view, but rather a
collection of green "shrubs" growing around your house.  As you add
more garbage, the shrubs just get larger.

Our garbage bags come in four sizes, ranging from the tiny "Azalea"
to our very popular "Sequoia" model for large families.  We even
have red, gold, and white varieties for those locales that
experience seasonal color changes in the fall and winter months.
```

A:\SAMPLE1   Doc 1 Pg 1 Ln 1.5" Pos 1"

WP

You may also want to remove, or *delete*, text from your document. As Figure WP1–18 shows, you can delete one character at a time, or as many pages as you like. You will now use some simple techniques to remove the words marked in Figure WP1–19.

Deleting Text

Using the Delete Key. The **Delete key** deletes a character at the position of the insertion point. Each time you press the Delete key, one character is deleted and any text to its right moves left to fill in the gap. Try this:

1. Use the arrow keys to move the insertion point to the comma after "Boulevard" in the third line of the address

2. Press **Delete**

Notice that the comma has been deleted and the text "Suite 876" has moved left.

3. Press `Delete` ten times to delete "Suite 876"

Use the Del key to remove the word "completely" on the third line of the first paragraph as follows:

4. Move the insertion point to the "c" in the word "completely"

5. Press `Delete` until you have deleted the word and the space after it

6. Save the document again as **SAMPLE1**

Using the Backspace Key.   The **Backspace** key deletes a character *to the left* of the insertion point and moves the point one space to the left. Try using the Backspace key to remove the word "brand" in the first line of the second paragraph as follows:

1. Move the insertion point to the letter "g" in the word "garbage" in the first line of the second paragraph (*after* the word you want to delete)

2. Press `← Backspace`

Notice that the space before the "g" has been deleted and the word "garbage" has moved left.

3. Press `← Backspace` five times to delete "brand"

Use the Backspace key to remove the word "growing" *and the space* on the fifth line of the second paragraph as follows:

4. Move the insertion point to the "a" in the word "around"

5. Press `← Backspace` until you have deleted the space and the word "growing"

6. Save the document again as SAMPLE1

Deleting Words with the Ctrl and Backspace Keys.   You can delete one character at a time with the Delete or Backspace key. You can also delete an entire word at a time (and the space that follows it) by combining keystrokes. To do this, position the insertion point at any letter in the word to be deleted, hold the Ctrl key, press the Backspace key, and then release both. Try deleting the phrase "in the fall and winter months" using this technique as follows:

1. Move to the letter "i" in the word "in" on the last line of the third paragraph

2. Press `Ctrl` + `← Backspace`

Notice that the word "in" *and the space after it* are gone.

3. Hold `Ctrl` and press `← Backspace` five more times to delete the next five words

4. Press `←`

5. Type `.` (a period) to complete the sentence

6. Resave the document as **SAMPLE1**

Other Delete Techniques.   WordPerfect offers other ways to delete text quickly. Although you will not use them now, you may want to examine these on your own. For example, the Ctrl and End keys will delete all text to the end of the current line; the Ctrl and Pg Dn keys will delete all text to the end of the current page. In the next chapter, you will also learn how to delete large blocks of text easily.

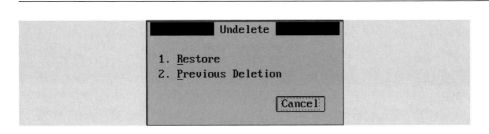

Figure WP1—20
The "Undelete" Dialog Box

Invoked with the Esc key. "Undelete" allows you to restore text that was inadvertently removed. (partial screen)

"Undeleting" Text.   As you have seen, the Esc key can "undelete" text. That is, you can restore text that was deleted by mistake. Try this.

1. Press **Esc**

☞ **Tip: You could also select Edit, Undelete from the menu, but it is much faster to use the Esc key.**

Notice that the text you deleted most recently appears on the screen highlighted for easy recognition, and a dialog box appears on the screen as in Figure WP1–20. If you wanted to restore the text to the current cursor location, you could press *R* (or *1*) to select *Restore*, or you could press the Enter or Esc key to cancel.

2. Press **↵** to cancel the undelete for now

Use the "undelete" option whenever you need to retrieve text that was inadvertently removed.

Basic Format Enhancements

It is easy to make formatting changes to enhance or emphasize portions of text. You may want to center headings or have text bolded or underlined. These formatting features can be specified either before or after text is typed. In this chapter, you will practice three format enhancements—center, bold, and underline—*before* typing text. The next chapter will examine enhancements to text that has already been typed.

Centering.   Headings or titles are often centered. The **Center feature** leaves equal margins on both sides of the text. The following exercise demonstrates how to request centering before typing the text to be centered. You will place the heading shown in Figure WP1–21 at the beginning of your document.

1. Start WordPerfect and open SAMPLE1 if needed
2. Move to the beginning of your document
3. Make sure that WordPerfect is in the insert mode

Remember, the word "Typeover" should *not* appear at the lower left of the screen.

4. If "Typeover" appears, press **Insert**

Now, create some blank lines at the beginning of your document as follows:

5. Press **↵** twice

6. Press **↑** twice to return to the top

7. To center, select <u>L</u>ayout, <u>A</u>lignment, <u>C</u>enter   [Shift + F6]

Figure WP1—21

Centering Exercise

This heading is about to be placed at the beginning of your document—automatically centered by the program.

```
                        Shrub-Garb Products
                         1234 Clean Street
                         Anytown, IL 67890


        November 1, 199X


        Mr. Phil D. Basket
        People Against Littering
        2000 Environment Boulevard
        Seattle, WA  98101
```

Figure WP1—22

Underlining Exercise

The following sentence with underlined text is about to be added to the end of your document.

```
        P.S. All of us at Shrub-Garb greatly appreciate your concern.
```

Notice how the insertion point moves to the center of the line.

☞ **Tip: In this case, it is much easier to use the function keys to center, rather than to press Alt + L, A, C. Learn to use the simpler approach for common commands.**

8. Type **Shrub-Garb Products** and press ⏎

The text has been centered automatically. Center the next two lines as follows:

9. Select <u>L</u>ayout, <u>A</u>lignment, <u>C</u>enter   [Shift + F6]

10. Type **1234 Clean Street** and press ⏎

11. Select <u>L</u>ayout, <u>A</u>lignment, <u>C</u>enter   [Shift + F6]

12. Type **Anytown, IL 67890** and press ⏎

13. Save the document with the new name of **SAMPLE2**

Underlining.   Underline—placing an underscore beneath text—is another text enhancement. Unlike a typewriter, WordPerfect can underline as you type. It is simply a matter of turning the underline toggle on before you type, and then off when you are finished. The following exercise demonstrates this technique. You will place the sentence shown in Figure WP1—22 at the end of your document.

1. Open SAMPLE2 if needed

2. Move to the end of your document

3. Press ⏎ to create a new line

4. Type **P.S. All of us at Shrub-Garb**

Figure WP1—23
Underlining Text

(a) A color change or underline of the position number indicates that the underline toggle is on. (b) The desired text has been underlined and the position number has returned to normal, showing that underline is no longer active.

```
Your Name
Regional Sales Manager


P.S.  All of us at Shrub-Garb
A:\SAMPLE2                                    Doc 1 Pg 1 Ln 8.33" Pos 4"
```
(a)

```
Your Name
Regional Sales Manager


P.S.  All of us at Shrub-Garb greatly appreciate your concern.
A:\SAMPLE2                                    Doc 1 Pg 1 Ln 8.33" Pos 7.2"
```
(b)

(Make sure you press the space bar after the word "Garb" to separate it from the next word.) You are now ready to "toggle on" the underlining feature. To toggle underline on,

5. Select F**o**nt, **U**nderline   [F8]

☞ **Tip: It is easier to use the F8 key here than the pull-down menus.**

Notice how the position number on the status line is underlined (or has changed color) on your screen, as in Figure WP1–23a, indicating that the underline toggle is on.

6. Type **greatly appreciate**

Note how these words appear underlined (or a different color) on your screen. To toggle the underline off,

7. Select F**o**nt, **N**ormal   [F8]

The position number has returned to normal, showing that underline is no longer active. Note that when using the menu, you must select "Normal," whereas you need only press F8 again if you use the keyboard.

8. Type a space and **your concern.**

The line on your screen should resemble Figure WP1–23b.

9. Resave the document as **SAMPLE2**

Bolding.   **Bold,** or boldface, is a text enhancement that emphasizes text by making it darker when it is printed. Like underlining, bolding is easily achieved by turning the bold toggle on before you type, and off when you are done. In this exercise, you will place the sentence shown in Figure WP1–24 at the end of your document.

1. Open SAMPLE2 if needed
2. Move to the end of your document

The insertion point should be at the end of the sentence after the word "concern," as in Figure WP1–25a.

3. Press **Space** twice to start a new sentence

4. Type **We have enclosed a**

Figure WP1—24

Bolding Exercise

The following sentence with bold text is about to be added to the end of your document.

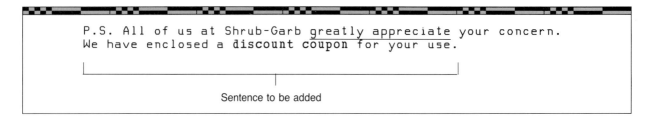

P.S. All of us at Shrub-Garb greatly appreciate your concern. We have enclosed a discount coupon for your use.

Sentence to be added

Figure WP1—25

Bolding Text

(a) The insertion point has been positioned to add the additional sentence. (b) The desired text has been bolded and the position number has returned to normal, showing that BOLD is no longer active.

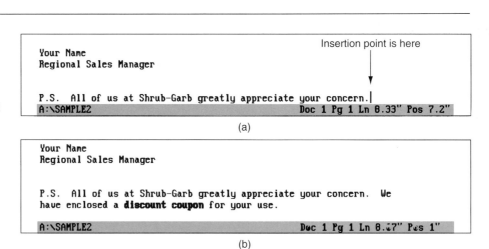

(a)

(b)

(Make sure to press the space bar after the word "a" to separate it from the next word.) You are now ready to "toggle on" the bolding feature. To toggle bold on,

5. Select F̲ont, B̲old   [F6]

☞ **Tip: It is easier to use the F6 key than the pull-down menus.**

Notice how the position number is brighter (or has changed color) on your screen. As with underline, this indicates that the bold toggle is on.

6. Type **discount coupon**

The words will appear darker (or a different color depending on the screen mode).

☞ **Tip: If you cannot see the brightness change, adjust the brightness and contrast controls on your monitor until the text difference is apparent. You can also select Font and see which enhancement is checked, then Esc.**

To toggle bold off,

7. Select F̲ont, N̲ormal   [F6]

The position number has returned to normal to show that the bold mode is no longer active.

```
                    Shrub-Garb Products
                     1234 Clean Street
                     Anytown, IL 67890


November 1, 199X


Mr. Phil D. Basket
People Against Littering
2000 Environment Boulevard
Seattle, WA 98101

Dear Mr. Basket:

Thank you for your recent letter regarding Shrub-Garb products.
Our company takes great pride in being the first to develop a
garbage disposal product that is not only biodegradable, but
environmentally pleasing as well.

As you know, our durable and popular Shrub-Garb garbage bags are
made to resemble bushes and shrubs that are native to each
geographic area in the United States.  On garbage day, there are
no unsightly plastic containers to mar your view, but rather a
collection of green "shrubs" around your house.  As you add more
garbage, the shrubs just get larger.

Our garbage bags come in four sizes, ranging from the tiny
"Azalea" to our very popular "Sequoia" model for large families.
We even have red, gold, and white varieties for those locales
that experience seasonal color changes.

Enclosed please find our new Price List.  We look forward to your
order and appreciate your interest in Shrub-Garb.  If I can be of
further assistance, do not hesitate to contact me.

Sincerely,



Your name
Regional Sales Manager

P.S.  All of us at Shrub-Garb greatly appreciate your concern.
We have enclosed a discount coupon for your use.
```

Figure WP1—26
The Printed Document

This is how the final document appears when printed with all insertions, typeovers, deletions, as well as underlined and bold text. (Your margins may vary slightly.)

WP

8. Press **Space** and type **for your use.**

9. Press ⏎

Your screen should now resemble Figure WP1–25b.

10. Resave this document as **SAMPLE2**

Your final screen document should resemble the printed version shown in Figure WP1–26. Note that you will not see all of the document on your screen at once. Press the Pg Dn key to view the bottom of your document, and the Pg Up key to view the top. Also note that underlined or bold text may appear differently on your screen than it will when printed.

Checkpoint

☐ Open the EXAMPLE document. Skip a line under the date. Center and type the heading "Adding New Text." Indent a new paragraph; type the first paragraph of the "Adding New Text" section from page WP22 into your document. Save the amended file.

☐ Delete the parentheses and the words within them from the paragraph you have just typed.

☐ Underline the word "document" where it appears two times in the paragraph. Set the heading in bold. Save the file again.

Printing a Document

The ultimate destination of most documents is paper. Although you work with documents on the screen, and save documents on disk for editing and future use, your goal is usually to produce a printed copy of the finished document.

WordPerfect has several commands for printing. You will examine the most common techniques in this exercise; later chapters will present others. Before you print, verify that:

1. Your computer is connected to a printer
2. The printer is turned on
3. The paper is correctly aligned in the printer

Now, you are ready to print.

4. Open SAMPLE2 if it is not on your screen

Printing a Full Document

The most frequently used PRINT command is the one that prints your full document (all of its pages). This is done as follows:

1. Select File, Print   [Shift + F7]

A print menu appears as in Figure WP1–27.

2. Press **F** or **1** to select *Full Document* if needed

3. Press **↵** (or **R**) to begin printing

You will be returned to your document as it is printing. Compare the printed version with Figure WP1–26.

Figure WP1–27
WordPerfect's Print/Fax Menu

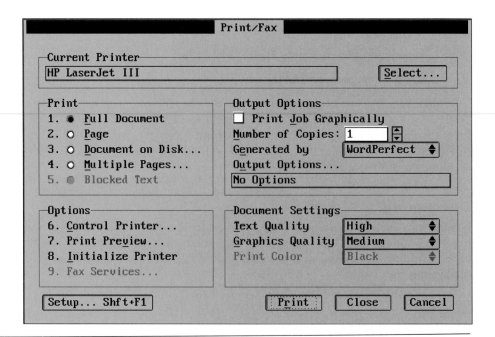

There will be times when you make a correction on one page and do not need to reprint an entire document. Instead, you can print a single page as follows:

1. Position the insertion point on the desired page

(In this example, there is only one page.)

2. Verify that the printer is ready

3. Select File, Print   [Shift + F7]

4. Press **P** or **2** to select *Page*

5. Press **↵** or **R** to begin printing

The single page will print. In the current one-page document, there is no difference between printing the full document and printing one page.

Printing One Page

Checkpoint

☐ Print the entire SAMPLE1 document.

☐ Using the Page feature, print only page 1 of your document (there is only one page).

☐ Use the EXIT command to save your document and exit WordPerfect.

- Word processing is the use of computer technology to create, manipulate, save, and print text materials such as letters, reports, and other documents. Most word processing packages offer the same basic capabilities.
- WordPerfect can be used with a hard-disk drive by first changing to the subdirectory in which WordPerfect is stored; or it can be used in a dual-diskette system by using WordPerfect program disks. It can also be selected from a network menu. The command to initiate WordPerfect is WP.
- The WordPerfect work screen displays an insertion point or cursor, which shows the current typing position, and a status line, which includes messages regarding the document number, page, line, and position of the insertion point in your document.
- The Ln message indicates the vertical position of the insertion point within the current page. The Pos message shows the current horizontal position of the insertion point and also displays the status of Caps Lock, underline, bold, and other enhancement features.
- The left side of the status line may display the filename, the typeover mode status, and other indicators, such as type style.
- The function keys can be used alone or in combination with either the Shift key, the Ctrl key, or the Alt key to invoke 48 different commands. A keyboard template can help you keep track of all the combinations.
- The arrow keys can be used alone to move the insertion point one character in any direction, or in combination with the Home and Ctrl keys to produce larger movements throughout the document.
- Entering text in WordPerfect is much like typing, except that the Enter key should be used only to skip lines or end paragraphs. The Enter key places a hard return in the document, which ends the line and moves the insertion point to the next line.
- Wordwrap occurs when the text that you are entering reaches the right margin. A soft return is automatically added to the text to move the next word onto the next line.

Summary

WP

- The Save command copies the current version of your document from RAM to disk. The Open command copies a file from disk back into RAM.
- WordPerfect can be set to function in either the insert mode or the typeover mode. When WordPerfect is in the insert mode, existing text on the screen is moved to the right to make room for new text that is entered. When the insert toggle is off, the typeover mode allows new text to replace old text on the screen character for character. The word "Typeover" appears on the screen to show that the typeover mode is active.
- Text can be deleted using the Delete key or the Backspace key. The Delete key removes characters at the cursor position and adjusts the remaining characters on the right to fill in. The Backspace key moves the cursor to the left and deletes any character there. The Ctrl and Backspace keys hit together delete one word at a time.
- Text can be enhanced through centering, underlining, and bolding. Centering leaves equal margins on both sides of the text; underlining places an underscore beneath characters; bolding prints characters darker.
- The ultimate destination of most documents is paper, in the form of a printed copy. WordPerfect allows you to print either the full document or selected pages.
- Some of the commands that were presented in this chapter include CANCEL, Help, Clear Screen, Change default drive, Save, Open, Center, Underline, Bold, Print, and Exit.

Key Terms

Shown in parentheses are the page numbers on which key terms are bold.

Backspace key (WP28)
Bold (WP31)
CANCEL command (WP9)
Center feature (WP29)
Delete key (WP27)
Document number (WP6)
Hard return (WP21)

Help feature (WP9)
Insert mode (WP22)
Insertion point (WP6)
Ln message (WP7)
Menu bar (WP6)
Open (WP17)
Pg message (WP7)
Pos message (WP7)
Pull-down menus (WP10)

Soft return (WP21)
Status line (WP6)
Typeover mode (WP25)
Underline (WP30)
Word processing (WP4)
Wordwrap (WP21)

Quiz

True/False

1. The command to start the WordPerfect program is WP.
2. The message "Pos 12" indicates that the Caps Lock toggle is on.
3. The status line is a visual indication of margins and tabs.
4. Pressing the Enter key produces a hard return.
5. The Ins key is used to switch between the insert and typeover modes.
6. The insert mode is on if you can see a filename in the lower left corner of the screen.
7. If you know your document's name, you can retrieve it by pressing the F10 key.
8. The screen should be cleared before retrieving a document.
9. The Enter key should be pressed at the end of each line.
10. WordPerfect lets you print selected pages from a document.

Multiple Choice

11. Which screen component does not normally appear when WordPerfect is started?
    a. dialog box
    b. insertion point
    c. document number
    d. position indicator

12. Which key activates WordPerfect's Help feature?
    a. F10
    b. F1
    c. F5
    d. F7

13. Which key is used to invoke the CANCEL command?
    a. Delete
    b. F7
    c. Esc
    d. End

14. Which function key initiates the WordPerfect Save routine?
    a. F1
    b. F5
    c. F7
    d. F10

15. What is the result of selecting "File, Close" and then the N key twice?
    a. The WordPerfect program is exited.
    b. The screen is cleared.
    c. A document is saved.
    d. A dialog box appears.

16. You need not press the Enter key when you reach the right margin because of the _____ feature.
    a. wordwrap
    b. hard return
    c. typeover
    d. insert

17. Which key deletes text at the insertion point and then moves text from the *right* to fill in?
    a. Backspace
    b. F1
    c. Typeover
    d. Delete

18. After pressing the F5 key in WordPerfect, which key would you next press to change the default drive?
    a. =
    b. /
    c. F1
    d. *

19. WordPerfect's PRINT command is initiated by pressing
    a. F7   c. F10
    b. Shift and F7   d. PrtSc

20. After pressing the F7 key, what is the correct keystroke sequence to exit WordPerfect *without* saving a document?

    a. Y, Y
    b. Y, N
    c. N, N
    d. N, Y

Matching

Select the term that best matches each phrase below:

a. Insertion point
b. Typeover mode
c. Pg message
d. Soft return
e. Hard return
f. Backspace
g. Delete key
h. Center
i. Insert mode
j. Status line
k. Pos message
l. Underline

21. A screen feature that provides information about the insertion point's current location and the modes selected for text entry
22. Displays the current horizontal location of the insertion point and indicates the status of Caps Lock
23. A visual indication of the current position
24. Produced by pressing the Enter key to end a line and move the insertion point to the next line
25. Produced by the automatic wordwrap feature at the end of each line
26. Deletes a character to the left of the insertion point and moves the insertion point one space to the left
27. Positioning text so that the spaces to its left and right are equal
28. A condition in which existing text on the screen moves to the right to make room for new characters being entered
29. A condition in which existing text is replaced character for character by new text
30. A text enhancement in which characters are underscored

Answers

True/False: 1. T; 2. F; 3. F; 4. T; 5. T; 6. T; 7. F; 8. T; 9. F; 10. T
Multiple Choice: 11. a; 12. b; 13. c; 14. d; 15. b; 16. a; 17. d; 18. a; 19. b; 20. d
Matching: 21. j; 22. k; 23. a; 24. e; 25. d; 26. f; 27. h; 28. i; 29. b; 30. l

Exercises

I. Operations

Provide the WordPerfect sequence of keystrokes required to do each of the operations shown below. For each operation, assume a hard-disk system with a floppy disk in Drive A, and further assume the WordPerfect program is in a subdirectory named \WP60. You may wish to verify each command by trying it on your computer system.

1. At the C:\> prompt, start the WordPerfect program.
2. Type your name and date in the upper left of the screen.
3. Insert your class between your name and date. Then, skip a line.

4. Center the words "MASTERING BUSINESS SOFTWARE."

5. Skip two lines.

6. Change the default drive to Drive A.

7. Add the word "PRODUCTIVITY" after the word "BUSINESS" from Exercise 4.

8. Type the word "underlined" underlined, and the word "bold" bold.

9. Save this document as EXWP1–1.

10. Clear the screen.

11. Open the document named EXWP1–1.

12. Save the document as EXWP1–2.

13. Exit the WordPerfect program.

II. Commands

Describe fully, using as few words as possible in each case, what command is initiated, or what is accomplished, in WordPerfect by pressing each series of keystrokes given below. Assume that each exercise part is independent of any previous parts.

Function Key Commands

1. `F8`

2. `Home` , `F7` , `M`

3. `Shift` + `F7`

4. `← Backspace`

5. `Insert`

6. `F1`

7. `↵`

8. `F7` , `N` , `N`

9. `F5` , `=`

10. `F10`

11. `Shift` + `F10`

Pull-Down Menus

1. Font, Underline

2. File, Exit, WP, M

3. File, Print

4. `← Backspace`

5. `Insert`

6. Help

7. `↵`

8. File, Close

9. File, File Manager, `=`

10. File, Save

11. File, Open

III. Applications

Perform the following operations using your computer system. You will need a hard drive or a network with WordPerfect on it, or a DOS disk and WordPerfect program disks. You will also need one additional disk to store the results of this exercise. In a few words, describe how you accomplished each operation, and its result.

Application 1: Job Inquiry

1. Boot your computer, initiate the WordPerfect program, and, if needed, set the default to the drive that contains your data disk.

2. Type the following letter. Make sure to center, underline, and bold as shown. Don't worry if the lines of text do not wrap exactly as shown in the sample. Instead, let wordwrap take effect to control your line breaks within paragraphs.

3. Save this letter as WORK1–1A.

```
                        Hugh Ken Hierme
                    123-456 Job Search Lane
                      New Job, CA 98765


         (Type today's date here)


         Anita Worker
         Mar-Park Consulting Services
         7546 Pleasant Beach Avenue
         San Dinmyshoos, CA 98766


         Dear Ms. Worker:


         In response to your advertisement in yesterday's
         Employment Times, enclosed please find my resume in
         application for the position of cliff diver.

         Although I haven't jumped professionally, I am sure
         that my enclosed history of falling off the Golden Gate
         Bridge, and the Eiffel Tower, will be of interest to
         you.

         I will be available for a job interview as soon as my
         splints and body cast are removed. I look forward to
         hearing from you at your earliest convenience.


         Sincerely,
```

4. Print a copy of the letter.

5. Clear your screen.

6. Open the WORK1–1A document from your data disk.

7. Make the following changes to the second paragraph:

   a. Add the words "off cliffs" after "jumped."

   b. Delete the word "enclosed."

   c. Change the word "falling" to "plummeting."

   d. After the last word, "you," add the sentence "Fortunately, I landed in water both times, which gives me some related experience to the job being offered by your firm."

8. Save this modified letter as WORK1–1B.

9. Print a copy of this new letter.

10. Clear your screen or exit the program.

Application 2: Employer Response

1. Boot your computer, initiate the WordPerfect program, and, if needed, set the default to the drive that contains your data disk.

2. Type the letter on the next page. Make sure to underline and bold as shown. Don't worry if the lines of text do not wrap exactly as shown in the sample. Instead, let wordwrap take effect to control your line breaks within paragraphs.

```
                    Mar-Park Consulting Services
                    7546 Pleasant Beach Avenue
                    San Dinmyshoos, CA 98766


(Type today's date here)

Mr. Hugh Hierme
123-456 Job Search Lane
New Job, CA 98765


Dear Mr. Hierme:


Thank you for your response to our advertisement in
the Employment Times, for the position of cliff
diver. We have had over 400 inquiries from well-
qualified applicants.

Your experience falling off the Golden Gate Bridge
and the Eiffel Tower is of interest to us for two
reasons: it displays your willingness to travel
and shows that you have no fear of extreme heights.

We would like to schedule an interview with you for
next week and will arrange to send a limousine to
bring you, and your body cast, to our offices.
Please call my secretary at 1-800-JUMPNOW to arrange
a time that is convenient. I look forward to meeting
you.


Sincerely,


Anita Worker
Human Resources Director
```

3. Save this letter as WORK1–2A.
4. Print a copy of the letter.
5. Clear your screen.
6. Open the WORK1–2A document from your data disk.
7. Make the following changes to second paragraph:
    a. Add the word "great" before "interest."
    b. Delete the word "extreme."
    c. Change the word "falling" to "plunging."
    d. After the last word, "heights," add the sentence "We would be interested in learning about any bungee jumping or parachuting that you may have done as well. A copy of your current health plan would also be of interest."
8. Save this modified letter as WORK1–2B.
9. Print a copy of this new letter.
10. Clear your screen or exit the program.

Application 3: Memo

1. Boot your computer, initiate the WordPerfect program, and, if needed, set the default to the drive that contains your data disk.

2. Type the following memo. Make sure to center, underline, and bold as shown. Don't worry if the lines of text do not wrap exactly as shown in the sample. Instead, let wordwrap take effect to control your line breaks within paragraphs.

```
                    Mar-Park Consulting Services
                    Inter-Office MEMORANDUM


          TO:  Phil D. Pool, Director
               Cliff Divers Training Center

          FROM:  Anita Worker, Director
                 Human Resources

          DATE:  (insert today's date here)

          SUBJECT:  Interviews for Cliff Divers


          ------------------------------------------------------


          The response to our advertisement in the Employment
          Times has been overwhelming. To date, we have
          received over 400 letters applying for the position
          of cliff diver.

          My staff has finished the initial screening and
          recommends that we invite the top 20 applicants
          to participate in the first round of interviews to
          be held next week.

          We will require the use of the gym and your 40-foot
          model cliff for the performance portion of the
          interview. Please make sure to fill the pool before
          the first test dive.
```

3. Save this memo as WORK1–3A.

4. Print a copy of the memo.

5. Clear your screen.

6. Open the WORK1–3A document from your data disk.

7. Make the following changes to second paragraph:

   a. Add the words "on Tuesday and Wednesday" after "held."

   b. Delete the words "round of."

   c. Change "20" to "25."

   d. After the last word, "week," add the sentence "Please adjust your schedule to join us at that time."

8. Save this modified letter as WORK1–3B.

9. Print a copy of this new memo.

10. Clear your screen or exit the program.

Expanding Word Processing: Enhancing Document Appearance

WP

OBJECTIVES

After completing this chapter you will be able to:

1 Use File Manager to copy, delete, rename, open, print, and look at documents.

2 Describe the purpose of the REVEAL CODES screen and use it to locate and delete text enhancement codes.

3 Explain the use of the BLOCK commands to copy, move, delete, or enhance text blocks.

4 Describe how to change layout parameters (such as margins, tabs, line spacing, justification, and paragraph indentation) and text attributes (base font, appearance, and size).

5 Describe how to search for text strings or replace text with new text throughout the document.

6 Use the WordPerfect auxiliary programs—Speller, Thesaurus, and Grammatik—to modify words in your document.

O V E R V I E W   This chapter extends your use of word processing by presenting additional techniques to understand the screen and to modify text. First, you will learn to use the File Manager screen to manipulate disk files. Then you will examine the hidden codes embedded in your document with REVEAL CODES.

BLOCK commands are introduced to expand your ability to move or adjust large areas of text quickly. You will then learn how to modify layout parameters, including margins, tabs, spacing, justification, and text attributes. The chapter then presents search-and-replace techniques for changing text. Finally, the chapter examines three WordPerfect auxiliary programs—Speller, Thesaurus, and Grammar Check—which can locate potential errors and improve the vocabulary of your document.

Using File Manager

WordPerfect offers a number of useful file management commands that let you manage your files without having to return to DOS. These commands are contained in one easy-to-use screen, invoked by the File Manager command. **File Manager** is a WordPerfect feature that provides a file directory and menu from which file management commands may be selected.

First, boot your computer and get to a blank WordPerfect screen. In a network, start WordPerfect normally. Here's a reminder of the steps in other systems:

Hard-Disk System

1. Boot up the system and get to the C:\> prompt

2. Insert your data disk into Drive A

3. Type **CD \WP60** (or the name of *your* subdirectory)

4. Press ⏎

5. Type **WP** and press ⏎

Now change the default drive to A as follows:

6. Press **F5** **=**

7. Type **A:** and press ⏎ **Esc**

Dual-Diskette System

1. Place your DOS start-up disk in Drive A, boot up the system, and get to the A> prompt

2. Insert the WordPerfect program disk 1 into Drive A

3. Insert your data disk into Drive B

4. Type **WP** and press ⏎

5. Replace the WordPerfect program disk 1 with the WordPerfect program disk 2 when instructed to do so

6. Press ⏎

Now change the default drive to B as follows:

7. Press **F5** **=**

8. Type **B:** and press ⏎ **Esc**

To initiate the File Manager screen, do the following:

1. Select File, File Manager [F5]

Your screen should display the proper default drive as the directory.

2. If it doesn't, change it now

3. Press ⏎

A File Manager screen should appear as in Figure WP2–1. Although your screen contents may differ, the screen should display the files contained on your data disk. At the top left is the current disk (and subdirectory, if any) being displayed— in this example, the root directory of the disk in Drive A. The second line shows the current sort order of the file display (in this case, filename). The bottom line shows the number of files on the disk, total disk space available, and space used.

As seen in Figure WP2–1, the left part of the screen displays up to 17 filenames at one time. Notice, too, that the files are listed in alphabetical order. Subdirectories are listed first, followed by files. *Note:* The "Current" and "Parent" lines at the top of the list are *not* column headings. They are used to change directories (as you will soon see).

A menu appears at the right of the screen. To issue commands in File Manager, press the arrow keys to highlight the file you want to use, and then press the number (or letter) of the desired menu selection. The following exercises demonstrate a few of these commands. *Note:* To stop at any time, press the Esc key to cancel the File Manager.

☞ **Tip: Because File Manager has its own menu, the menu bar does not work in this screen.**

Initiating the File Manager Screen

WP

Use *Copy* to copy the highlighted file into this, or another, disk or directory. Try this exercise:

1. Press the arrow keys to move the highlight to the SAMPLE1 file

Copying a File

Figure WP2–1

The File Manager Screen

The File Manager Screen displays files in the current directory and a list of command options at the right of the screen. (Your list may differ.)

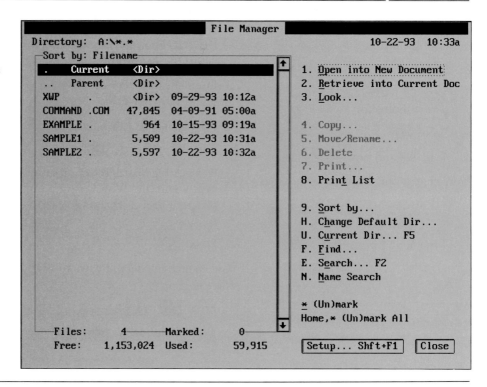

2. Press **C** or **4** for *Copy* (or click the *Copy* line with a mouse)

The screen asks "Copy Highlighted File to:_" and awaits your reply.

3. Type **TEST** and press **↵**

The file will be copied into the same directory. Of course, you could copy a file to another directory or disk by including the complete path in the filename (as in *A:\XWP\TEST*).

Now that you have created a new file, its name appears in the list in proper order.

Moving/ Renaming a File

Use *Move/Rename* to change a file's name or move it to another disk or directory. This example will rename the TEST file.

1. Highlight the TEST filename

2. Press **M** or **5** for *Move/Rename* (or click it)

3. Type **NEWTEST** and press **↵**

Notice that "NEWTEST" replaces "TEST" on the list (in alphabetical order). If you had added a disk or directory identifier to the name (such as A:\XWP\NEWTEST), the file would have been moved to the new location.

Looking at a File

The **Look** function lets you view the highlighted file *without* opening it in WordPerfect. This is useful if you simply want to see a document's contents. It will not change the document, nor will it alter the document on which you are currently working.

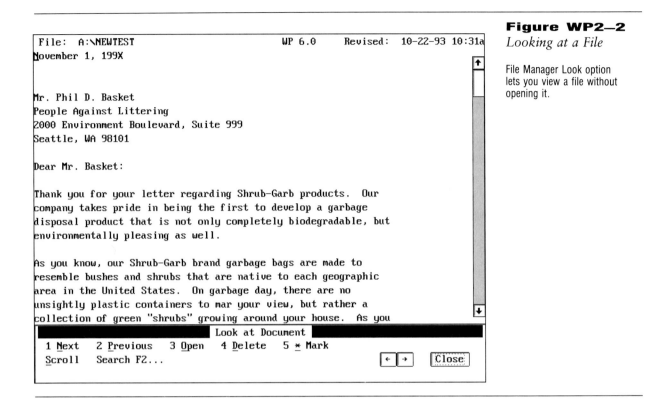

Figure WP2–2
Looking at a File

File Manager Look option lets you view a file without opening it.

1. Highlight the NEWTEST file

2. Press **L** or **3** or **↵** to *Look*

A screen similar to Figure WP2–2 appears. Notice that it looks different from the normal WordPerfect screen. The menu at the bottom lets you look at other documents (next or previous on the list). You can also open or delete the current document on the screen.

To move through the document,

3. Press **↓** (or **Pg Dn**)

You can use the Up and Down arrow keys (or other arrow keys with Home or Ctrl) to look through the document as much as you want.

4. Press **↵** to return to the File Manager

You can view another directory easily in File Manager. Try this:

Viewing Another Directory

1. Highlight the **XWP <DIR>** line

☞ **Tip: The XWP directory was created earlier, see p. WP4.**

☞ **Tip: The XWP directory was created earlier, see p. WP4.**

2. Press **↵**

This tells WordPerfect to read the XWP directory. No files are currently saved in it, as you can see. To return to the root directory of your disk,

3. Highlight **Parent <DIR>** in the list

4. Press **↵**

Figure WP2–3
Printing Selected Pages

(a) The Print Multiple Pages
screen is usually set to print all
pages. (b) The screen has been
set to print page 1. (partial
screens)

```
┌──────────────────────────────────────────────────┐
│███████████████  Print Multiple Pages  ████████████│
│                                                    │
│  1. Page/Label Range:   │(all)                   │ │
│  2. Secondary Page(s):  │                        │ │
│  3. Chapter(s):         │                        │ │
│  4. Volume(s):          │                        │ │
│                                                    │
│  5. Odd/Even Pages  │Both ◆│                      │
│                                                    │
│  6. ☐ Document Summary                            │
│  7. ☐ Print as Booklet                            │
│  8. ☐ Descending Order (Last Page First)          │
│                                                    │
│                          │ OK │  │Cancel│          │
└──────────────────────────────────────────────────┘
```
(a)

```
┌──────────────────────────────────────────────────┐
│███████████████  Print Multiple Pages  ████████████│
│                                                    │
│  1. Page/Label Range:   │1                       │ │
│  2. Secondary Page(s):  │                        │ │
│  3. Chapter(s):         │                        │ │
│  4. Volume(s):          │                        │ │
│                                                    │
│  5. Odd/Even Pages  │Both ◆│                      │
│                                                    │
│  6. ☐ Document Summary                            │
│  7. ☐ Print as Booklet                            │
│  8. ☐ Descending Order (Last Page First)          │
│                                                    │
│                          │ OK │  │Cancel│          │
└──────────────────────────────────────────────────┘
```
(b)

Printing a File

In the last chapter, you learned how to print your current document. You can also print documents directly from the File Manager. Use the *Print* function to send one (or more) of these documents to the printer. You can print an entire document or select a range of pages.

First, make sure that your printer is ready—that its power is on and it is connected to your computer. The following exercises show you how to print either the entire NEWTEST document or just one page.

Printing a Complete Document.   To print the entire NEWTEST document, do the following:

1.   Highlight NEWTEST

2.   Press **P** or **7** to *Print*

A "Print Multiple Pages" menu appears. Note the "(all)" that is shown in item 1, as in Figure WP2–3a.

3.   Press **↵** to print all pages

The File Manager screen returns and the document will begin to print. You may now continue without waiting for it to finish. This is called **background printing**.

Option	Example	The Program Will Print:
X	2	Page X only
X Y or X,Y	2 6 or 2,6	Pages X and Y
X-	6-	From Page X to the end
X-Y	3-8	Pages X through Y
-X	-9	From the beginning through Page X

Figure WP2—4
Some Examples of Printing Selected Page Ranges

WordPerfect keeps a copy of the document in a special printer *buffer* (memory area), freeing the program for your continued work. You may open a document, continue to use File Manager, or even select other files to print. WordPerfect will store additional files in the order you select them, and print them in sequence.

Selecting Pages.   To select specific pages to print (in this example, page 1 of NEWTEST), do the following:

1.   Highlight NEWTEST

2.   Press **P** or **7** to *Print*

As before, "(all)" appears on the screen. To indicate the first page only,

3.   Type **P** for *Page/Label Range*

4.   Type **1** and press **↵** as in Figure WP2–3b

5.   Press **↵**

The page will be printed. Of course, you could indicate any page range in Step 4 by typing one or more of the commands displayed in Figure WP2–4. For example, typing *2,8,11-16,20-* prints page 2, page 8, pages 11 through 16, and all the pages from page 20 to the end of the document.

Deleting a File

Use the *Delete* function to remove a file from the disk. Try deleting the NEWTEST file as follows:

1. Highlight NEWTEST

2. Press **D** or **6** to *Delete*

Your screen asks if you really want to delete the file. Pressing the Enter key (or the N key) would cancel the DELETE command. Instead,

3. Press **Y** to delete

The file is deleted and its name is immediately removed from the list.

☞ **Tip: You can also press the Delete key to delete the highlighted file.**

Marking Files

At times, you may want to use an option on more than one file at a time. To do this, use an asterisk (*) to *mark* several files before you select an option. When you invoke the option, it will be performed on all the marked files in succession.

Figure WP2–5

Marking Multiple Files

SAMPLE1 has been marked for use with an asterisk.

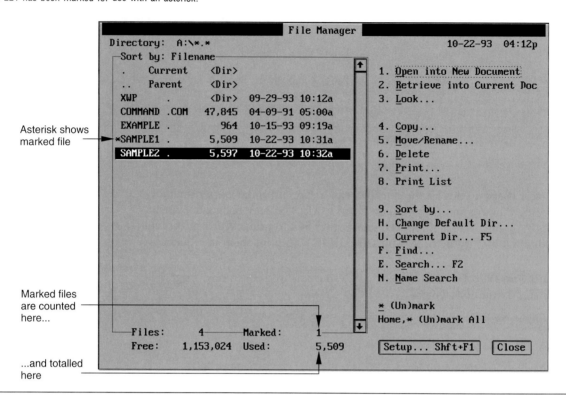

Asterisk shows
marked file

Marked files
are counted
here...

...and totalled
here

In this exercise, you will practice marking two files for copying to another subdirectory:

1. Move to SAMPLE1

2. Press **Space** or ***** to mark it

The SAMPLE1 file should now be marked with an asterisk as in Figure WP2–5. Note that as files are marked, they are counted in the *Marked* area and their sizes are totaled in *Used*.

3. Move to SAMPLE2 if needed

4. Press **Space** or *****

☞ **Tip:** If you change your mind, you can *unmark* a file by repeating the procedure (high-light the filename and press the space bar or asterisk key) to remove the asterisk mark. You can also press Home * to mark (or unmark) *all* files.

Now, copy the two marked files to the \XWP subdirectory:

5. Press **C** or **4** to *Copy*

The screen asks "Copy marked files?"

6. Press **Y** to select "Yes"

When the screen responds with "Copy Marked Files to:"

7. Type **\XWP** and press **↵**

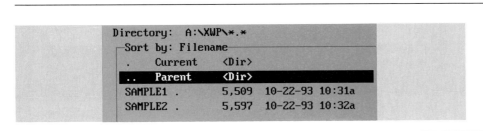

Figure WP2—6
Changing Directories

The \XWP subdirectory is
displayed. (partial screen)

The files will be copied to the \XWP subdirectory. Now, delete these new files using the marked files approach. First, change the directory:

8. Press **Home** and then ***** to unmark the files

9. Highlight "XWP <Dir>" and press **↵**

The \XWP directory should appear as in Figure WP2–6.

10. Mark SAMPLE1 and SAMPLE2 with asterisks (or press **Home** ***** to mark both)

11. Press **D** or **6** (or **Delete**)

The screen asks "Delete marked files?"

12. Press **Y**

The screen warns "Marked files will be deleted. Continue?"

13. Press **Y**

The marked files are gone. Now change the default back to the root directory before continuing. Here's a quick way:

14. Highlight the line ". . Parent <Dir>"

15. Press **↵**

☞ **Tip: To move to another directory, highlight its name and press the Enter key. To move to the root directory, use "Parent <Dir>."**

Searching for a Filename

As you have seen when selecting a file, you can use the arrow keys (or mouse) to highlight a desired filename. However, this is cumbersome when there are many files on your disk. One alternative is to press the PgDn key to "jump" a screen at a time. You can also use WordPerfect's *Name Search* feature to quickly locate files. Even though the current disk list is small, you can practice the technique to locate the SAMPLE2 file. While in File Manager,

1. Press **N** for *Name Search*

A box appears at the lower left of your screen.

2. Type **SAMPLE2**

As you type each character, the highlight moves to the first file that matches the search criteria.

3. Press **↵** to end the search

Once you end the search, you can choose the option you want to perform, move the highlight to another file, or exit the File Manager.

Figure WP2–7
Sorting a File List

(a) The File Manager setup
screen lets you change the sort
order (partial screen). (b) The
File List has been sorted by
extension.

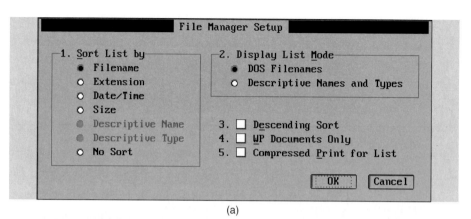

(a)

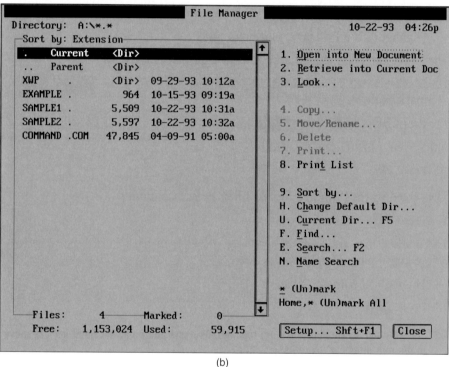

(b)

**Sorting a
File List**

By default, File Manager presents files in alphabetical order by filename. However,
you can easily rearrange the list by extension, date and time, or size as needed.
For example, in the File Manager,

1. Press **S** (or **9**) to select *Sort by* . . .

A "File Manager Setup" box appears as in WP2–7a. Note that the current sort
setting is "Filename."

2. Press **S** (or **1**) to select *Sort List by* . . .

You can now choose the new sort pattern. In this example,

3. Press **E** (or **2**) to select *Extension*

4. Press **↵** to accept

As shown in Figure WP2–7b, the filename list has been rearranged appropriately and a "Sort by: Extension" message appears at the top of the list.

5. Switch back to filename order (press **S** **S** **F** and **↵**)

Searching for Text

Another useful feature of File Manager is its ability to search files for specific text and restrict the file list to only those files that contain the desired text. For example, what if you wanted to find all files that contained the name "Basket." Try this:

1. Invoke the File Manager if needed

2. Press **F** to select *Find*

A "Find" box appears.

3. Press **E** (or **4**) to select *Entire Document*

You can now type the desired text. In this example,

4. Type **Basket** and press **↵**

When the program finishes its search, the File Manager list will display only those files that contain the search phrase. You could then continue to use File Manager normally. *Note:* The effects of the search will be canceled when you exit from the File Manager.

Opening a File

You already know that File Manager can be used to open a document. This exercise opens your SAMPLE2 document:

1. Move the highlight to **SAMPLE2**

2. Press **O** or **1**

If the query "Retrieve into current document?" appears, then you still have a document in memory. Press N to answer "no," press the Esc key to exit, then clear your screen, reenter File Manager, and repeat Steps 1 and 2.

You are now back in the work screen with SAMPLE2 ready to be edited.

Checkpoint

☐ Use File Manager to copy SAMPLE1 to CHECK1 on the XWP subdirectory; then switch to the \XWP directory.

☐ Rename CHECK1 as CHECK2; print CHECK2.

☐ Delete CHECK2, return to the parent directory, and exit File Manager.

Understanding REVEAL CODES

Before tackling format changes, you should understand the hidden codes that determine your document's appearance. WordPerfect does not normally display formatting codes, but "hides" them within your document. These codes are generated every time you issue commands for such effects as hard return, bold, underline, center, line spacing, and margins. They take effect *at the insertion point location at which they are invoked* until they are removed or superseded by another command. Understanding the placement of these codes, and how to remove them, is essential, and you must learn to recognize and locate them in

Figure WP2–8

REVEAL CODES

Some of the codes used by
WordPerfect to format text.

Code	Definition
[-Hyphen]	Hyphen character
[Block]	Beginning of block
[Bold On/Off]	Bold (on or off)
[Cntr on Mar]	Center (on Margin)
[Font]	Font
[Footer A or B]	Footer (A or B)
[Footnote]	Footnote
[Header A or B]	Header (A or B)
[HPg]	Hard page break (forced)
[HRt]	Hard return (Enter key)
[Italc On/Off]	Italics (on or off)
[Lft Indent]	Indent
[Just]	Justification
[Ln Spacing]	Line spacing setting
[L/R Mar]	Left and right margins
[Pg Num]	New page number
[Pg Numbering]	Page numbering
[SPg]	Soft page break
[SRt]	Soft return (wordwrap)
[T/B Margins]	Top and bottom margins
[Lft Tab]	Left Tab
[Tab Set]	Tab setting
[Und On/Off]	Underline (on or off)

your document. WordPerfect's **REVEAL CODES** feature makes it easy by displaying these hidden codes. Figure WP2–8 presents a few of the WordPerfect codes.

Although you may invoke the REVEAL CODES command at any point in a document, this exercise requires that you be at the start of SAMPLE2, so prepare your computer as follows:

1. Open SAMPLE2 if it is not on your screen
2. Move to the start of the document

The REVEAL CODES screen
displays the original document at
the top and reveals all hidden
codes in the bottom half of the
screen.

```
 File  Edit  View  Layout  Tools  Font  Graphics  Window  Help
                          Shrub-Garb Products
                          1234 Clean Street
                          Anytown, IL 67890


          November 1, 199X


          Mr. Phil D. Basket
          People Against Littering
          2000 Environment Boulevard
          Seattle, WA 98101

          Dear Mr. Basket:

          Thank you for your recent letter regarding Shrub-Garb products.
          Our company takes great pride in being the first to develop a
          garbage disposal product that is not only biodegradable, but
          environmentally pleasing as well.

          As you know, our durable and popular Shrub-Garb garbage bags are
          made to resemble bushes and shrubs that are native to each
  {    ▲    ▲    ▲    ▲    ▲    ▲    ▲    ▲    ▲    ▲    ▲    ▲    }
 [Open Style:InitialCodes][Just][Cntr on Mar]Shrub[- Hyphen]Garb Products[HRt]
 [Cntr on Mar]1234 Clean Street[HRt]
 [Cntr on Mar]Anytown, IL 67890[HRt]
 [HRt]
 [HRt]
 A:\SAMPLE2                              Doc 1 Pg 1 Ln 1" Pos 1"
```

To initiate the REVEAL CODES feature as shown in Figure WP2–9,

1. Select <u>V</u>iew, Reveal <u>C</u>odes   [Alt + F3]

☞ **Tip: The F11 key on the extended keyboard will also invoke REVEAL CODES.**

REVEAL CODES can be turned off just as easily. To return to the normal work
screen,

2. Select <u>V</u>iew, Reveal <u>C</u>odes   [Alt + F3 or F11]

*Initiating
and
Exiting
REVEAL
CODES*

Turn REVEAL CODES on again so that you can examine it closely:

1. Press **F11** this time

As shown in Figure WP2–9, REVEAL CODES divides your screen in two: the
top of the screen is the normal work screen; the bottom part displays your text
with the hidden codes revealed. A ruler line divides the two parts.

Note that the insertion point is resting on Line 1″, Pos 1″ of your document.
Although the top screen does not show them, there are a few codes in the lower
part of the screen that should be recognizable to you. On the first line alone,
there are three: the [*Cntr on Mar*] code centers the line; there is a hyphen
[*-Hyphen*] in "Shrub-Garb"; and there is a hard return [*HRt*] (generated when
you pressed the Enter key to end the line). As shown by the highlighting, the
cursor is now resting on the [Cntr on Mar] code.

You can move freely throughout the REVEAL CODES screen without harm-
ing your document. Use the arrow keys to see this effect:

2. Press ↓ 14 times to move below the salutation

*Reading
the
REVEAL
CODES
Screen*

Figure WP2—10

Deleting Formatting Codes

The [Center on Mar] code has been highlighted prior to its deletion in REVEAL CODES.

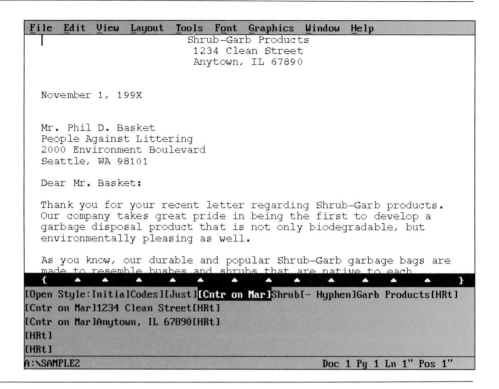

As you move, note how both screens *scroll*, or roll upward, to reveal each new line. You can see a soft return [SRt] or a hard return [HRt] at the end of each line.

3. Press **Home** **Home** **↓** to go to the document's end

Note the [*Bold On*] code, which shows the start of the bold text enhancement, and [*Bold Off*], which shows where bold ends.

4. Press **F11**

to return to the regular screen.

Deleting Text Enhancements

REVEAL CODES can be used effectively to locate and remove unwanted codes, such as those for centering, underlining, bolding, and hard returns. Any code displayed in REVEAL CODES can be deleted by positioning the cursor appropriately and then pressing the Del or Backspace key, just as you would to delete "normal" text.

☞ **Tip: You can leave REVEAL CODES on as you work. Insert, delete, or modify text as you normally would, while watching the changes both on the upper part of the screen and in the lower, "revealed codes," part as well.**

Try the following exercises:

1. Invoke the REVEAL CODES feature (by key or menu)

2. Move to the start of your document

3. Highlight the [Cntr on Mar] code in the lower part of the screen, as in Figure WP2—10

4. Press `Delete`

The [Cntr on Mar] code disappears from the screen and, because the code is gone, the first heading line is no longer centered.

5. Highlight and delete the other two [Cntr on Mar] codes

One more:

6. Highlight the [Bold On] code on the last line of your document

(Note that the code, once highlighted, also displays the type style and size.)

7. Press `Delete`

The [Bold On] and [Bold off] codes have both been removed, and the bold text in your document has returned to its normal state. You can use this technique to locate and remove any format change that you no longer want in your document, including all the features listed in Figure WP2–8.

8. Turn off REVEAL CODES
9. Save this amended document as **SAMPLE3**

Checkpoint

☐ On a clear screen, type a few sentences, including some centered, bold, and underlined words. Print the page.

☐ Use REVEAL CODES to locate and delete the text enhancements (bold, underline, center). Print the page.

☐ Clear the screen without saving.

BLOCK Commands

BLOCK commands allow you to edit or format complete words, sentences, paragraphs, or entire documents at one time. A **block** is a segment of contiguous text. It can be as small as one character or as large as a document. The following exercises let you experiment with BLOCK commands for moving, copying, deleting, formatting, and saving. To prepare for these exercises,

1. Start WordPerfect or clear the screen
2. Open SAMPLE2 for use

Identifying a block is a three-step process: (1) move to the start of the block; (2) turn on the Block feature; and then (3) move to the end of the block. Try this:

Identifying a Block

1. Move your insertion point to the "M" in "Mr. Phil D. Basket" (as shown in Figure WP2–11a)

To turn on the Block feature,

2. Select <u>E</u>dit, <u>B</u>lock   [Alt + F4]

☞ **Tip: The F12 key on the extended keyboard will also invoke the Block feature (and is recommended).**

Figure WP2—11
Using BLOCK Commands

(a) The insertion point is positioned at the start of a text block. (b) Moving the insertion point after invoking the BLOCK command highlights the desired block.

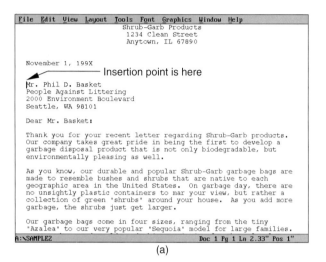
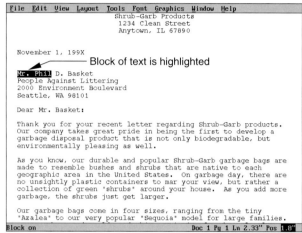

(a)　　　　　　　　　　　　　　　(b)

The words "Block on" appear in the lower left corner of your screen, showing that the Block feature is active. Note, too, the Pos number indicates highlighting.

3.　Press →　eight times

This positions your insertion point past the word "Phil," as in Figure WP2–11b, with the block of text highlighted on your screen. You have successfully identified a block.

4.　Press ←　eight times to move back to the "M"

Notice that the highlight shrinks as you move back. You may change the amount of text included in a block by moving the cursor until you are satisfied. In fact, you can mark blocks with any cursor movement you know. For example, to highlight the entire line,

5.　Press ↓

If you change your mind, you can press the Esc key to cancel the command, or just turn off the Block feature as follows:

6.　Select Edit, Block　　　　　　　　　　　　　　　　　　[Alt + F4]

Once a block has been identified, you can then invoke other commands that will affect the entire block. The following exercises demonstrate various commands that work with blocks of text. (*Note:* You can also use a mouse to identify a block. Simply point to the start, press and hold the left mouse button, and move to the end and release.)

Cutting and Pasting a Block

Cutting and pasting (or "block move") is a process that lets you identify a block of text and move it anywhere in a document (or into another file). In this exercise, you will move Phil's name beneath the name of the company in the address.

1.　Open SAMPLE2 if it is not on your screen

Now identify the entire name line as a block:

2. Move to the "M" in "Mr. Phil D. Basket"

3. Invoke the Block feature (with Edit, Block)   [Alt + F4]

4. Press ↓

The line is highlighted as a block. Now invoke the cut and paste command as follows:

5. Select Edit   [Ctrl + F4]

If you used the menu, an Edit menu will appear as in WP2–12a. (If you used Ctrl + F4, a "Move Block" box will appear as in WP2–12b.)

6. Select Cut and Paste (**E** in menu or **T** in Move box)

At this point, the block disappears from the screen, and the message "Move cursor . . ." appears. In effect, you have "cut" the block from your document and placed it into a temporary holding area. It is not lost, but merely awaiting your command to "paste" it back in.

7. Press ↓ to go to the next line

8. Press ↵

The block is now in its new location, as in Figure WP2–13a.

9. Save this document as **SAMPLE4**

Copying a Block

A *block copy* is a process that lets you identify a block of text and duplicate it anywhere in the document (or in another file). It is identical to block move except that the original block stays where it is; it is not cut before it is pasted elsewhere. To perform a block copy, follow the same steps as for a block move, but select *Copy and Paste* instead of *Cut and Paste* in Step 6. For example,

1. Open SAMPLE4 if it is not on your screen
2. Position the insertion point at the "M" in "Mr. Phil"
3. Block the "Mr. Phil D. Basket" line
4. Select *Copy and Paste* (**Y** in menu or **C** in Move box)

This time, the block does not disappear from the screen, but you are instructed (as before) to "Move cursor."

5. Press ↑ twice

6. Press ↵ to accept the new position

The block is copied, as in Figure WP2–13b. (If you have an extra line beneath "Phil," delete it.)

7. Save this document again as **SAMPLE4**

Moving or Copying "Standard" Blocks

More often than not, your text block may be a "standard" size—a complete sentence, paragraph, or a page. If so, WordPerfect provides an easy way to move or copy it. Simply skip the block identification and go right to the MOVE command. Try this example:

1. Open SAMPLE4 if it is not on your screen
2. Move to the "T" in "Thank" at the beginning of the first paragraph
3. Select Edit, Select   [Ctrl + F4]

Figure WP2–12
Cutting and Pasting

(a) An Edit menu appears if you used the menu. (b) A "Move Block" box appears if you used Ctrl + F4.

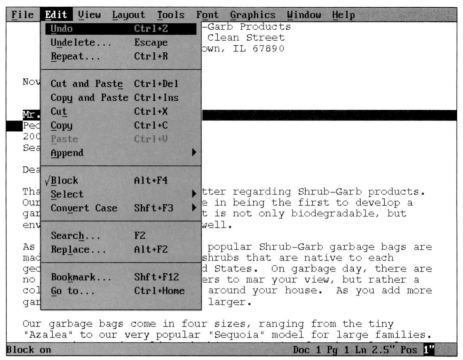

(a)

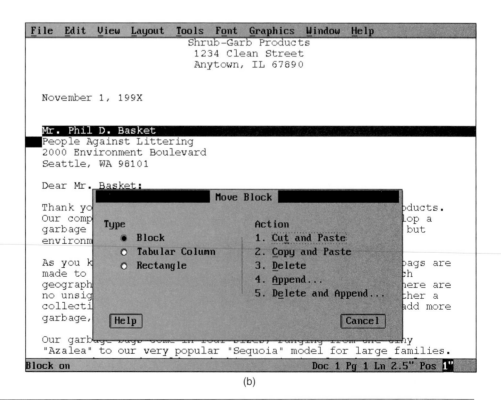

(b)

```
File   Edit   View   Layout   Tools   Font   Graphics   Window   Help
                         Shrub-Garb Products
                          1234 Clean Street
                          Anytown, IL 67890


        November 1, 199X


        People Against Littering
        Mr. Phil D. Basket
        2000 Environment Boulevard
        Seattle, WA 98101

        Dear Mr. Basket:

        Thank you for your recent letter regarding Shrub-Garb products.
        Our company takes great pride in being the first to develop a
        garbage disposal product that is not only biodegradable, but
        environmentally pleasing as well.
```

(a)

```
File   Edit   View   Layout   Tools   Font   Graphics   Window   Help
                         Shrub-Garb Products
                          1234 Clean Street
                          Anytown, IL 67890


        November 1, 199X


        Mr. Phil D. Basket
        People Against Littering
        Mr. Phil D. Basket
        2000 Environment Boulevard
        Seattle, WA 98101

        Dear Mr. Basket:

        Thank you for your recent letter regarding Shrub-Garb products.
        Our company takes great pride in being the first to develop a
        garbage disposal product that is not only biodegradable, but
        environmentally pleasing as well.

        As you know, our durable and popular Shrub-Garb garbage bags are
        made to resemble bushes and shrubs that are native to each
        geographic area in the United States.  On garbage day, there are
        no unsightly plastic containers to mar your view, but rather a
        collection of green "shrubs" around your house.  As you add more
        garbage, the shrubs just get larger.

        Our garbage bags come in four sizes, ranging from the tiny
```

(b)

Figure WP2–13
Moving and Copying Text Blocks

(a) Moving the block.
(b) Copying the block.

A menu asks you which standard block you want to move: "Sentence, Paragraph, Page."

4. Press **S** or **1** for *Sentence*

Notice how the entire sentence is highlighted, as in Figure WP2–14. As before, the menu asks what to do with the block: Cut and Paste, Copy and Paste, Delete, Append, and so on. The rest of the procedure is the same as you've already learned. For now,

5. Select *Cut and Paste*

Typically, you would now move to a new location, but for this exercise,

6. Press **↵**

Figure WP2–14

Marking Standard Text Blocks

Standard-sized blocks can be easily marked directly with Ctrl + F4.

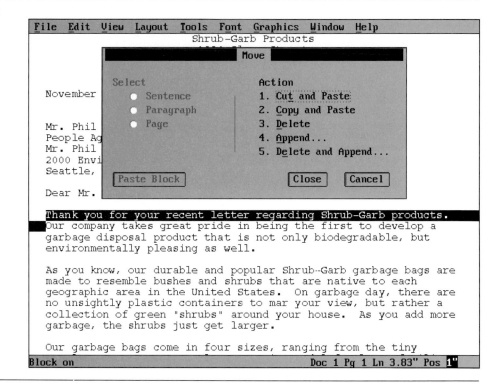

This puts the sentence back in the same place. You can use this technique to move, copy, or even delete entire sentences, paragraphs, or pages.

Deleting a Block

A *block delete* is a process that lets you identify a block of text and remove it. It is similar to a block move except that the block is simply cut from the document; it is not pasted back. Although you could follow the same steps as for a block move, except select *Delete*, there is a simpler way. Try this exercise:

1. Open SAMPLE4 if it is not on your screen

To block the *second* "Mr. Phil D. Basket" line as in Figure WP2–15a,

2. Move to the "M" at the start of the block

3. Select Edit, Block   [Alt + F4]

4. Press ↓

5. Press **Delete**

The block is deleted, as in Figure WP2–15b. As with any other deleted text, if you make a mistake in block deletions, you can always press the Esc key and 1 to restore the last cut you made.

☞ **Tip: You can also retrieve the last block placed into the temporary holding area by pressing the Ctrl and F4 keys and then P (for Paste).**

Block Enhancements

A **block enhancement** is a process that lets you identify a block of text and change its formatting. Perhaps you want to underline or bold text, or center an existing heading. First,

1. Clear your screen
2. Open SAMPLE3

Figure WP2–15

Deleting a Block

(a) The block is marked. (b) The block is deleted.

```
 File   Edit   View   Layout   Tools   Font   Graphics   Window   Help
                          Shrub-Garb Products
                            1234 Clean Street
                            Anytown, IL 67890


         November 1, 199X


         Mr. Phil D. Basket
         People Against Littering
         Mr. Phil D. Basket
         2000 Environment Boulevard
         Seattle, WA 98101

         Dear Mr. Basket:

         Thank you for your recent letter regarding Shrub-Garb products.
         Our company takes great pride in being the first to develop a
         garbage disposal product that is not only biodegradable, but
         environmentally pleasing as well.

         As you know, our durable and popular Shrub-Garb garbage bags are
         made to resemble bushes and shrubs that are native to each
         geographic area in the United States.  On garbage day, there are
         no unsightly plastic containers to mar your view, but rather a
         collection of green "shrubs" around your house.  As you add more
         garbage, the shrubs just get larger.

         Our garbage bags come in four sizes, ranging from the tiny
 Block on                                     Doc 1 Pg 1 Ln 2.83" Pos 1"
```

(a)

```
 File   Edit   View   Layout   Tools   Font   Graphics   Window   Help
                          Shrub-Garb Products
                            1234 Clean Street
                            Anytown, IL 67890


         November 1, 199X


         Mr. Phil D. Basket
         People Against Littering
         2000 Environment Boulevard
         Seattle, WA 98101

         Dear Mr. Basket:

         Thank you for your recent letter regarding Shrub-Garb products.
         Our company takes great pride in being the first to develop a
         garbage disposal product that is not only biodegradable, but
         environmentally pleasing as well.

         As you know, our durable and popular Shrub-Garb garbage bags are
         made to resemble bushes and shrubs that are native to each
         geographic area in the United States.  On garbage day, there are
         no unsightly plastic containers to mar your view, but rather a
         collection of green "shrubs" around your house.  As you add more
         garbage, the shrubs just get larger.

         Our garbage bags come in four sizes, ranging from the tiny
         "Azalea" to our very popular "Sequoia" model for large families.
 A:\SAMPLE4                                   Doc 1 Pg 1 Ln 2.67" Pos 1"
```

(b)

WP

The following exercises demonstrate each of these techniques.

Center. This document's heading is no longer centered. You can use the BLOCK command to center it once again.

1. Put the insertion point on the "S" in "Shrub-Garb"

2. Select <u>E</u>dit, <u>B</u>lock   [Alt + F4 or F12]

3. Press ↓ three times

The entire heading is now identified as the block.

4. Select <u>L</u>ayout, <u>A</u>lign, <u>C</u>enter   [Shift + F6]

The block is centered.

5. Save the document as **SAMPLE5**

Underline and Bold. Block enhancements of underline and bold are performed in a similar manner—just identify the block and invoke the enhancement. For example,

1. Open SAMPLE5 if needed
2. Move to the "e" in "environmentally" in the last line of the first paragraph
3. Identify the block "environmentally pleasing"
4. Select <u>F</u>ont, <u>U</u>nderline   [F8]
5. Save this document again as **SAMPLE5**

Uppercase and Lowercase. If you want to change all the letters in a block to uppercase or lowercase form without having to retype them, you can use WordPerfect's Switch feature. Try this:

1. Open SAMPLE5 if needed
2. Move to the "S" in "Shrub-Garb" in the heading
3. Identify the block "Shrub-Garb Products"
4. Select <u>E</u>dit, Con<u>v</u>ert Case   [Shift + F3]

A menu appears offering "Uppercase, Lowercase, Initial Caps."

5. Press **U** for *Uppercase*

The text has been changed accordingly. (You can also switch text to lowercase or initial caps—first letter capitalized—the same way.)

6. Resave as **SAMPLE5**

Saving a Block

Sometimes you may want to save a block of text so that you can recall it for later use. In the SAMPLE5 document, assume that you want to save the second paragraph (the one that starts with "As you know. . .").

1. Open SAMPLE5 if needed
2. Move the insertion point to the first character in the second paragraph—the "A" in "As"
3. Block the entire paragraph and the line beneath it

Your screen should resemble Figure WP2–16. If it does not, press the Esc key and repeat these steps.

4. Select <u>F</u>ile, Save <u>A</u>s   [F10]

```
 File  Edit  View  Layout  Tools  Font  Graphics  Window  Help
                       SHRUB-GARB PRODUCTS
                         1234 Clean Street
                         Anytown, IL 67890


    November 1, 199X


    Mr. Phil D. Basket
    People Against Littering
    2000 Environment Boulevard
    Seattle, WA 98101

    Dear Mr. Basket:

    Thank you for your recent letter regarding Shrub-Garb products.
    Our company takes great pride in being the first to develop a
    garbage disposal product that is not only biodegradable, but
    environmentally pleasing as well.

    As you know, our durable and popular Shrub-Garb garbage bags are
    made to resemble bushes and shrubs that are native to each
    geographic area in the United States.  On garbage day, there are
    no unsightly plastic containers to mar your view, but rather a
    collection of green "shrubs" around your house.  As you add more
    garbage, the shrubs just get larger.

    Our garbage bags come in four sizes, ranging from the tiny
    "Azalea" to our very popular "Sequoia" model for large families.
 Block on                                Doc 1 Pg 1 Ln 5.5" Pos 1"
```

Normally, the F10 key saves the entire document. However, when the Block feature is active, the F10 key will save only the highlighted block. A "Save Block" dialog box will appear.

5. Type **GARBAGE** as the block's filename

6. Press ⏎ to save it

7. Clear your screen

Stored text blocks can be opened just like any other disk file.

1. Select <u>F</u>ile, <u>O</u>pen   [Shift + F10]

2. Type **GARBAGE** and press ⏎

The paragraph appears on your screen.

You can also add text blocks to an existing document by invoking the RETRIEVE command while the document is on the screen:

3. Move to the bottom of the document

4. Select <u>F</u>ile, <u>R</u>etrieve   [Shift + F10]

5. Type **GARBAGE** and press ⏎

There are now two paragraphs on your screen: the one that was there, and the block that was just added to it.

☞ **Tip: Block files can also be retrieved with the File Manager as any file can. To add new material to a document already in memory, highlight a file and then select *Retrieve* from the menu.**

6. Clear the screen

WP

Checkpoint

☐ Use the F5 key to retrieve the GARBAGE file. Copy the first sentence to the end of the document.

☐ Block underline and then block uppercase the words in the last sentence.

☐ Block save the last sentence only as GARBAGE2; then clear the screen.

Changing Layout Format

WordPerfect includes commands that let you control the final layout of your document. **Layout** refers to the appearance of text on the page—the combination of print and white space. Until now, you have been using WordPerfect's default settings for such layout settings as margins, tabs, line spacing, and justification.

You will now create a short document that will include a number of these layout features. Remember that all layout changes, like other formatting adjustments, take effect *at the insertion point* and affect all following text until another format change is made. To begin:

1. Start WordPerfect if needed
2. Clear the screen

Margins

The default margins are set at one inch on both the left and right sides of the document. Often, you may want to make margins larger or smaller.

Setting Margins.   For example, to change the left margin to 1.5″ and the right margin to 2″, try the following:

1. Select <u>L</u>ayout   [Shift + F8]

You will see a Layout menu as shown in Figure WP2–17a (or a pop-up Format box as in Figure WP2–17b if you use Shift + F8).

2. Select <u>M</u>argins (press **M**)

The "Margin Format" box will appear as shown in Figure WP2–18.

3. Press **L** or **1** to select *Left Margin*

Your insertion point will move to the current left margin setting, which displays *1″*.

4. Type **1.5** **↵**

5. Press **R** or **2** for *Right Margin*

The insertion point now moves to the current right margin setting.

6. Type **2** **↵**

7. Check the margin settings to see if they are correct; repeat the process if they are not

8. Press **↵** to exit this menu and accept the changes

9. If a Format box appears, press **↵** to close it (the box will appear if you started with Shift + F8)

The screen will now return, ready to use the new margins. You may notice that the current cursor position is now 1.5″—the new left margin setting. You can use REVEAL CODES to see the *Margin* command.

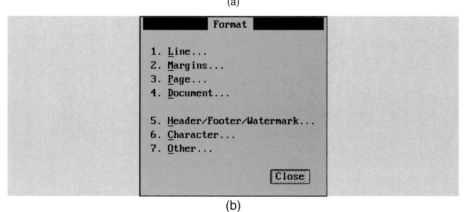

File   Edit   View   **Layout**   Tools   Font   Graphics   Window   Help

Character...	Shft+F8
Line...	Shft+F8
Page...	Shft+F8
Document...	Shft+F8
Columns...	Alt+F7
Tables	Alt+F7 ▶
Envelope...	Alt+F12
Special Codes...	
Other...	Shft+F8
Margins...	Shft+F8
Justification	▶
Tab Set...	
Alignment	▶
Header/Footer/Watermark...	
Footnote	Ctrl+F7 ▶
Endnote	Ctrl+F7 ▶
Comment	Ctrl+F7 ▶
Styles...	Alt+F8

(a)

Format

1. Line...
2. Margins...
3. Page...
4. Document...

5. Header/Footer/Watermark...
6. Character...
7. Other...

Close

(b)

Figure WP2—17
Changing the Layout

(a) ⁻he Layout menu. (b) The
Format pop-up box (partial
screen).

WP

To see the effect of the new margins,

10. Type the document shown in Figure WP2–19

Remember to press the Tab key at the beginning of each paragraph, but do *not* press the Enter key until you reach the end of each paragraph, as shown

11. Save this document as **LAYOUT1**

You can change the margins whenever you want by moving the cursor to the desired position and following the procedure for setting margins. This can be done before you type or after text has been entered. The text following the change will be reformatted automatically to conform to the new margins. For example,

12. Move to the start of paragraph 2 (at Pos 1.5″)

13. Select Layout, Margins   [Shift + F8, M]

14. Press   **L**   and type **2.5**   ↵

Figure WP2–18

The "Margin Format" Box (partial screen).

```
┌──────────────── Margin Format ────────────────┐
│                                                │
│  ┌─Document Margins──────────────────────────┐ │
│  │ 1. Left Margin:               [1"      ]   │ │
│  │ 2. Right Margin:              [1"      ]   │ │
│  │                                            │ │
│  │ 3. Top Margin:                [1"      ]   │ │
│  │ 4. Bottom Margin:             [1"      ]   │ │
│  └────────────────────────────────────────────┘ │
│  ┌─Paragraph Margins─────────────────────────┐ │
│  │ 5. Left Margin Adjustment:    [0"      ]   │ │
│  │ 6. Right Margin Adjustment:   [0"      ]   │ │
│  │                                            │ │
│  │ 7. First Line Indent:         [0"      ]   │ │
│  │ 8. Paragraph Spacing:         [1.0    ]▲▼  │ │
│  └────────────────────────────────────────────┘ │
│                              [  OK  ] [Cancel] │
└────────────────────────────────────────────────┘
```

Figure WP2–19

Margin Practice Document

Press the Tab key when you see "[Tab]" and press the Enter key when you see "¶."

```
Word Publishing ¶
¶
[Tab] It is clear that the current distinctions
made among word processing, desktop publishing,
and presentation graphics programs will soon die
out. It is likely that all three will merge into
one "word publishing" software package including
sophisticated text entry, editing, layout, and
graphics capabilities.¶
[Tab] Yet, the increased power offered by such
programs places more emphasis on the artistic
training and skills of potential users. We must
remember that like an artist's brush, these
programs can just as easily produce junk as
masterpieces. It is still the human who must
creatively apply these tools and be held
accountable for their end product. The ease
afforded by technology does not eliminate our
responsibility for its use--in fact, it places
higher demands on our skills and vigilance.¶
¶
Source: Martin/Burstein. COMPUTER SYSTEMS
FUNDAMENTALS, The Dryden Press, 1990.¶
```

15. Press **R** and type **2.5** ↵

16. Press ↵ (and another ↵ if needed to close the box)

Examine the new margins that take effect in paragraph 2.

Deleting Margins.   As with other format changes, you can use REVEAL CODES to locate and remove margin settings. The previous margin setting in the

Figure WP2–20
Deleting Margin Settings

(a) The margin code is marked for deletion. (b) When the current margin setting is deleted, the text reverts to the preceding margin setting (or the default).

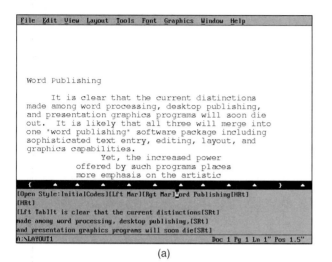

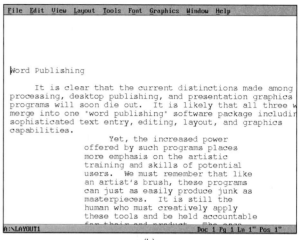

(a)   (b)

text will then take effect. If there is none, the text will reformat to the default margins. Try this:

1. Press **Home** **Home** ↑

2. Activate REVEAL CODES (Select <u>V</u>iew, Reveal <u>C</u>odes)   [F11]

Your screen should resemble Figure WP2–20. The cursor is on the "W" of "Word" and the ruler line shows the current margin settings of 1.5″ and 2″.

3. Press ← twice

The left margin setting is now highlighted on the lower screen.

4. Press **Delete** to remove the left margin setting

5. Press **Delete** to remove the right margin setting

6. Exit REVEAL CODES (Select <u>V</u>iew, Reveal <u>C</u>odes)   [F11]

The text has been restored to the default margin settings, as in Figure WP2–20b.

7. Use the same procedure to delete the other left and right margin settings at the beginning of paragraph 2
8. Save this document as **LAYOUT2**

The default setting for line spacing is single spacing. This can be changed easily using a procedure similar to that for changing margins. For example, double space your document as follows:

Spacing

1. Open LAYOUT2 if needed

2. Move to the beginning of the first paragraph

3. Select <u>L</u>ayout   [Shift + F8]

Figure WP2—21

The Line Format Dialog Box

The Line Format dialog box allows you to modify tabs, justification, spacing, and other text layout factors (partial screen).

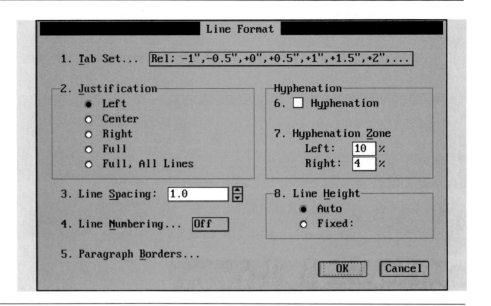

4. Select Line (press **L**)

A "Line Format" box appears as in WP2–21.

5. Select Line Spacing

Your insertion point will move to the current line spacing setting.

6. Type **2** to set double spacing

7. Press **↵**

8. Press **↵** (or "OK") to return to your document (If you started with Shift + F8, press **↵** again to close the box)

The document is now double-spaced from the cursor position until the end.

9. Save the document as **LAYOUT3**

As with margins, line spacing changes can be placed anywhere in a document and can be removed with REVEAL CODES.

Justifi-cation

Justification aligns words neatly at the margin. In WordPerfect, documents can have four different justification settings: *left* margin only, *right* margin only, *full* (both margins justified), or *center* (neither margin justified). As shown in Figure WP2–22, the two most popular justification options are *left* and *full*. In **full justification**, WordPerfect places extra spaces between words to ensure that the last letter of each line aligns with the lines above it when the document is printed.

With a typical dot-matrix printer, extra spaces may appear between some words. Newer printers, such as laser and ink-jet, spread the spaces evenly throughout the line, so that they are hardly noticeable (as in Figure WP2–22b).

Margins that are not justified are *ragged*—they do not have added spaces and, as in normal typing, may not line up at the margin edge. Thus, left justification (also called *ragged-right*) leaves a ragged right edge; full justification leaves no ragged edges at all. The default setting for WordPerfect 6.0 is left justification.

Figure WP2–22
Justification

```
        This paragraph displays an example of left justification in
WordPerfect. The left margin is justified but the right margin
is left "ragged." Extra spaces are not inserted between words by
the program, but are left as if typed on a typewriter. Left
justification is also known as "ragged-right."

                                    (a)

        This paragraph displays an example of full justification in
WordPerfect. Notice that the left margin and the right margin are
both justified. Extra spaces are inserted as needed between words
on each line by the program, to ensure that the last letter of each
line aligns neatly with the lines above it.

                                    (b)
```

Changing Justification. Of course, justification can be changed easily. Do the following:

1. Move the insertion point to the beginning of the document

Note that justification is typically set at the start of your document so that the justification of the entire document is consistent.

2. Select Layout   [Shift + F8]

3. Press **L** for *Line*

4. Press **J** for *Justification*

The Justification box is activated as in Figure WP2–23.

5. Press **F** or **4** for *Full Justification*

6. Press **↵** to return to your document (press **↵** again if needed)

The document is now full-justified from the insertion point until the end (as you will see shortly).

7. Save the document as **LAYOUT4**

Using the Print Preview Option. It may be difficult to understand full justification if you use the text mode, because its effect is not shown on the normal work screen (which displays a ragged right margin). To see full justification, you must be in graphics or page mode, print your document, or use the *Print Preview* feature. **Print Preview** allows you to see a document on screen as it will appear when printed.
    Try this:

1. Open LAYOUT4 if needed

2. Move the insertion point to the start of the document

3. Select File   [Shift + F7]

4. Press **V** to select *Print Preview*

5. Press **1** for *100%*

Figure WP2–23

The WordPerfect Justification Menu (partial screen)

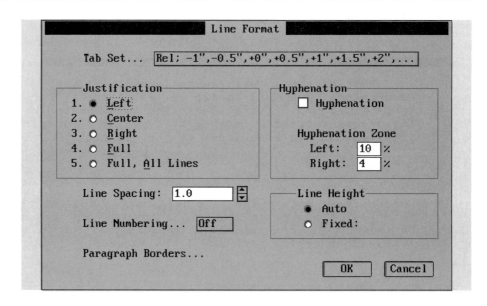

Figure WP2–24

The Print Preview *Screen*

The Print Preview screen displays a screen representation of a printed document page.

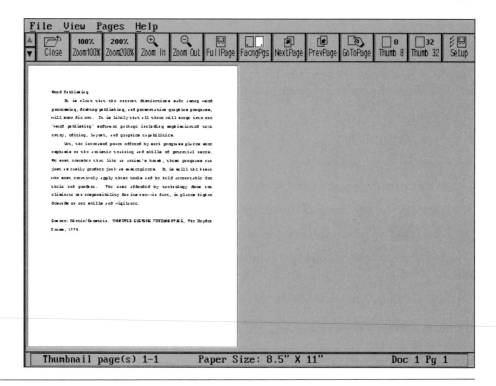

A screen similar to Figure WP2–24 appears. This screen simulates how your document will look when it is printed. Notice that both margins are justified. You may use Print Preview whenever you want to see the layout of a document. Experiment with the menu options to change the detail level of the view.

6. Press **F7** to exit when you are done

As with margins and line spacing, justification can be set anywhere in the document or removed easily with REVEAL CODES.

Figure WP2—25
*Paragraph Indent
Practice Document*

```
 File   Edit   View   Layout   Tools   Font   Graphics   Window   Help
      The following criteria should be used when considering new
      applicants for job openings in your department:

      1.    The qualified applicant should possess skills in fundamental
            microcomputer concepts and terminology.
      2.    The qualified applicant should possess at least a two-year
            degree in computer science, business, or a related field.
            An official college transcript will be required before a
            final decision can be made.
      3.    He/she should have a working knowledge of basic DOS
            techniques on an IBM-compatible or Apple Macintosh
            microcomputer, as well as experience with word processing
            and spreadsheet applications.  The applicant may be required
            to demonstrate stated skills on our equipment.
      4.    He/she should have excellent written and oral communication
            skills.
```

Changing the Display Mode. Now is a good time to see the effect of a different view mode, if you haven't already switched. Try this:

1. Clear the screen and open the LAYOUT4 document

2. Select <u>V</u>iew   [Ctrl + F3]

3. Press (or select) **T** for *Text Mode*

As you have learned, the text mode is the fastest mode for editing because it only displays mono-spaced characters. There are no graphics, which take time to generate. Note, too, that full justification is not displayed in this mode. Now, change to the next display level:

4. Select <u>V</u>iew   [Ctrl + F3]

5. Press (or select) **G** for *Graphics Mode*

Graphics mode imitates a WYSIWYG environment by displaying text and graphics as they will appear when printed. Note that full justification appears in this mode.

📚 **Tip: Page mode (invoked by selecting View, Page mode) enhances the graphics mode by adding the ability to see the entire printed page, including top and bottom margins, headers, footers, and page numbers.**

The display mode you select depends on what type of text and graphics you are using, and how fast your screen reacts to your commands. You may leave your screen in graphics mode for the remainder of this chapter, or switch to page mode if you prefer.

Paragraph Indent

At times, you may want to create an itemized list similar to that shown in Figure WP2—25. Pressing the Tab key indents only the first line of each item, but it will not indent the entire paragraph as shown. WordPerfect provides an INDENT command for this purpose. **INDENT** lets you indent an entire paragraph without changing the margins. Try this example, using Figure WP2—25 as a guide:

1. Clear your screen

2. Type the first sentence of the text

3. Press ↵ twice after "department:"

4. Type **1.** at the left margin

5. Select Layout, Alignment, Indent   [F4]

The F4 key—which is easier to invoke—(or the menu sequence) invokes WordPerfect's INDENT command, and the insertion point moves to the first tab.

6. Type the sentence after "1."

Notice that the second line of the sentence does not return to the left margin but is automatically indented.

7. Press ⏎ after typing "terminology."

The Enter key adds a hard return that breaks you out of the Indent feature.

8. Continue to type the remaining items in the list, pressing F4 (or the menu sequence) to indent after each item number, and ⏎ after each complete item

9. Save this document as **LAYOUT5**

☞ **Tip: The Shift and F4 keys (or the pull-down menu sequence Layout, Alignment, Indent) will paragraph indent from both margins at the same time.**

Tabs

Tabs are used to place text in specific positions on each line, typically every half inch. Each time you depress the Tab key, the insertion point moves a half inch to the right.

At times, you may want to remove some tab settings so that pressing the Tab key once would send you directly to a desired location. You may also need to adjust positions of the tabs, or want to change the type of tab available.

There are four options for tab settings:

L for Left	Text is aligned at the tab stop
C for Center	Text is centered over the tab setting
R for Right	Text is right-aligned at the tab stop
D for Decimal	Text is aligned on a decimal point at the tab stop

These tabs can also be set with a *dot leader* that fills the space up to the tab with a line of dots. This is useful in such lists as a table of contents, where the eye must move across the line to find a corresponding number.

Tabs can be measured from the left page edge or from the left margin. **Absolute tabs** are measured from the left page edge regardless of the current margin setting. That is, an absolute tab setting of 2″ is two inches from the left edge. **Relative tabs**, the default, are measured from the left margin. For example, if the left margin is 1.5″, then a relative tab of +.5″ is one-half inch to its right, or a total of two inches from the page edge. Relative tabs include a plus or minus sign to show their position from the left margin.

1. Clear your screen

2. Type the first paragraph of Figure WP2–26

3. Press ⏎ twice after the word "positions:"

You can now change the tabs:

4. Select Layout   [Shift + F8, L]

5. Select *Tab set* (press B in the menu or T in the Line Format box)

Figure WP2–26

Tab Practice Document

```
At present, we have the following job openings. Applicants
displaying the stated criteria above should be given priority in
placement for these positions:

        Data Entry . . . . . . . . . . . 7.50/hr
        WordPerfect Assistant  . . . . . 10.50
        Lotus 1-2-3 Assistant  . . . . . 11.25
        Senior Programmer  . . . . . . . 15.75
        Systems Analyst  . . . . . . . . 25.35
```

A "Tab Set" screen appears similar to the one in Figure WP2–27. At the top of the screen is a tab ruler line. This ruler, marked in inches, shows all current tab settings (each indicated by an "L"). Notice that each inch is divided into tenths with short "tick" marks.

If your tabs are not in relative form (the "Relative" box is not marked and no plus signs show on the ruler line), change them as follows:

6. Press **Tab** to see the mnemonic codes

7. Press **E** for Relative tabs

Tabs can now be set by moving the insertion point to the desired position on the tab ruler and then pressing L, C, R, or D for the type of tab desired.

☞ **Tip: You can set repeating tabs by pressing P, typing a number, and pressing the Enter key.**

Try this exercise:

8. Press **A** to clear all tabs

The *L*s disappear from the ruler line.

9. Press **→** until you move the insertion point to the large center line (fifth tick mark) between *+1″* and *+2″*

This corresponds to +1.5″ past the margin.

10. Press **L** to place a left-aligned tab here

Now try the other method to set a tab:

11. Press **S** to *Set Tab*

The cursor moves to the "Set Tab" entry line.

12. Type **5** and press **↵**

13. Now press **D** to make this a decimal tab

Although you could leave this tab as is, add a dot leader to it for practice, as follows:

14. Press **.** (period)

The "D" will now be shown in reverse video on the screen, indicating that a dot leader has been added to this tab position. Also note that the "Dot Leader" and "Decimal" boxes are marked (as in Figure WP2–27b). If not, repeat as needed.

Figure WP2—27

The "Tab Set" Screen

(a) The default screen. (b) New tabs are set.

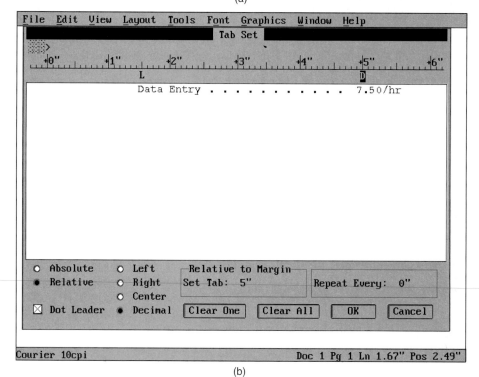

```
File   Edit   View   Layout   Tools   Font   Graphics   Window   Help
 At present, we have the following job openings.  Applicants
 displaying the stated criteria above should be given priority in
 placement for these positions:

        Data Entry . . . . . . . . . . . 7.50/hr
```
(a)

```
File   Edit   View   Layout   Tools   Font   Graphics   Window   Help
 At present, we have the following job openings.  Applicants
 displaying the stated criteria above should be given priority in
 placement for these positions:

        Data Entry . . . . . . . . . . 7.50/hr
        WordPerfect Assistant. . . . . 10.50
        Lotus 1-2-3 Assistant. . . . . 11.25
        Senior Programmer. . . . . . . 15.75
        Systems Analyst. . . . . . . . 25.35
```
(b)

Figure WP2–28
Selecting Tabs

Selecting the proper tabs can determine whether text is left-, right-, or decimal-aligned; centered; or preceded by dot leaders.

15. Press **F7** once to exit

Notice that item 1 (Tab set) on the menu shows relative tabs at approximately +1.5″ and +5″. If it does not, press **T** and repeat Steps 8 through 15.

16. Press **↵** to exit the menu (press **↵** again if needed)

Once tabs have been set, you can proceed to type and see the effect immediately. Using Figure WP2–26 as a guide:

17. Press **Tab** once to move to the first tab column

18. Type **Data Entry**

19. Press **Tab** again to get to the second tab column

20. Type **7.50/hr** and press **↵**

Your screen should now resemble Figure WP2–28a. Text is left-aligned at approximately Pos 2.5″ (1.5″ from the left margin). The second column has dot leaders and its decimal point is at a point close to Pos 6″ (5″ from the left margin). Your numbers may differ slightly.

21. Enter the remaining lines in the table, pressing **Tab** before each column

    and **↵** at the end of the line

The completed screen should resemble Figure WP2–28b. Note how the decimal points align.

22. Save this document as **LAYOUT6**

Tabs can be set anywhere in the document or removed with REVEAL CODES.

Checkpoint

☐ On a clear screen, set justification to Left and both margins to 2″. Type a paragraph of your choice.

☐ Beneath the paragraph, reset tabs as follows: an L-Tab at +3″ and an R-Tab with dot leader at +5″. Type a price list of five items.

☐ Beneath the list, type a paragraph using the paragraph indent feature. Save as **LAYOUT7.** Clear the screen.

Figure WP2–29
Font Practice Document

Text enhancements have not
yet been added.

```
 File   Edit   View   Layout   Tools   Font   Graphics   Window   Help
 Word Publishing

      It is clear that the current distinctions made among word
 processing, desktop publishing, and presentation graphics
 programs, will soon die out.  It is likely that all three will
 merge into one "word publishing" software package including
 sophisticated text entry, editing, layout, and graphics
 capabilities.
 |
```

Changing Text Attributes

Until now, you have been using the default WordPerfect text setting, modifying it slightly to create bold or underlined characters. However, if your printer has the capability, you can change the overall type style and also enhance text appearance and size to greatly improve the look of your document.

To prepare for this exercise,

1. Start WordPerfect or clear your screen.
2. Open the LAYOUT2 document

(If you do not have this document, or want to practice, type the text as in Figure WP2–29, then skip to Step 6.)

3. Position the insertion point at the left margin at the beginning of the second paragraph (to the left of "Yet")

4. Press **Ctrl** + **PgDn** to delete the rest of the page's text

In response to "Delete remainder of page?"

5. Press **Y**

Your screen should resemble Figure WP2–29. This small amount of text is sufficient to demonstrate the techniques that affect text appearance.

6. Save the document as **FONT1**

Although you can use fonts in text mode, it is easier to work with fonts if you are in graphics or page mode.

7. Select View, Graphics to change to graphics mode

Setting the Base Font

A *font* is a style of type. The **base font** (or *current font*) is the type style in which WordPerfect prints normal text. Typically, WordPerfect uses a font called Courier 10 (the "10" indicates 10 characters per inch) as a base font, although any font and size can be used (if it is available to WordPerfect and your printer can produce it). The base font determines the overall type style—all other text enhancements (in size or appearance) simply provide variations.

Changing the Base Font.   Like with other WordPerfect commands, base font settings take effect at the current insertion point position and determine the style of the text that follows. Assume that you want to change the base font for the entire document.

```
 File   Edit   View   Layout   Tools   Font   Graphics   Window   Help
                                     Font
   Type  Built-In                          HP LaserJet III

   1. Font   Courier 10cpi                      ▼  2. Size   12pt      ▼

  ┌3. Appearance──────────────────────────────┐   ┌5. Position─────┐
  │ □ Bold          □ Italics     □ Small Caps │   │ ● Normal       │
  │ □ Underline     □ Outline     □ Redline    │   │ ○ Superscript  │
  │ □ Dbl Undline   □ Shadow      □ Strikeout  │   │ ○ Subscript    │
  └────────────────────────────────────────────┘   └────────────────┘
  ┌4. Relative Size───────────────────────────┐   ┌6. Underline────┐
  │ ● Normal      ○ Small      ○ Very Large    │   │ ⊠ Spaces       │
  │ ○ Fine        ○ Large      ○ Extra Large   │   │ □ Tabs         │
  └────────────────────────────────────────────┘   └────────────────┘
  ┌Resulting Font──────────────────────────────────────────────────┐
  │                                                                 │
  │          The Quick Brown Fox Jumps Over the Lazy Dog            │
  │                                                                 │
  ├─────────────────────────────────────────────────────────────────┤
  │ Courier 10cpi                                                   │
  └─────────────────────────────────────────────────────────────────┘

  [Setup... Shft+F1]  [Normal]  [Color...]          [ OK ]   [Cancel]


 A:\FONT1                              Doc 1 Pg 1 Ln 1" Pos 1"
```

1. Move the insertion point to the start of the document (**Home**   **Home**

   ↑)

2. Select Font, Font   [Ctrl + F8]

A *Font menu* appears on the screen, as in Figure WP2–30. This menu allows you
to change font style, size, and appearance, and then view the change in the
"Resulting Font" box near the bottom.

3. Press **F** or **1** for *Font*

A list of all available fonts appears on your screen as in Figure WP2–31a. For
example, the current list displays fonts typically available with a popular laser
printer: CG Times and Courier. (Your font list may differ.) A highlight indicates
the current base font, in this case, Courier 10cpi.

   Fonts typically offer character widths that are either of *fixed size* or *proportionally spaced*. Fixed-size text characters all have the same width; an "i" occupies
the same width as an "m." However, the widths of proportionally spaced characters (such as those in this book) vary depending on the letter; an "i" is much
narrower than an "m."

   The notation "cpi" that follows some font names identifies a fixed-size font,
whereas no entry indicates proportionally spaced fonts. To select a new base
font,

4. Move the highlight bar to the desired font using the **↓** or **↑** keys

In this case, select "CG Times" if you have it. If you do not, select a different
font than the current base font.

5. Press **↵** to select the font

Figure WP2–31

Changing the Base Font

(a) Available fonts appear when you select "Font." (b) Changing font size.

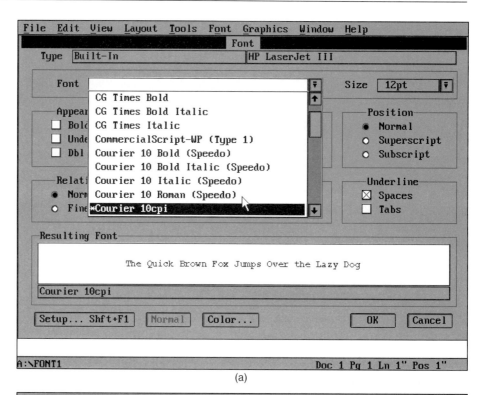

(a)

(b)

File Edit View Layout Tools Font Graphics Window Help
Word Publishing
It is clear that the current distinctions made among word processing, desktop publishing, and presentation graphics programs, will soon die out. It is likely that all three will merge into one "word publishing" software package including sophisticated text entry, editing, layout, and graphics capabilities.

Figure WP2—32
The FONT2 Document

The base font has been changed to a CG Times 12-point style.

The name appears in the font entry line, and the new font is shown in the "Resulting Fonts" box. If you selected a scalable font, you can now adjust the point size if you want. A **point** is a typesetting measurement of height (equal to about 1/72nd of an inch). The larger the point size, the bigger the text that is produced. The average 12-point font is approximately 1/6″ high.

6. Press **S** for *Size*

7. Press **↓** to see available sizes

Note the current size of 12 points is highlighted as in Figure WP2—31b.

8. Move the highlight to "14"

(Note the size increase in the "Resulting Font" Box.)

9. Press **↵** to accept

10. Press **↵** to leave the Font screen

Figure WP2—32 displays the document as it would appear in graphics mode if the base font were changed to a CG Times, 12-point, proportionally spaced font. (Your document's appearance may differ based on the font you have chosen.)

11. Save the document as **FONT2**

Removing Base Font Settings. As with other text enhancements, base font settings can be changed by specifying another base font or deleting the current base font setting.

1. Press **Home** **Home** **↑** to move to the start of the document

2. Invoke REVEAL CODES (Select View, Reveal Codes)   [F11]

3. Press **←** to highlight the [Font: CG Times] specification

4. Press **Delete** to delete the base font setting

5. Highlight the [Font Size: 14 pt] specification

6. Press **Delete**

The text returns to the preceding base font setting or (if none exists) to the default base font (Courier 10cpi).

7. Exit from REVEAL CODES
8. Clear the screen

You can also modify the appearance and relative size of any text, using procedures similar to underlining or boldfacing. The following exercises examine two techniques: adjusting the appearance of text that already exists in your document and adjusting the appearance of new text as it is entered.

Adjusting Text Appearance

WP

Figure WP2—33
Sample Text Enhancements

WordPerfect offers a number of text enhancements to emphasize text.

Bold
Underline
Double Underline
Italic
Shadow
SMALL CAPS
Redline
Strikeout

Bold
Underline
Double Underline
Italic
Outline
Shadow
SMALL CAPS
Redline
Strikeout

Adjusting the Appearance of Existing Text. Most often, you will want to change the appearance of text that you have already entered into your document. This is easily done, as you might expect, with the block command. For example, you will now change the appearance of the title "Word Publishing" in the FONT1 document.

1. On a fresh screen, open FONT1

2. Block the words "Word Publishing" (**F12** , or <u>E</u>dit, <u>B</u>lock in the menu)

3. Select F<u>o</u>nt, F<u>o</u>nt   [Ctrl + F8]

4. Press **A** for *Appearance*

   The list of nine text enhancements is activated. (Samples of each appear in Figure WP2–33.) You now select the enhancement you want to use. For example, to set the title in small capital letters,

5. Press **C** for *Small Caps*

The text will appear in the "Resulting Fonts" box to show the change.

6. Press **↵** to accept and return to the work screen

Another way to adjust appearance is to use the Font menu as follows: Let's say you want to double underline the words "will soon die out" in the third line.

7. Block the words "will soon die out"

8. Select F<u>o</u>nt   [Alt + O]

Note the enhancements in the menu list.

9. Press **D** to *Double Underline*

The change is made.

10. Save this document as **FONT2**

(replacing the old FONT2 document).

Adjusting the Appearance of New Text.   Using a technique similar to bold-facing or underlining, you can also adjust text appearance as you type. In this case, you invoke the text change, type the text, and then return to normal text. For example, you will now type some italicized text at the end of the FONT2 document.

1.   On a fresh screen, open FONT2 if needed
2.   Move to the end of the document (**Home** **Home** **↓**)
3.   Press **↵** to skip a line

Now, invoke the font change:

4.   Select F<u>o</u>nt, <u>I</u>talics [Ctrl + F8, A, I, Enter]
5.   Type **This is italicized text.**

The new text will appear italicized (or in a new color in text mode) to show that its appearance has been altered. You must now return the appearance setting to normal so that additional text will not be affected.

6.   Select F<u>o</u>nt, <u>N</u>ormal   [Ctrl + F8, A, I, Enter]
7.   Type two spaces and then **This is normal text.**

Note that the new text appears nonitalicized.

8.   Resave this document as **FONT2**

☞ **Tip: You can use Ctrl + I to turn on italics; Ctrl + N returns to normal. Similarly, you can use Ctrl + U for underline and Ctrl + B for bold.**

Adjusting Text Size

WordPerfect also allows you to change relative text size within a font to em-phasize, deemphasize, superscript (above line), or subscript (below line). The technique is similar to adjusting text appearance.

For text already typed, block the text to be changed, select F<u>o</u>nt, <u>S</u>ize (or press the Ctrl and F8 keys) then press **R** for Relative *Size*. You can then choose from among the seven sizes offered on the screen, from "Fine" to "Extra Large" by pressing the desired mnemonic letter and exiting the menu.

Of course, you can also adjust the size of text as you type, using the same technique, but remember to select "Normal" text when you are finished.

Deleting Text Enhancements.   As with other text enhancements, appearance and size settings can be deleted using the REVEAL CODES screen to locate the unwanted enhancement and then deleting it from the document.

Try adding some enhancements to your document, including style and size changes. Then, delete a few, but do *not* save the document.

Checkpoint

☐ Open a document of your choice or type a few sentences. At the start of the document, change the base font to a different style and size from its current setting and then save the document at TEXT1.

☐ Using TEXT1, change the text appearance of the first sentence to italics.

☐ While in TEXT1, change the relative size of the second sentence to "small." Save the document as TEXT2.

Global Editing

Most word processing programs let you locate specific blocks of text and, if you want, replace them with others. In word processing, a "block" of text is called a **text string**—a collection of contiguous characters or words. Such strings may be a few characters long or consist of several neighboring words. The following exercises provide some insight into searching for, or replacing, these strings. First, create a practice document as follows:

1. Clear your screen
2. Type the text shown in Figure WP2–34
3. Save the document as **SEARCH1**

Searching

The **SEARCH** feature allows you to specify a text string, or series of keystrokes, and have the program locate each occurrence of the string in your document. This exercise allows you to search for the word "data" in your document:

1. Move the insertion point to the beginning of the document

☞ **Tip: Searches start at the current insertion point position. Moving to the beginning of your document ensures that the entire text will be searched.**

To initiate a search,

2. Select Edit, Search   [F2]

A "Search" box appears on the screen as in Figure WP2–35a and awaits your entry.

3. Type **data** and press ↵

4. Press **F2** to start the search

☞ **Tip: You can also press the Tab key or the down arrow to move to the Search button and then press Enter. Of course, you can also click "Search" with a mouse.**

The program will locate the first occurrence of the word "data" and move the insertion point just past it.

Note that entering a search string in all lowercase letters (as in "data") will locate *all* occurrences of the string, even if some or all of its letters are uppercase (as in "Data" or "DATA"). However, if you want to restrict the search to exact matches only ("Data" will locate only "Data"), press **C** to select *Case Sensitive Search* before starting the search.

5. Press **F2** twice to continue the search

Figure WP2—34

Search-and-Replace Practice Document

```
File  Edit  View  Layout  Tools  Font  Graphics  Window  Help
|      Data and information are not the same.  Data are the raw
facts that you input into a computer system.  Information, on the
other hand, is the result of processing data into a more useful
form.
      Decisions are never made on data, but rather on the
information that can be produced by manipulating the data in a
way that helps solve a problem.  For example, you can organize
data, sort data, select from data, perform math on data, group
data, and summarize data.
```

Figure WP2—35
Searching for Text

a) The Search dialog box. b) The Search and Replace dialog box. (partial screens).

```
┌─────────────────────────── Search ───────────────────────────┐
│                                                               │
│  Search For: ┌──────────────────────────────────────────────┐│
│              │_                                             ││
│              └──────────────────────────────────────────────┘│
│                                                               │
│     ☐ Backward Search          ☐ Find Whole Words Only       │
│     ☐ Case Sensitive Search    ☐ Extended Search (Hdrs, Ftrs, etc.)│
│                                                               │
│  [Codes... F5] [Specific Codes... Shft+F5]    [Search F2] [Cancel]│
└───────────────────────────────────────────────────────────────┘
```

(a)

```
┌──────────────────── Search and Replace ──────────────────────┐
│                                                               │
│  Search For:  ┌─────────────────────────────────────────────┐│
│               │data                                         ││
│               └─────────────────────────────────────────────┘│
│                                                               │
│  Replace With: ┌────────────────────────────────────────────┐│
│                │<Nothing>                                   ││
│                └────────────────────────────────────────────┘│
│                                                               │
│     ☐ Confirm Replacement      ☐ Find Whole Words Only       │
│     ☐ Backward Search          ☐ Extended Search (Hdrs, Ftrs, etc.)│
│     ☐ Case Sensitive Search    ☐ Limit Number of Matches:    │
│                                                               │
│  [Codes... F5] [Specific Codes... Shft+F5]   [Replace F2] [Cancel]│
└───────────────────────────────────────────────────────────────┘
```

(b)

You could continue to press the F2 key twice to find every occurrence of "data," or stop whenever you want. Note that the insertion point will remain at the most recent match. You can also search *backwards* through a file (always from the current insertion point position) by selecting the "Backward Search" option after entering your search text. The insertion point would then move back to a previous match of "data."

☞ **Tip: If you can't think of a particular word when typing a document, type *zzz* (or something similar) in its place and continue. Later, you can search for all the *zzz*'s and then type in the words you want in their place.**

Replacing

The **REPLACE** feature lets you locate a specific text string, or series of keystrokes, and replace it with another string. The new string need not be the same length as the one it replaces. This exercise replaces the word "data" in your document with the word "porcupines":

1. Open SEARCH1 if needed
2. Move to the beginning of the document

Like SEARCH, REPLACE starts at the current insertion point position.

3. Select Edit, Replace   [Alt + F2]

A "Search and Replace" box appears as in Figure WP2–35b.

☞ **Tip: The previous search string always reappears when you issue a new SEARCH or REPLACE command.**

4. Type **data** (unless it already appears on screen)

5. Press ⏎ to move to the "Replace With" entry line

Figure WP2—36

Search and Replace

The string "data" has been replaced with "porcupines."

File Edit View Layout Tools Font Graphics Window Help
Porcupines and information are not the same. Porcupines are the raw facts that you input into a computer system. Information, on the other hand, is the result of processing porcupines into a more useful form.   Decisions are never made on porcupines, but rather on the information that can be produced by manipulating the porcupines in a way that helps solve a problem. For example, you can organize porcupines, sort porcupines, select from porcupines, perform math on porcupines, group porcupines, and summarize porcupines▌

6. Type **porcupines**

7. Press **F2** (or select "Replace") to replace all "data" with "porcupines"

The screen responds with "11 Replacements made."

8. Press **↵** to accept

The program has located and replaced *all* occurrences of the word "data," as in Figure WP2–36. Of course, replacing text is not as simple as it appears. You have to be concerned with the agreement of verbs, vowels, and gender in any changes you produce. You must also watch out for text strings that are part of larger words. For example, replacing "in" with "out" could create words like "outner," "woutdow," and "thout." In these cases, it is wiser to search for a whole word. To do this, you would select the "Find Whole Words Only" option (by pressing **W**).

9. Save this document as **SEARCH2**

You may also choose which strings get replaced and which do not by selecting the "Confirm Replacement" option. As the program locates each matching string, it will ask you to confirm the change. You can then respond with *Y* or *N*, or press the Esc key to cancel the rest of the routine.

    Change *every other* "porcupine" to "hamster" using the confirm technique as follows:

10. Move to the start of the SEARCH2 document

11. Select <u>E</u>dit, Re<u>p</u>lace   [Alt + F2]

12. For *Search* type **porcupine** and press **↵**

13. For *Replace* type **hamster** and press **↵**

14. Now press **F** to choose the "Confirm" option

An "X" appears in the confirm box.

15. Press **↵** or **F2** to continue

The program stops at the first "porcupine" and asks "Confirm Replacement?"

16. Press **Y** to change it to "hamster"

The program stops at the second "porcupine" and asks "Confirm Replacement?"

17. Press **N** to leave it as "porcupine"

Get the idea?

18. Continue to answer Y or N alternately until there are no more "por-cupines" to change, or press Esc now to stop

19. When done, press ↵ to continue

20. Clear the screen but do *not* save this document

Checkpoint

☐ Type items 14–17 in the REPLACE procedure (exactly as they appear in this text) onto a clear screen, then replace all "press" with "tap."

☐ Use the *Confirm* option to replace only the second and third "tap" words with "depress."

☐ Save as SEARCH3. Clear the screen.

Using Auxiliary Programs

WordPerfect offers a number of useful auxiliary programs—especially, a speller, a thesaurus, and a grammar check. These programs are not part of the main word processor but can be invoked on command.

A spelling checker, or **Speller,** enables you to check each word in your document for correct spelling. It is especially useful if you are a poor speller or typist, since the list used by most speller programs will identify most typographical errors and misspelled words (WordPerfect's speller contains over 115,000 words).

Speller

To prepare for this exercise, do the following:

1. Start WordPerfect or clear the screen
2. Type the text in Figure WP2–37

Make sure to type all six errors as they appear in the figure. Although you would not deliberately make these errors, they will allow you to practice some speller techniques.

3. Save the document as **WPSPELL1**

Figure WP2–37
Speller Practice Document (with six errors)

```
          This is an exmaple of WordPerfect's spel check. I don't
     really typ this poorly. I am am only prakticing so that I can
     learnhow to use it.

     Make sure you type these six errors:
          1st line: exmaple, spel
          2nd line: typ, am am, prakticing
          3rd line: learnhow
```

Speller is probably installed with the WordPerfect program and is immediately available.

4.   Select <u>T</u>ools, <u>W</u>riting Tools, <u>S</u>peller   [Ctrl + F2]

After a few moments, the status line displays the menu shown in Figure WP2–38a.

☞ **Tip: Although you can check one word at a time, it is wiser to wait until you have finished your document, and then run the entire file through Speller once.**

In this example, to check the entire file,

5.   Press   **D**   or   **3**   to select *Document*

The Speller Screen.   WordPerfect will now check each word in your document against its list. The first word that does not appear in its list will be highlighted, as shown in Figure WP2–38b. Note, too, that a line separates the document from the Spell portion of the screen. In this area, the program indicates that the word was "Not Found" and lists some options at the right. The screen may also display some suggested spellings at the left—one of which may be the spelling you desire. Your choices include these:

- Press the letter shown to the left of the choice on the Speller screen if the corresponding word contains the correct spelling of the highlighted word (the program will replace the highlighted word with your selection).
- Press O or 1 to *skip* the highlighted word *once* without correcting it. The program will highlight this word again if it appears later in the document.
- Press S or 2 to *skip* the highlighted word now and for the remainder of the document. This is usually chosen for proper names that are not contained in the list.
- Press T or 3 to *add* this word to the dictionary. This is useful for words that are spelled correctly and used often. You should not attempt to add words to a list if you are not using your own computer system.
- Press W or 4 to *edit* the word yourself. This will move the cursor into the document area and allow you to make any changes you want (you'll have to press the F7 key when you are done to return to the speller).

Examine Figure WP2–38b. Notice that "exmaple" is highlighted at the top of the screen and that one suggested spelling, "example," is listed on the screen.

1.   Press   **A**   to select "example"

The next incorrect word, "spel," is highlighted. After a short delay, eight or so alternatives are offered by the program.

2.   Press   **D**   to select "spell"

In response to the next highlighted misspelling,

3.   Press   **E**   to select "type"

Your screen should now highlight the second "am" in "am am." Here is a different probable error—two words in a row spelled exactly the same, without any punctuation between them. Doubling words is a common typing error that can be identified by the Speller program.

4.   Press   **D**   or   **3**   to delete the second double word

5.   Press   **A**   to select "practicing"

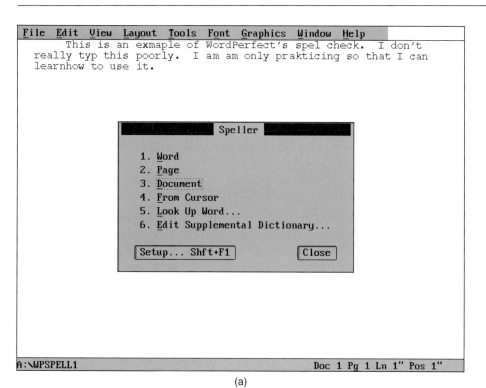

(a)

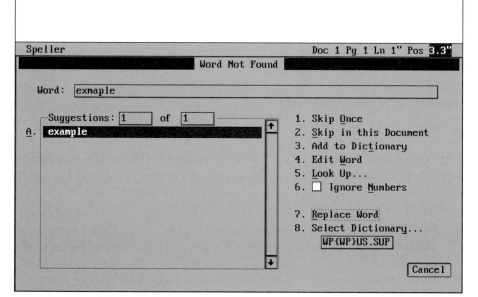

(b)

Figure WP2—38
Speller

(a) The Speller menu. (b) Speller has located a misspelled word and offers a suggestion.

WP

Your screen should now highlight "learnhow." This is clearly a typographical error. To fix it,

6. Press `W` or `4` to *Edit*

7. Move the cursor to the "h" in "how"

8. Press `Space` to separate the words

9. Press `F7` to return to the Speller

Finding no more incorrect words to highlight, Speller ends. At this time,

10. Press `↵` to leave Speller

11. Save the corrected document as **WPSPELL2**

Speller is a useful auxiliary to word processing, but it is not infallible. It will find most mistakes, but it will not look for capitalization, nor will it find words that are spelled correctly *but used incorrectly,* as in "Eye herd ewe wore hear" instead of "I heard you were here." *You* are still responsible for checking your own documents for proper usage, spelling, and grammar.

Thesaurus

An electronic **thesaurus** suggests synonyms—words with similar meaning—to the one at the current insertion point position. Some programs also list antonyms—words with opposite meaning—as well. A thesaurus operates much like a spelling checker but allows you to examine different nuances, or (as the thesaurus itself suggests), different hints, shades, and subtleties of meaning. In this way, it enhances your vocabulary and allows you to express your thoughts more precisely (or should we say accurately, exactly, or directly?). The thesaurus is a separate program that can be invoked from the keyboard. To prepare for this exercise, do the following:

1. Start WordPerfect or clear the screen
2. Type the sentence **Too many cooks spoil the broth.**

You will now use this well-known quote to examine the Thesaurus feature.

3. Place the insertion point anywhere within the word "many"

The thesaurus is probably installed with the WordPerfect program and is immediately available by command.

4. Select <u>T</u>ools, <u>W</u>riting Tools, <u>T</u>hesaurus   [Alt + F1, T]

The Thesaurus Screen.   After a few moments, the thesaurus will present a screen resembling Figure WP2–39. Synonyms will appear in the boxed area, the first choice marked with a highlighting bar. The screen may also display a second column of selections. Your choices include these:

- Press <u>R</u> to *replace* the word with one highlighted on the screen. The program will then replace the highlighted word with your selection and return to the document.
- Press <u>V</u> to *view* your document. This is done if you want to reread a sentence in context before choosing a synonym. (You will have to press the F7 key to return to the thesaurus when you're done.)
- Press <u>L</u> to *look* up another word for which you want to find synonyms (you could then press Enter or type a new word).
- Press the Right arrow key to switch to another displayed column of choices. (You can always press the Left arrow key to return to the first column.)

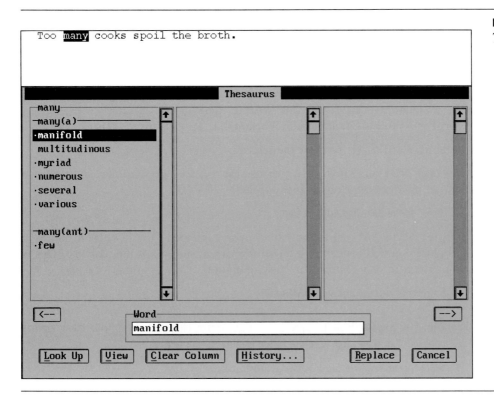

Figure WP2–39
The Thesaurus Screen

- Press C to *clear* the current column if you need to free some space for more word searches.
- Press the Esc key to cancel the thesaurus without making any change.

Try some of the following thesaurus commands. Examine Figure WP2–39. Notice that one choice is "numerous."

1. Move the highlight to "numerous" using the arrow keys

2. Press **R** to select "numerous" as the replacement

The word "many" is replaced by "numerous" on the screen.

3. Move the insertion point to "cooks"

4. Invoke Thesaurus (Tools, Writing Tools, Thesaurus)   [Alt + F1,T]

5. Press **↓** to move to the choices below

6. Find and highlight "chef"

7. Press **R** to *Replace*

8. Type an **s** onto the end of "chef" on the screen to make it plural

Continue the process: move to a word, invoke the thesaurus, and select a synonym (or cancel).

9. Move the cursor to "spoil"

10. Invoke Thesaurus

11. Highlight "putrefy" and select it as the replacement

12. Change the word "broth" on your own

The sentence might now read, "Too numerous chefs putrefy the consomme." Obviously, a thesaurus can be overused, but it can also offer helpful suggestions when you want your vocabulary to be precise.

Grammar Checker

WordPerfect also includes a **grammar checker**—an auxiliary program that checks for grammatical errors in your writing. The grammar checker offered in WordPerfect 6.0 is Grammatik 5, Version 1.1. To prepare for this exercise,

1. Start WordPerfect or clear the screen

You now need some text on which to practice, so type the following sentence with all its mistakes, exactly as it appears:

2. Type **is the best things in lif free.**

Be sure to type "is" without a capital letter, misspell "life" (without the "e"), and place a period instead of a question mark at the end of the sentence. This is enough text to demonstrate the basic operation of the grammar checker.

3. Save this document as **GRAMMAR1**

☞ **Tip: It is a good idea to save documents before changing them with the grammar checker. You may want to return to the original in the future.**

4. Select Tools, Writing Tools, Grammatik   [Alt + F1, G]

The Grammatik program appears on your screen, offering three options: (I) interactive check, (T) statistics check, and (Q) quit. You can also adjust various conditions using the menus at the top of the screen. For example, you could change preferences by pressing Alt + P, change check parameters with Alt + C, or select another file with Alt + F. However, for now,

5. Press **I** to select *Interactive Check*

As shown in Figure WP2–40, the screen splits in two: the upper portion diplays the document; the lower portion provides messages and advice. If the grammar checker finds a potential error, it highlights it on the upper screen and offers advice at the bottom.

The first error found is the spelling error. Note that the word "lif" is highlighted at the top and a "Spelling error" message appears at the bottom. The program offers a menu of actions that you can take to fix (or ignore) the problem. In this case, the program suggests that you use the REPLACE command to view some of its spelling suggestions.

6. Press **F2** (Replace) to list the replacement words.

7. Highlight *life* if needed and press **↵** to select it

8. Press **F10** to scan for the next error

The next problem is capitalization. In this instance, there is only one suggested replacement.

9. Press **F2** to replace "is" with "Is"

10. Press **F10** to continue

☞ **Tip: You can also press F9 to edit problems yourself, or F10 to continue without fixing the text at all.**

The program next finds the missing question mark. Again, it suggests only one remedy.

```
 Edit  Quit                                        F1=Help
┌──────────── A:\GRAMMAR1 - General (Standard Formality) ────────────┐
│   is the best things in │lif│ free.◄                                │
│                                                                     │
│                                                                     │
│                                                                     │
│                                                                     │
│                                                    100% checked     │
├──────────────── Rule Class: Spelling ──────────────────────────────┤
│  Check:    │lif│                                                    │
│                                                                     │
│  Advice:   Spelling error.                                          │
│                                                                     │
│                                                                     │
│  Replacement: (Use Replace command to see spelling guesses.)        │
├─────────────────────────────────────────────────────────────────────┤
│  F10: Next problem    F6: Ignore rule class   F3: Replace/Next  F2: Replace │
│  F9: Edit problem     F5: Ignore word         F7: Learn word               │
└─────────────────────────────────────────────────────────────────────┘
```

Figure WP2—40
Using the Grammar Checker

The grammar checker has detected a potential error and offers advice in the lower half of the screen.

11. Press **F2** to replace the period with a question mark

12. Press **F10** to continue

Finally, the grammar checker evaluates the subject–verb agreement and offers advice and a choice of two corrections.

13. Press **F2** to list the suggested replacements

14. Highlight *Are* and press **↵** to select it

15. Press **F10** to continue

When all errors have been found, you will be returned to the initial Grammatik screen. At this point,

16. Press **Q** to quit and return to your document

After a moment, the selected changes will appear in your document.

17. Save the corrected document as GRAMMAR2

Explore the techniques you have learned in this chapter. Create a few documents; change margins, tabs, and spacing; and try out the intricacies of the Speller Thesaurus, and Grammatik programs until you are satisfied with your mastery of each.

Checkpoint

☐ Type a paragraph with at least 10 spelling or typographical errors; save it as WPSPELL3.

☐ Use the Speller to correct all the errors, and save the corrected version as WPSPELL4.

☐ Use the thesaurus to change at least 10 words to their synonyms; save as WPSPELL5. Clear the screen.

Summary

- The File Manager screen feature offers a number of useful file management commands, including *Copy, Rename, Move, Delete, Print, Look,* and *Open.*
- The PRINT command can be used to send entire documents or selected pages to the printer. Once the pages are sent, WordPerfect uses background printing to free the program for continued use.
- The REVEAL CODES feature displays normally hidden format codes in the current document for easy reference. This feature can be used to locate and delete unwanted formatting or text enhancements.
- Almost all WordPerfect commands and enhancements take effect at the insertion point position where they were issued.
- A text block is a segment of contiguous text. BLOCK commands can be used to move, copy, delete, or enhance text blocks. Text enhancements include centering, bolding, underlining, and shifting to uppercase and lowercase letters.
- Layout refers to the arrangement of text and white space on a page. Layout changes include margins, tabs, spacing, justification, and paragraph indent.
- Justification aligns words neatly at a margin. The two most popular justification options are left and full justification. Margins that are not justified are called *ragged.*
- Tabs are used to position text in specific locations on each line. Tabs can be set left, center, right, or decimal. They can also be measured relative to the left margin or set an absolute distance from the left page edge.
- WordPerfect allows you to adjust the base font (type style) or change the appearance or size of text as needed.
- Print Preview is a PRINT option that lets the user see a document on screen as it will appear when printed.
- Paragraph Indent allows an entire paragraph to be indented without changing the margins elsewhere in a document.
- The SEARCH feature locates each occurrence of a specific text string in a document. The REPLACE feature adds the ability to replace each found text string with another one.
- Auxiliary programs include Speller, Thesaurus and Grammatik. Speller identifies words that might be misspelled. The thesaurus suggests synonyms for words selected by the user. The grammar checker (Grammatik) evaluates the grammar of your text.

Key Terms

Shown in parentheses are the page numbers on which key terms are boldfaced.

Absolute tab (WP74)
Background printing (WP48)
Base font (WP78)
Block (WP57)
BLOCK commands (WP57)
Block enhancement (WP62)
File Manager (WP44)
Full justification (WP70)
Grammar Checker (WP92)
INDENT (WP73)

Justification (WP70)
Layout (WP66)
Look (WP47)
Point (WP81)
Relative tab (WP74)
REPLACE (WP85)
REVEAL CODES (WP54)
SEARCH (WP84)
Speller (WP87)
Tab (WP74)
Text string (WP84)
Thesaurus (WP90)
View Document (WP71)

Quiz

True/False

1. The File Manager screen is invoked by typing *DIR*.
2. Background printing frees up WordPerfect for further use.
3. The Print Preview and File Manager Look features are similar in effect.
4. In REVEAL CODES, [Und on] indicates the start of underlined text.
5. Text enhancements can be removed by deleting them in the REVEAL CODES screen.
6. Text blocks are identified on the screen through the use of highlighted text.
7. A block enhancement is used to change the format of text that is about to be typed on the screen.
8. WordPerfect can change blocks of text to uppercase and lowercase letters.
9. The default setting for line spacing is single spacing.
10. Paragraph Indent is invoked with the Tab key.

Multiple Choice

11. Which function allows a file to be viewed without opening it in the work screen?
    a. Print Preview
    b. Copy
    c. Block
    d. Look
12. What pages will print if "2,10-" is specified in the print page command?
    a. Page 2 and Page 10
    b. all pages between Page 2 and Page 10
    c. Page 2 and from Page 10 to the end of the document
    d. Page 2 and the next 10 pages
13. A segment of contiguous text is called a
    a. block.
    b. hidden code.
    c. document.
    d. highlight.
14. "Cut and Paste" is the editing term for which word processing function?
    a. Copy
    b. Delete
    c. Block
    d. Move
15. When a block is highlighted on the screen, pressing the F10 function key will do which of the following?
    a. save the highlighted block to disk
    b. retrieve a block from disk
    c. save the entire document to disk
    d. produce an error message
16. Which one of these is *not* a justification setting in WordPerfect?
    a. left justification
    b. midjustification
    c. full justification
    d. right justification

17. The left-margin-only justification style is also known as
    a. ragged-left.
    b. ragged-right.
    c. left indented.
    d. completely justified.
18. Which type of tabs are measured with reference to the left margin?
    a. referenced tabs
    b. decimal tabs
    c. relative tabs
    d. absolute tabs
19. A collection of contiguous characters specified in a search or replace function is called a
    a. revealed code.
    b. layout feature.
    c. dot leader.
    d. text string.
20. Which of the following series of words will be considered entirely correct by the Speller program?
    a. I went to to the store.
    b. He soar The plain fly in thee ski.
    c. She heard a loudnoise.
    d. We waited for the airplain to land.

Matching

Select the term that best matches each phrase below:

a.	Absolute tab	g.	Text string
b.	Full justification	h.	Thesaurus
c.	Layout	i.	REVEAL CODES
d.	Print Preview	j.	INDENT
e.	Look	k.	Justification
f.	Speller	l.	Tab

21. A feature that allows the user to see a screen representation of a document as it will appear when printed
22. A program that suggests synonyms for selected words
23. A feature that allows the user to see hidden formatting codes in a document
24. A feature that allows text to be placed in specific positions on a line
25. A feature that indents an entire paragraph without changing margins elsewhere in the document
26. A setting measured from the left edge of the page
27. A function invoked from the File Manager that allows a file to be viewed without opening it
28. A collection of contiguous characters or words
29. The arrangement of text and white space on a page
30. Alignment of text so that it falls exactly at a margin

Answers

True/False: 1. F; 2. T; 3. F; 4. F; 5. T; 6. T; 7. F; 8. T; 9. T; 10. F
Multiple Choice: 11. d; 12. c; 13. a; 14. d; 15. a; 16. b; 17. b; 18. c; 19. d; 20. b
Matching: 21. d; 22. h; 23. i; 24. l; 25. j; 26. a; 27. e; 28. g; 29. c; 30. k

Exercises

I. Operations

Provide the WordPerfect sequence of keystrokes and actions required to do each of the operations shown below. For each operation, assume a system with a hard disk and a diskette in Drive A. Further assume that the default drive has been set to Drive A earlier, and that a file called NOTES1 is on the data disk. If you want to verify each command by trying it on your computer system, you will have to type a few words in WordPerfect and then save it as a document called NOTES1 on your disk before you begin.

1. See a list of files for the disk in Drive A.
2. Copy the NOTES1 file to a file called NOTES2.
3. Rename the NOTES2 file to TESTNOTE.
4. Print the NOTES1 file.
5. Delete the TESTNOTE file.
6. Open the NOTES1 file onto the work screen.
7. Activate the REVEAL CODES screen, and then exit it.
8. Underline any text with the BLOCK UNDERLINE command.
9. Move the underlined text to the bottom of your document.
10. Save the underlined block as a file called NOTES2.
11. Change the spacing of the entire document to double-spaced.
12. Change the margins to left 2″ and right 1.5″.
13. Save the document as NOTES1 and quit WordPerfect.

II. Commands

Describe fully, using as few words as possible in each case, what command is initiated, or what is accomplished, in WordPerfect by pressing each series of keystrokes given below. Assume that each exercise part is independent of any previous parts.

Function Key Commands

1. `F4`
2. `Shift` + `F8`
3. `Alt` + `F4`
4. `Ctrl` + `F4`
5. `Alt` + `F2`
6. `F2`
7. `Ctrl` + `F2`
8. `F5`
9. `Alt` + `F3`
10. `Ctrl` + `F8`

Pull-Down Menus

1. Layout, Alignment, Indent
2. Layout
3. Edit, Block
4. Edit, Cut and Paste
5. Edit, Replace
6. Edit, Search
7. Tools, Writing Tools, Speller
8. File, File Manager
9. View, Reveal Codes
10. Font, Font

III. Applications

Perform the following operations using your computer system. You will need a hard drive or network with WordPerfect on it, or a DOS disk and two WordPerfect program disks. You will also need your data disk for retrieval and to store the results of this exercise. In a few words, describe how you accomplished each operation, and its result. Save the document after each operation is completed so that you can always return to these exercises later.

WP

Application 1: Job Inquiry

1. Boot your computer, initiate the WordPerfect program, and, if needed, set the default to the drive that contains your data disk.

2. Use the File Manager screen to open the WORK1–1A file you prepared earlier, or type it now as in Application 1 in the previous chapter. Your letter should resemble the following sample.

```
                        Hugh Ken Hierme
                    123-456 Job Search Lane
                      New Job, CA 98765

Today's Date

Anita Worker
Mar-Park Consulting Services
7546 Pleasant Beach Avenue
San Dinmyshoos, CA 98766

Dear Ms. Worker:

In response to your advertisement in yesterday's
Employment Times, enclosed please find my resume in
application for the position of cliff diver.

Although I haven't jumped professionally, I am sure
that my enclosed history of falling off the Golden Gate
Bridge, and the Eiffel Tower, will be of interest to
you.

I will be available for a job interview as soon as my
splints and body cast are removed. I look forward to
hearing from you at your earliest convenience.

Sincerely,
```

3. If you just typed it, save it as WORK1–1A.

4. Use File Manager to copy it to a file called WORK2–1A.

5. Use REVEAL CODES to remove the bold enhancement from the text in the third paragraph.

6. Use the *Text Block* command to move the second paragraph beneath the third paragraph. Fix the spacing between paragraphs if needed.

7. Number each paragraph at the left margin and then use the PARAGRAPH INDENT command to indent each paragraph one tab stop in after the number.

8. Use the BLOCK: UPPERCASE command to change "Mar-Park Consulting Services" to all uppercase letters.

9. Move to the start of the first paragraph and change the line spacing to double spacing for the rest of the document.

10. Change the margins for the entire letter to left 1.5″ and right 1.5″.

11. Save this letter as WORK2–1B.

12. Print a copy of this new letter using the File Manager print technique.

13. Clear your screen and exit WordPerfect.

Application 2: Employer Response

1. Boot your computer, initiate the WordPerfect program, and set the default to the drive that contains your data disk.

2. Use the File Manager screen to open the WORK1–2A document you prepared earlier, or type it now by following the Application 2 exercise in the previous chapter. Your letter should resemble the sample below.

```
                    Mar-Park Consulting Services
                     7546 Pleasant Beach Avenue
                     San Dinmyshoos, CA 98766


       (Type today's date here)

       Mr. Hugh Hierme
       123-456 Job Search Lane
       New Job, CA 98765


       Dear Mr. Hierme:


       Thank you for your response to our advertisement in
       the Employment Times for the position of cliff diver.
       We have had over 400 inquiries from well-qualified ap-
       plicants.

       Your experience falling off the Golden Gate Bridge
       and the Eiffel Tower is of interest to us for two
       reasons: it displays your willingness to travel
       and shows that you have no fear of extreme heights.

       We would like to schedule an interview with you for
       next week and will arrange to send a limousine to
       bring you, and your body cast, to our offices.
       Please call my secretary at 1-800-JUMPNOW to arrange
       a time that is convenient. I look forward to meeting
       you.


       Sincerely,


       Anita Worker
       Human Resources Director
```

3. If you just typed it, save it as WORK1–2A.

4. Use File Manager to copy it to a file called WORK2–2A.

5. Use REVEAL CODES to remove the bold enhancement from the text in the third paragraph. Boldface the "Golden Gate Bridge" and "Eiffel Tower" in the second paragraph

6. Use the text BLOCK commands to move the second paragraph beneath the third paragraph. Fix the spacing between paragaphs if needed.

7. Number each paragraph at the left margin and then use the PARAGRAPH INDENT command to indent each paragraph one tab stop in after the number

8. Use the BLOCK uppercase command to change "Mar-Park Consulting Services" to all uppercase letters.

9. Move to the start of the first paragraph and change the line spacing to double spacing for the rest of the document.

10. Change the margins for the entire letter to left 1.2″ and right 1.2″.

11. Save this letter as WORK2–2B.

12. Print a copy of this new letter using the page print technique.

13. Clear your screen and exit WordPerfect.

Application 3: Memo

1. Boot your computer, initiate the WordPerfect program, and set the default to the drive that contains your data disk.

2. Use the File Manager screen to open the WORK1–3A document you prepared earlier, or type it now by following the Application 3 exercise in the previous chapter. Your memo should resemble the sample below.

```
                      Mar-Park Consulting Services
                        Inter-Office MEMORANDUM


          TO:  Phil D. Pool, Director
               Cliff Divers Training Center

          FROM:  Anita Worker, Director
                 Human Resources

          DATE:  (insert today's date here)

          SUBJECT:  Interviews for Cliff Divers


          -----------------------------------------------------------


          The response to our advertisement in the Employment
          Times has been overwhelming. To date, we have
          received over 400 letters applying for the position
          of Cliff diver.

          My staff has finished the initial screening and
          recommends that we invite the top 20 applicants
          to participate in the first round of interviews to
          be held next week.

          We will require the use of the gym and your 40-foot
          model cliff for the performance portion of the
          interview. Please make sure to fill the pool before
          the first test dive.
```

3. If you just typed it, save it as WORK1–3A.

4. Use File Manager to copy it to a file called WORK2–3A.

5. Use REVEAL CODES to remove the bold enhancement from the text in the first paragraph.

6. Use the text BLOCK commands to move the second paragraph beneath the third paragraph. Fix the spacing between paragraphs if needed.

7. Number each paragraph at the left margin and then use the PARAGRAPH INDENT command to indent each paragraph one tab stop in after the number.

8. Use the BLOCK uppercase command to change "Mar-Park Consulting Services" to all uppercase letters.

9. Move to the start of the first paragraph and change the line spacing to double spacing for the rest of the document.

10. Change the margins for the entire memo to left 2″ and right 2″. Remove the line between "Mar-Park Consulting Services" and "Inter-Office MEMORANDUM."

11. Save this memo as WORK2–3B.

12. Print a copy of this new memo using any print technique.

13. Clear your screen and exit WordPerfect.

3

WordPerfect 6.0 for DOS

Advanced Word Processing: Multipages, Multidocuments, Automation, Graphics, and Data Transfer

WP

OUTLINE

OBJECTIVES

After completing the modules in this chapter you will be able to do any or all of the following:

1 Demonstrate techniques for managing multipage documents, to include page breaks, page numbering, page jumps, headers, and footers.

2 Work with two documents at the same time, both in separate screens and on the same screen.

3 Create and merge primary and secondary files to create individualized letters.

4 Explain the purpose of macros and describe the procedures for creating, editing, and invoking them.

5 Create and modify text outlines and sorts.

6 Draw lines and boxes using the GRAPHICS command and Table feature and add graphic figures and captions to text.

7 Demonstrate the use of a mouse with the button bar and ribbon.

8 Explain ASCII files, and import data into and export data from WordPerfect.

O V E R V I E W   This chapter provides an advanced set of word processing techniques, including managing larger documents, using two documents at once, merging files, creating outlines, automating commands, and using tables and graphics. Each procedure is presented as a separate module that can be studied independently.

You will be using files available on disk and others created by you. The chapter first examines concepts related to multipage documents, such as automatic headers, footers, and page numbering. Techniques for using two documents are presented next, including copying between files and merging. Creating, using, and editing macros are introduced next, followed by procedures for managing footnotes, outlines and sorts. The chapter then examines the advanced word processing procedures involved in creating tables and combining text and graphics, concluding with techniques for importing and exporting files.

Preparing for This Chapter

This text includes a separate data disk that contains files for use with this chapter. These files reduce the amount of keystroking you must do. If you do not have this disk (or want extra practice), you can create the files yourself.

The files must first be copied to your data disk so they will be available for use. Check with your instructor or lab technician, or follow the appropriate procedure below for your system (it is assumed that you are already at the DOS prompt). *Note:* If you have two diskette drives (even in a hard-disk system), follow the dual-diskette system instructions.

Hard-Disk System (with one disk drive)

Create a subdirectory to hold the files for copying:

1. Type **MD C:\FILES** ⏎

2. Place the Dryden File Diskette in Drive A

3. Type **COPY A:\WP\ *.* C:\FILES** ⏎

4. Remove the Dryden File Diskette and replace it in its envelope

5. Place your data diskette in Drive A

6. Type **COPY C:\FILES\ *.* A:** ⏎

Now remove the hard disk subdirectory:

7. Type **ERASE C:\FILES\ *.*** ⏎

8. Type **RD C:\FILES** ⏎

Dual-Diskette System

1. Place the Dryden File Diskette in Drive A

2. Place your data diskette in Drive B

3. Type **COPY A:\WP\ *.* B:** ⏎

4. Remove the Dryden File Diskette from Drive A and replace it in its envelope

Module 1: Managing Multipage Documents

WordPerfect's basic commands are sufficient for preparing short documents, such as letters and memos. As documents become larger, however, you can call upon advanced features to help you move around the file and manage the final output. Such features include page breaks, headers and footers, page numbering, and insertion point movements.

A two-page document (EXWP3–1) has been prepared for your use. Open the document as follows:

1. Start WordPerfect
2. Open the EXWP3–1 document

The complete document is shown in Figure WP3–1. If you do not have EXWP3–1 available (or want the practice), type it in now, copying the text shown in the figure. Then save it as EXWP3–1.

Just as WordPerfect inserts soft returns each time you reach the right margin, it also creates **soft page breaks** each time you reach the end of a text page. These breaks are shown by a single line extending across the width of the screen. They are *soft* because, like soft returns, they are not locked into one particular spot but change their location as you edit your document. Move to the first soft page break as follows:

Soft Page Breaks

1. Press **Pg Dn** to move to page 2

2. Press **↑** once

Figure WP3–1
The EXWP3–1 Document

(a) First half.

REPORT DEADLINES

Andrea sat nervously in front of the microcomputer screen.
She stretched her fingers over the keyboard while Elissa Roberts,
manager of Freddy Johnson's Travel Agency, looked on. Andrea had
skipped lunch to finish this work, stopping only when the
stiffness in her neck and fingers forced her to take a break.
This was her first big assignment since completing the word
processing course at Oakridge University. She could have used
more practice with the word processor--especially on this
keyboard, which differed from the one she used at school. Her
fingers kept pressing the wrong key for SHIFT, forcing her to
backspace and retype more often than usual. If only she was
better acquainted with the layout, she'd be fine. But there was
no time for that now. Andrea knew that time was short, and
excuses wouldn't help. The job simply had to be completed.
    Andrea had arrived at work earlier that morning to learn
that an important meeting had been moved up, well ahead of
schedule. With only hours left before the meeting, Andrea had
been asked to put her word processing training to the test--a
typewriter was clearly too slow for all the work that had to be
done. After four hours of straight typing, she was tired, but
could not let Elissa down.
    After her brief rest, Andrea searched through the filenames
on disk and retrieved the first ten pages of the proposal she had
saved a few minutes ago. Even though she was under intense
pressure, her training had taught her to constantly make backup
copies of her work for safekeeping. She couldn't afford to lose
any part of this report if something unforeseen happened to the
computer.
    "There's still so much to do," she thought. "Even if I can
read Freddy's handwritten notes, the current margins and spacing
are all wrong, the paragraphs must be changed around, the
itinerary is incomplete, and typing errors must be corrected."
Not being the best speller, she also dreaded the editing which
would follow after the rest of the report had been typed. But
there was no turning back. The meeting could not be postponed,
and the report must be ready. Andrea began to type.
    Elissa joined Andrea a few minutes later. She began
deciphering Freddy's handwriting and dictating it to Andrea.
Andrea didn't stop to fix mistakes, but just typed it into the
word processor as quickly as possible.

Your screen should now resemble Figure WP3–2. The insertion point is positioned on the last line of the page. The soft page break is shown by the solid line beneath the insertion point. (Page mode also displays top and bottom page margins.)

3. Press ↓ once.

You should now be on the first line of page 2, directly beneath the soft page break.

If you were to change the text in some way (add text, delete text, adjust margins, or set line spacing, for example), the soft page break would automatically relocate to the proper position. Try this:

(b) Second half.

When she finished the rough draft, Andrea printed out the
itinerary portion and brought it to Elissa for review. She made
sure to print it triple-spaced, leaving more than enough room for
written additions. While Elissa filled in the missing data,
Andrea went back to the computer and started the built-in
spelling checker. As each error appeared on the screen, she
corrected it herself or selected one of the computer's correct
spelling choices. Elissa returned with the completed itinerary
that Andrea used to fill in the missing sections of the document.
Now it was time for "clean up." Andrea ran her punctuation
and style program. It found a few run-on sentences, some missing
punctuation, and a repeated word. Andrea corrected these flaws
quickly. Next, she printed a double-spaced draft of the entire
document on her dot-matrix printer and made copies on the
photocopier. Freddy, Elissa and Andrea got together to review
their copies for style and content. Freddy felt that the word
"fantastic" was overused and would have negative results at the
meeting. Elissa didn't like the order of paragraphs on page
twenty. Andrea spotted an error, "we hope you enjoy your tip,"
that the speller could not pick up. Andrea made note of the
changes.
Retrieving the document once more, Andrea located each
appropriate page and altered the document to match her notes.
She moved the paragraphs around, deleted a few sentences, and
used the on-line thesaurus to replace "fantastic" with
"fabulous," "fanciful," "marvelous," and just plain "great." She
almost forgot to change "tip" to "trip."
Now, after a quick command to change the left margin to
allow space for a binder, and adding headers and page numbers,
Andrea was ready to print. She saved the document on disk, and
took it into Elissa's office where the laser printer was located.
A few commands later and the report was being printed,
letter-perfect, at twelve pages a minute. Within three minutes,
it was done.
Andrea ran to the photocopier, made ten copies, and inserted
them into presentation binders. Five minutes after the meeting
started, Andrea walked in with a stack of impressive reports--one
for each participant. Then she calmly walked out and collapsed
at her desk!

4. Press **Home** **Home** **↑**

5. Select <u>L</u>ayout   [Shift + F8]

6. Press **L** **S** **2** **↵** to set double spacing

7. Press **↵** to exit (press **↵** again if needed to close the Format box)

8. Move to the first line of page 2

Note that the soft page break now occurs earlier in the text.

9. Save this document as **EXWP3–1A**

Figure WP3—2
A Soft Page Break

A soft page break is placed automatically by WordPerfect and shown with a single line across the page. (Page margins are also shown in page mode.)

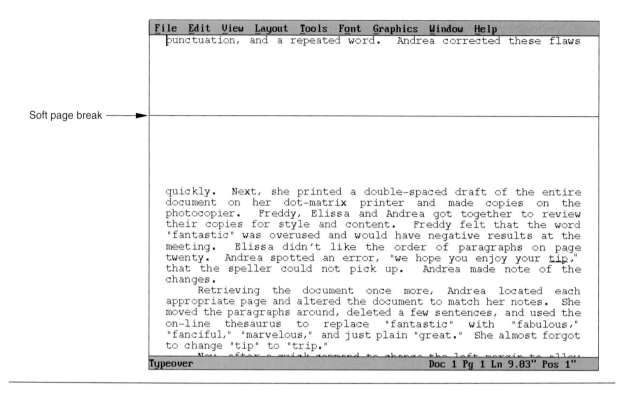

Soft page break

> ☞ **Tip: You cannot remove or adjust soft page breaks. They are placed automatically by the program and will be moved, or eliminated, as you make changes in your document.**

Hard Page Breaks

There are times when you will want to force a page break before reaching the physical end of the page. Perhaps you want to separate a title page from the rest of a document, or make sure a report section starts on a new page. You can do this by using the Ctrl plus the Enter keys to insert a hard page break, which appears as a double dashed line extending across the screen. Like a hard return, a **hard page break** remains fixed at a specific location in the text. It does not change its location unless you change it.

Creating Hard Page Breaks.   Try creating the following hard page break:

1.   Open EXWP3–1A
2.   Move your insertion point to Ln 1.33″

This is just below the title. Your screen should resemble Figure WP3–3. To insert a hard page break,

3.   Select Layout, Alignment, Hard Page   [Ctrl + Enter]

> ☞ **Tip: The Ctrl + Enter key combination is the easier method.**

Figure WP3—3
*Creating a Hard
Page Break*

Place the insertion point where
you want the page to end and
press the Ctrl and Enter keys to
create a hard page break (shown
by a double line).

```
 File   Edit   View   Layout   Tools   Font   Graphics   Window   Help



                        REPORT DEADLINES

 |

       Andrea sat nervously in front of the microcomputer screen.
 She stretched her fingers over the keyboard while Elissa Roberts,
 manager of Freddy Johnson's Travel Agency, looked on.  Andrea had
 skipped lunch to finish this work, stopping only when the stiffness
 in her neck and fingers forced her to take a break.  This was her
 first big assignment since completing the word processing course at
 Oakridge University.  She could have used more practice with the
 word processor--especially on this keyboard, which differed from
 the one she used at school.  Her fingers kept pressing the wrong
 key for SHIFT, forcing her to backspace and retype more often than
 Typeover                              Doc 1 Pg 1 Ln 1.33" Pos 1"
```

A solid double line appears, showing that a hard page break has been inserted.
Page 1 now contains only the title, whereas page 2 starts the story. No matter
how you adjust your text, this page break will remain between the title and the
first paragraph of your document (unless you remove it).

Removing Hard Page Breaks.   Hard page breaks are removed like any other
text enhancement—with the Delete or Backspace key. Because the double line
clearly indicates the location of the hard page break on the screen, you do not
need to use REVEAL CODES as you might with other text codes. You have two
easier choices—either place the insertion point on the line below the hard page
break and press the Backspace key, or place the insertion point on the line above
it and press the Delete key. Try this:

1. Press   **↑**   to position the insertion point on Pg 1 Ln 1.33"

2. Press   **Delete**   to remove the hard page break

(You could have also placed the insertion point on the first line of page 2 and
pressed the Backspace key.) Try inserting and deleting a few hard page breaks
for practice.

Headers and Footers

Headers and **footers** are lines of text that usually appear on every page of a
multipage document. They contain descriptive information such as a document
title or a chapter name. In a long letter, they might indicate a topic and date.
Headers, the more common variety, are used at the top of the document, whereas
footers appear at the bottom.

WordPerfect allows up to two headers and footers on each page, designated as "A" or "B," respectively. A header or footer is usually positioned one inch from the top (or bottom) of the page, with one blank line between it and the main text. The remaining space is used for your document.

Creating a Header.   The following exercise creates a header for the EXWP3–1 document (a footer can be created in a similar fashion).

1. Start WordPerfect (or clear the screen) and open EXWP3–1

Usually you do not place a header (or footer) on a document's first page. Instead, you position the insertion point on the page where the header will begin.

2. Press `Pg Dn` to move to page 2

3. Select Layout   [Shift + F8]

Your screen should now display the Layout or Format menu (depending on which method you used to start).

4. Press `H` for *Header/Footer/Watermark*

A Header/Footer/Watermark menu appears as in Figure WP3–4a.

5. Press `H` for *Headers*

6. Press `A` for *Header A*

A number of placement options appear on the screen, as shown in Figure WP3–4b. You can place a header on every page, or place separate headers (A and B) on odd and even pages as in a book.

7. Press `A` to select placement on *All Pages*

8. Select Create (or just press `↵`)

A header entry screen appears. You can now fill in the header as follows:

9. Type **Word Processing**

10. Press `F7` to exit

The header has been placed into your document. It will appear when you print, but, like justification, it is not displayed on the screen unless you use page mode (as in Figure WP3–5a). To see the header as it will appear when printed, use *Print Preview*:

11. Select File   [Shift + F7]

12. Press `V` for *Print Preview*

13. Press `Alt` + `V` and then `1` to see the document at 100%

Your screen should resemble Figure WP3–5b. If you press Pg Up to move to page 1, you should see no header.

14. Press `Esc` to exit from *Print Preview*

15. Save the document as **EXWP3–1B**

The procedure to create a footer is identical, except that you press *F* in Step 5 to choose *Footers*.

☞ **Tip: Headers and footers reduce the number of text lines that can be printed on each page. This may cause text to "spill over" onto a new page. Therefore, use page mode or Print Preview to check proper text layout before printing.**

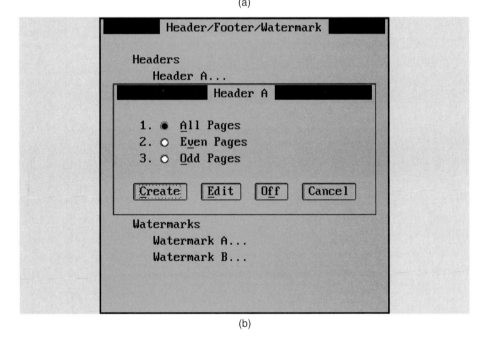

Figure WP3—4
Creating a Header

(a) The Header/Footer/Watermark menu is first selected.
(b) Choosing "Headers" invokes the placement options menu at the bottom of the screen.

Editing a Header.   A header or footer can be modified with almost the same procedure that created it. For example, to change the header "Word Processing" to "Word Processing Assignment," follow these steps:

1. Select Layout   [Shift + F8]

2. Press **H** **H** **A** for *Header A*

3. Press **E** for *Edit*

Figure WP3—5

The Header as It Appears in Your Document

(a) In page mode. (b) In Print Preview.

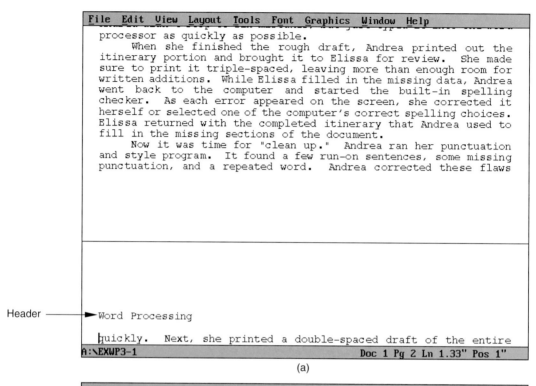

(a)

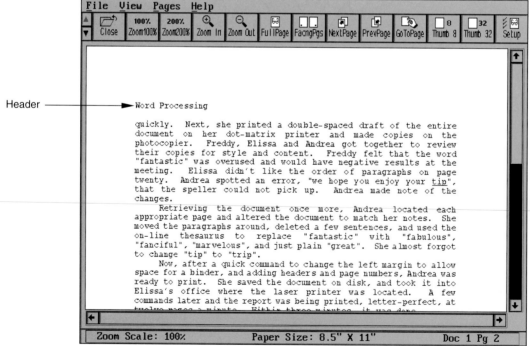

(b)

The header screen will appear as you left it earlier.

4. Move to the end of "Word Processing"

5. Press **Space** and type **Assignment**

6. Press **F7** to exit

The header has been modified; you can see it in page mode or use Print Preview to see it.

7. Save the document as **EXWP3–1C**

Note: Editing a footer is an identical process to that for editing a header, except that you press *HFA* instead of *HHA* in Step 2 to choose *Footers*.

Deleting a Header.   Headers and footers can be deleted if they are no longer needed in your document. The approach is the same as deleting any hidden code—move to the appropriate page, then find and delete the header code using REVEAL CODES.

However, you may want to simply turn off, or discontinue, a header at some point. To do this,

1. Select Layout   [Shift + F8]

2. Press **H** **H** **A** for *Header A*

3. Press **F** for *Off*

4. Press **↵** to exit (press **↵** again if needed to close the Format box)

The header will not appear in your document beyond the page on which you issued the *Off* command.

Page Numbering

When you are typing a multipage document, you may want to include page numbers. As with headers, page numbers typically start on page 2, leaving the first page unnumbered.

The following exercises will allow you to number pages in your document, position the number on the page, and modify the numbering scheme.

Positioning.   Creating page numbers is simply a matter of telling the program where you want them to appear.

1. Clear the screen and then open the EXWP3–1 document

Now move the insertion point to the page where numbering will begin.

2. Press **Pg Dn** to move to page 2

3. Select Layout   [Shift + F8]

4. Press **P** for *Page*

5. Press **N** for *Page Numbering*

A Page Numbering screen appears, as in Figure WP3–6a. Note that item 1 shows no page numbering has been set; item 2 shows the current page as page 2.

6. Press **P** for *Page Number Position*

A screen resembling Figure WP3–6b appears. This screen offers six locations for placing numbers on *every* page—namely, 1 (top left), 2 (top center), 3 (top right), 5 (bottom left), 6 (bottom center), or 7 (bottom right). Two additional positions

Figure WP3—6

Adding Page Numbers

(a) The Page Numbering screen.
(b) The Page Number Position
screen offers options for printing
numbers on every page (1–3,
5–7), alternating pages (4, 8),
or no page numbers (9).

```
┌──────────────────────────────────────────────────────────────┐
│                         Page Format                            │
│  ┌──────────────────────────────────────────────────────────┐ │
│  │                      Page Numbering                        │ │
│  │                                                            │ │
│  │  1. Page Number Position...  │None                       ││ │
│  │                                                            │ │
│  │  2. Page Number...           │2                          ││ │
│  │                                                            │ │
│  │  3. Secondary Page Number... │2                          ││ │
│  │                                                            │ │
│  │  4. Chapter...               │1                          ││ │
│  │                                                            │ │
│  │  5. Volume...                │1                          ││ │
│  │                                                            │ │
│  │  6. Page Number Format       │[page #]                   ││ │
│  │                                                            │ │
│  │  7. Insert Formatted Page Number                           │ │
│  │                                                            │ │
│  │  ┌─────────────────┐              ┌──────┐  ┌────────┐     │ │
│  │  │ Number Codes... F5 │            │  OK  │  │ Cancel │     │ │
│  │  └─────────────────┘              └──────┘  └────────┘     │ │
│  └──────────────────────────────────────────────────────────┘ │
└──────────────────────────────────────────────────────────────┘
```

(a)

```
┌──────────────────────────────────────────────────────────────┐
│                         Page Format                            │
│  ┌──────────────────────────────────────────────────────────┐ │
│  │                   Page Number Position                     │ │
│  │                                                            │ │
│  │  Page Number Position                      ┌─Page─┐        │ │
│  │  1.  ○  Top Left          Every            │1 2 3 │        │ │
│  │  2.  ○  Top Center        Page             │      │        │ │
│  │  3.  ○  Top Right                          │5 6 7 │        │ │
│  │  4.  ○  Alternating, Top                   └──────┘        │ │
│  │  5.  ○  Bottom Left                      ┌─Page─┐┌─Page─┐   │ │
│  │  6.  ○  Bottom Center     Alternating    │4     ││    4 │   │ │
│  │  7.  ○  Bottom Right      Pages          │Even  ││ Odd  │   │ │
│  │  8.  ○  Alternating, Bottom              │8     ││    8 │   │ │
│  │  9.  ●  None                             └──────┘└──────┘   │ │
│  │                                                            │ │
│  │  A.  Font/Attributes/Color...                              │ │
│  │                                                            │ │
│  │                              ┌──────┐  ┌────────┐          │ │
│  │                              │  OK  │  │ Cancel │          │ │
│  │                              └──────┘  └────────┘          │ │
│  └──────────────────────────────────────────────────────────┘ │
└──────────────────────────────────────────────────────────────┘
```

(b)

are offered for alternating pages—namely, 4 (top outside corner) or 8 (bottom outside corner). Choice 9 shuts off the page numbers.

7. Press |I| for *Top Right* numbering

8. Press |↵| (or select "OK") to accept your choice

9. Press |↵| twice more to exit

Numbers have been added to your document (but will appear only in the printed version or in page mode).

10. Save the document as **EXWP3–1D**

Renumbering. At times, a document's physical page number may not be the number you want to use. For example, if the first two pages of a report are a title page and table of contents, you may want numbering to start with the *third* page shown as page 1, not page 3. A minor change can accomplish this easily. To see the effect, first open document EXWP3–2 as follows:

1. Start WordPerfect or clear your screen
2. Open EXWP3–2

The first page should read "Thoughts about Word Processing." *Note:* If you do not have EXWP3–2, create it now by retrieving EXWP3–1 and modifying it by following the instructions listed in Figure WP3–7.

This document has a title page, which should not be numbered. Although page numbering has already been set to start on the second page, a quick look in page mode or with Print Preview reveals why this won't work:

3. View the document or switch to page mode if needed

4. Press `Pg Dn`

Your screen should resemble Figure WP3–8. Notice that page 2 is *numbered* as page 2! You must now renumber the pages, starting with page 2, so that it will begin as *page 1*. Here's how:

5. Exit Print Preview if needed

6. Select Layout   [Shift + F8]

7. Press `P` for *Page*

8. Press `N` for *Page Numbering*

Up to this point, this is the regular procedure for creating page numbers. Note that item 1 shows page numbers are set to "top right." Item 2 shows that this page will be numbered "2."

9. Press `N` to set a new page number

10. Press `N` and `1` to set page 1

11. Press `↵` three times to exit (and once more if Format box appears)

12. Press `Pg Up` and then `Pg Dn` to reset the screen

The page counter has been set to 1.

13. Save this document as **EXWP3–2a**

Page locations and page numbering are usually set at the same time. You may want to experiment with this by using REVEAL CODES to locate and remove the hidden page number command at the start of page 2. Then relocate numbers at the bottom center of each page and start numbering page 2 as page 10. Do *not* save this when you are finished.

Page Jumps

Normal arrow controls let you move easily on one page, but they can become tedious when working on a larger document. WordPerfect offers a few commands to move around multipage documents easily. The Pg Up and Pg Dn keys allow you to move one page at a time in either direction. Better yet, the **GO TO** command quickly relocates the insertion point on any page you name. In effect, it "jumps" directly to that page. Try this:

1. Start WordPerfect or clear your screen
2. Open EXWP3–2

Figure WP3—7
Creating the EXWP3–2 Document

If EXWP3–2 is not available, retrieve EXWP3–1 and follow these instructions to create it.

To create EXWP3–2 from EXWP3–1:

1. At start of document, change line spacing to 2.

2. Delete the title line.

3. Press the Enter key 10 times.

4. Center the heading ''Thoughts about Word Processing''

5. Create a hard page break.

6. Create page numbers on the top right.

7. Insert the following two paragraphs at the beginning of the new page:

```
     According to Charles Parker, "word processing is
the use of computer technology to create, manipulate,
and print text materials."  These materials include
such items as letters, memos, legal contracts, article
manuscripts, and other documents.  As Parker explains
it, word processing saves so much time that most people
stop using their typewriters once they learn word
processing.
     The following story, written by Edward Martin,
demonstrates why word processing is so valuable to a
typical office.  The story, reprinted here with
permission of the author, begins as follows:
```

8. Add this closing paragraph at the end:

```
     Clearly, this story demonstrates that word
processing can greatly benefit normal typing tasks.  It
can even make the impossible possible.  Even though
this is impressive, it would appear that this is only
the beginning.  If word processing is combined with
special graphics software and additional computer
equipment, it can create a desktop publishing system--
"a microcomputer-based publishing system that lets you
combine page elements such as text, art, and photos,
thus creating attractive-looking documents that look
like they came off a printer's press."  But that is
another story.
```

9. Save the document as EXWP3–2.

3. Select <u>E</u>dit, <u>G</u>oto   [Ctrl + Home]

The screen responds with "Go to_" and awaits your reply.

4. Type **3** to select the third page

5. Press ⏎

The insertion point is repositioned at the start of page 3.

Figure WP3—8
Changing Page Numbers

The first text page of the document will be numbered 2—and should be changed.

```
 File   Edit   View   Layout   Tools   Font   Graphics   Window   Help



                                        Page number──────────► 2

     According to Charles Parker, "word processing is the use of
computer  technology  to  create,  manipulate,  and  print  text
materials."  These materials include such items as letters, memos,
legal contracts, article manuscripts, and other documents.  As
Parker explains it, word processing saves so much time that most
people  stop  using  their  typewriters  once  they  learn  word
processing.
     The following story, written by Edward Martin, demonstrates
why word processing is so valuable to a typical office.  The story,
reprinted here with permission of the author, begins as follows:
     Andrea sat nervously in front of the microcomputer screen.
She stretched her fingers over the keyboard while Elissa Roberts,
manager of Freddy Johnson's Travel Agency, looked on.  Andrea had
skipped lunch to finish this work, stopping only when the stiffness
in her neck and fingers forced her to take a break.  This was her
first big assignment since completing the word processing course at
Oakridge University.  She could have used more practice with the
word processor--especially on this keyboard, which differed from
the one she used at school.  Her fingers kept pressing the wrong
key for SHIFT, forcing her to backspace and retype more often than
usual.  If only she was better acquainted with the layout, she'd be
 A:\EXWP3-2                              Doc 1 Pg 2 Ln 1.33" Pos 1"
```

☞ **Tip: If your document is shorter than the selected page, the insertion point will be positioned at the start of the *last* page.**

6. Clear the screen

Checkpoint

☐ Clear the screen and open EXWP3–1. Add a footer that places the words "Check Point" at the lower left.

☐ Change the page numbering to appear in the outer top corner of alternating pages.

☐ Renumber page 1 to start as page 10. Save the document as WPCHECK1, print it, and then clear the screen.

Module 2: Working with Two Documents

A powerful tool (and challenge) is the capability to work with two documents at once. Although this technique allows you to move freely between two documents as if they were one, it also places demands on your ability to keep track of where you are and what you are doing. The following exercises allow you to practice working with two documents.

Switching between Documents

Using two documents is a fairly straightforward procedure. First, you type (or open) a document normally. Then, you switch to a second screen and type (or open) a second document. From then on, you move back and forth between the documents as needed. The key to understanding where you are at any given time

---

Figure WP3—9

Entering the Documents

(a) Type the text in part a into Doc 1 and save it as EXWP3–3a. (b) Type the text in part b into Doc 2 and save it as EXWP3–3b.

```
(a) Text for Doc 1:

This sample illustrates how easily text can be copied from
one document into another by switching between two documents
in WordPerfect.  For example, this paragraph is part of the
first document.  It was typed into the Doc 1 screen and then
saved as EXWP3-3a.¶
¶
This paragraph was also typed into the first document.  If
you were to print out a copy of EXWP3-3a, you would only see
these two paragraphs.¶
¶
(b) Text for Doc 2:

This paragraph was typed into the Doc 2 screen and saved as
EXWP3-3b.  If you were to print out a copy of EXWP3-3b, you
would only see this paragraph.¶
¶
```

is to watch the document number—Doc 1 or Doc 2—on the status line. In the following exercise, you will create two short documents, copy a paragraph from one into the other, and then save the completed document. Of course, you can use these techniques to manage up to *nine* documents at a time.

Entering Doc 1. The first task is to open or create a document on the Doc 1 screen. In this example, you will create a short document as follows:

1. Clear your screen
2. Type the text shown in Figure WP3–9a

Remember to press the Enter key only when you reach each paragraph symbol (¶) in the figure.

3. Save this document as **EXWP3–3a**

Switching to Doc 2. With the document ready on the Doc 1 screen, switch to the second screen as follows:

1. Select Window, Switch   [Shift + F3]

☞ **Tip: This technique switches between the two most current documents. If you need to access more than two documents, select "Window, Switch to" instead. You can then select from a list of active documents.**

The new screen will be blank, and you will see *Doc 2* on the status line. Now enter the Doc 2 text:

2. Type the text shown in Figure WP3–9b
3. Save this document as **EXWP3–3b**

You now have two documents in memory at the same time. Selecting "Window, Switch" (or pressing the Shift plus F3 keys) will switch back and forth between the two documents, as shown in Figure WP3–10. Try it:

Figure WP3—10
Switching Document Screens

Pressing the Shift and F3 keys (in menu, Window, Switch) allows you to switch between the two most current documents in memory.

```
This sample illustrates how easily text can be copied from
one document into another by switching between two documents
in WordPerfect.  For example, this paragraph is part of the
first document.  It was typed into the Doc 1 screen and then
saved as EXWP3-3a.

This paragraph was also typed into the first document.  If
you were to print out a copy of EXWP3-3a, you would only see
these two paragraphs.

 A:\WP3-3A                                    Doc 1 Pg 1
```

```
This paragraph was typed into the Doc 2 screen and saved as
EXWP3-3b.  If you were to print out a copy of EXWP3-3b, you
would only see this paragraph.

 A:\WP3-3B                                    Doc 2 Pg 1
```

4. Select Window, Switch to switch to Doc 1   [Shift + F3]
5. Select Window, Switch to switch to Doc 2   [Shift + F3]

Manipulating Text in Two Documents.   You can now manipulate text between the two documents almost as easily as you do within one.

In normal use, you may choose to keep Doc 2 simply as a reference as you work on Doc 1, switching to it whenever necessary. You can also scroll each document independently to move to particular locations within each.

However, a more important reason for using two documents is the capability of copying (or moving) text from one document into the other. In this exercise, you will copy the paragraph in Doc 2 and place it after the first paragraph in Doc 1.

1. Switch your screen to Doc 2 if needed

Now block the paragraph for copying as follows:

2. Move the insertion point to the start of the paragraph, as shown in Figure WP3–11a

3. Select Edit, Block   [Alt + F4]

4. Press ↓ four times

This will highlight the paragraph and the line beneath it.

5. Select Edit, Copy + Paste   [Ctrl + Ins]

This procedure is similar to the normal copy routine up to this point. As expected, your screen now prompts you with "Move cursor; press Enter to retrieve." Since the "target" for the paragraph is in Doc 1, you must now switch to Doc 1 and complete the copy as follows:

6. Select Window, Switch to switch to Doc 1   [Shift + F3]

7. Move the insertion point to the beginning of the second paragraph

8. Press ↵ to complete the copy

Figure WP3–11

Copying between Two Documents

(a) The insertion point is positioned at the start of the first paragraph in Doc 2. (b) The block has been copied into the middle of Doc 1.

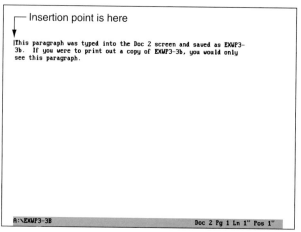

| (a) | (b) |

Your screen should now resemble Figure WP3–11b, with the paragraph from Doc 2 copied into Doc 1.

☞ **Tip: Although you can copy or move text from Doc 1 into Doc 2, it is good practice to keep Doc 1 as the main document and Doc 2 as the one from which you will always transfer text.**

Saving.   Now that you have copied successfully, save the new document as EXWP3–3C (as you would save any document).

1. Select <u>F</u>ile, Save <u>A</u>s   [F10]

2. Type **EXWP3–3C** and press ↵

You need not save Doc 2 since it is already on your disk. If you wanted to save it, however, you could switch to Doc 2 and invoke the SAVE command.

Clearing Doc 2.   You no longer need Doc 2 in the computer's main memory, so clear it as follows (remember that it is already saved on your disk as EXWP3–3B):

1. Select <u>W</u>indow, <u>S</u>witch to switch to Doc 2   [Shift + F3]

2. Select <u>F</u>ile, <u>E</u>xit   [F7]

3. Press **N** in answer to "Save document?"

4. Press **Y** in answer to "Exit Document 2?"

You will now be returned to the Doc 1 screen. Each time you want to add text to Doc 1 from another document, simply repeat the procedure: switch to Doc 2, open a document, mark its text block for copy, switch back to Doc 1, and complete the copy.

Until now, you have been viewing Doc 1 and Doc 2 on separate screens. It is also possible to display both documents on one screen at the same time. This is done by placing each document in a *frame* and then adjusting each frame to occupy less than its maximum size.

Tiling and Cascading.   Try the following exercise to show two (or more) documents on the screen at one time.

1. Clear the screen and open EXWP3–3A
2. Switch to Doc 2
3. Open EXWP3–3B
4. Switch back to Doc 1

Although both documents are now active, you can see only one at a time. An easy way to see both documents is to place each in a smaller frame, or window. You can then position them so that one occupies the top of the screen and the other occupies the bottom. This is easily done with the **tile** command, which places documents side-by-side with no overlapping.

5. Select <u>W</u>indow   [Ctrl + F3, W]

6. Press **T** to select <u>T</u>ile

Your screen should now resemble Figure WP3–12a. Notice that both documents can be seen at the same time. Doc 1 is displayed on the upper half of the screen, while Doc 2 occupies the lower half. The active document is indicated by the color of its title bar. Currently, the Doc 1 title bar is shown in color, indicating Doc 1 is active. To switch to Doc 2,

7. Select <u>W</u>indow, <u>S</u>witch   [Shift + F3]

Notice that the color shifts to Doc 2, showing that Doc 2 is active. The Switch, Copy, and Move procedures work the same way as before, but you can now see both documents as you work.

Another way to arrange documents is to *cascade* them. The **cascade** command overlaps document windows (as if they were in a pile) so that only their title bars appear. You can then select the window you want to make active and view on the screen. Try this:

8. Select <u>W</u>indow, <u>C</u>ascade   [Ctrl + F3, W, C]

Your screen should resemble Figure WP3–12b. Currently, Doc 2 is uppermost and thus the active window.

9. Switch to Doc 1

Note that it is brought to the top of the "pile" and becomes the active window.

10. Switch back to Doc 2

☞ **Tip: If you are using a mouse, you need only click the title bar of the document you want to make the active one.**

Resizing a Window.   If you are using a mouse, you can resize or reposition the windows as desired (see the Appendix for details). Although it is more cumbersome, the keyboard can also be used to change the size and position of document windows. This exercise adjusts both size and position using the keyboard:

1. Press **Ctrl** + **F3** for *Screen*

2. Press **W** for *Window*

3. Press **S** for *Size*

Figure WP3—12

*Using Tiling and
Cascading Windows*

(a) Tiling places windows side by
side. (b) Cascading overlaps
windows.

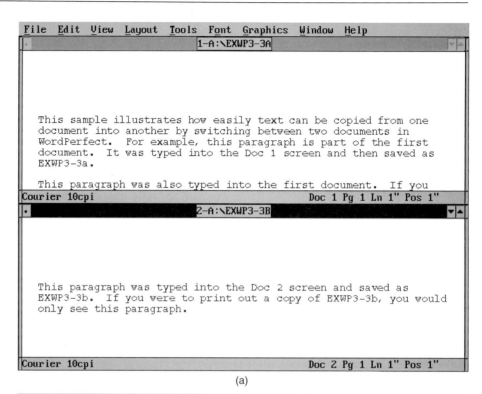

(a)

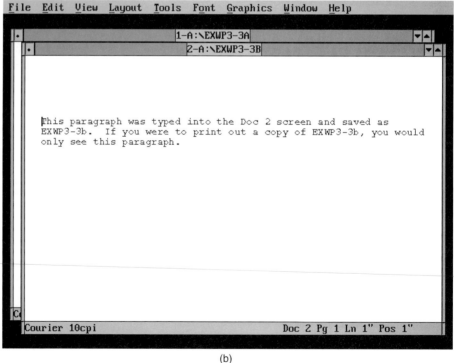

(b)

A dotted line appears as a rectangle around the active window displaying its
current size. You can now make the window smaller. Here, you will move the
right edge 20 spaces to the left, and then raise the bottom edge 8 spaces upward:

4. Press ← 20 times

The active window is shortened appropriately.

5. Press ↑ 8 times

Now, the active window shrinks in vertical size. (You could continue to change the horizontal and vertical size using the four arrow keys as needed.)

6. Press ↵ to accept the new size

Repositioning a Window.   Windows can also be moved to different locations on the screen as desired. Sometimes, repositioning a window allows you to view another window that might have been beneath it on the screen "pile." To reposition a window,

1. Press **Ctrl** + **F3** for *Screen*

2. Press **W** for *Window*

3. Press **M** for *Move*

The rectangular dotted line reappears, showing the current size and position. You will now relocate this window five spaces lower and six spaces to the right:

4. Press ↓ five times to move down

5. Press → six times to move right

6. Press ↵ to accept the new position

The window has been relocated as expected. You can adjust the size or position of any window as the need arises.

Resetting the Full Screen.   When you no longer need smaller windows, you can maximize the document windows. This exercise returns the screen to its full size:

1. Select <u>W</u>indow, <u>M</u>aximize   [Ctrl + F3, W, A]

This sets Doc 2 to its maximum size, leaving no space for another window.

2. Switch to Doc 1 (**Shift** + **F3**)

Repeat the maximize procedure as follows:

3. Select <u>W</u>indow, <u>M</u>aximize   [Ctrl + F3, W, A]

Each document is now again in its own full screen. Clear both documents before continuing, as follows:

4. Select <u>F</u>ile, <u>E</u>xit, N, Y   [F7, N, Y]

You will now be in Doc 2.

5. Select <u>F</u>ile, <u>E</u>xit, N, N   [F7, N, N]

Your screen is now clear.

Checkpoint

☐ Open EXWP3–1. Copy the first and last paragraphs into the Doc 2 screen.

☐ Switch to Doc 2. Save this document as WPCHECK2.

☐ Reset window frames (tiled) to show both documents. Use the Shift plus PrtSc keys to print a copy of the screen, then clear both screens.

Module 3: Merging Files

Merge is a process by which information from two sources is combined to produce a third document. This is extremely useful in creating customized letters. In this procedure, a standard form letter can be altered for each customer to include the customer's specific name, address, and so forth.

An easy way to merge is to create a form letter *without* any customer identification. Then, when you need a new letter, retrieve the form and type in the new name and address. Although useful for a few letters, this gets fairly tedious for a long list.

A better method uses two separate files: a primary file and a secondary file. The **primary file** contains text (such as a form letter) and instructions for merging. The **secondary file** contains the specific data to be merged into the primary file (such as a list of names and addresses). The following exercise creates both files and then merges them to produce individualized letters.

Creating the Primary File

The primary file you will create is displayed in Figure WP3–13. This primary file starts with a centered heading and date, and then leaves space for three data fields—namely, NAME, COMPANY, and ADDRESS. The salutation leaves space for TITLE, and the paragraph leaves spaces for ITEM, PRICE, and COMPANY. When the final letter is printed, these field names will be replaced with actual data. Create the primary file as follows:

1. Clear the screen
2. Type the centered heading as shown in Figure WP3–13
3. Skip a line and type today's date
4. Skip another line

Figure WP3–13

The Primary Merge File

The primary file uses field names to indicate the location of variable data.

```
 File   Edit   View   Layout   Tools   Font   Graphics   Window   Help




                              We Sell Anything, Inc.
                               1001 Knights Road
                              Mobius Strip, NM 12345

          November 1, 199X

          FIELD(NAME)
          FIELD(COMPANY)
          FIELD(ADDRESS)

          Dear FIELD(TITLE):

          Thank you for your letter inquiring about our product, FIELD(ITEM
          ).  The current price is FIELD(PRICE), plus appropriate tax.  We
          would be happy to fill your order upon receipt of a FIELD(COMPANY
          ) purchase order or check.

          Sincerely,


          Martin Parker
          Sales Manager
          |

 Courier 10cpi                                    Doc 1 Pg 1 Ln 4.67" Pos 1"
```

Figure WP3—14
Creating the Primary File

(a) The first field has been completed. (b) The complete address.

```
                      We Sell Anything, Inc.
                        1001 Knights Road
                      Mobius Strip, NM 12345

November 1, 199X

FIELD(NAME)
|
```
(a)

```
                      We Sell Anything, Inc.
                        1001 Knights Road
                      Mobius Strip, NM 12345

November 1, 199X

FIELD(NAME)
FIELD(COMPANY)
FIELD(ADDRESS)

|
```
(b)

You are now ready to create the first field marker for NAME.
To create a field:

5. Select <u>T</u>ools, <u>M</u>erge, <u>D</u>efine   [Shift + F9]

A screen appears asking you to select "Form" or "Data" type.

6. Press **F** **↵** to select *Form*

7. Press **F** for *Field*

8. Type **NAME** in answer to "Field:"

9. Press **↵** to accept this field

A field marker appears on the screen as in Figure WP3–14a. Use this procedure each time you create a field. Now continue with the letter.

10. Press **↵** to move to the next line

Now create fields for COMPANY and ADDRESS:

11. Create the **COMPANY** field (using Steps 5–9 as before)

12. Press **↵** to move to the next line

13. Create the **ADDRESS** field (using Steps 5–9)

14. Press **↵** twice

The complete address now resembles Figure WP3–14b. Continue with the salutation as follows:

15. Type **Dear** and press **Space**

16. Create the **TITLE** field (use Steps 5–9)

Figure WP3–15

The Secondary Merge File

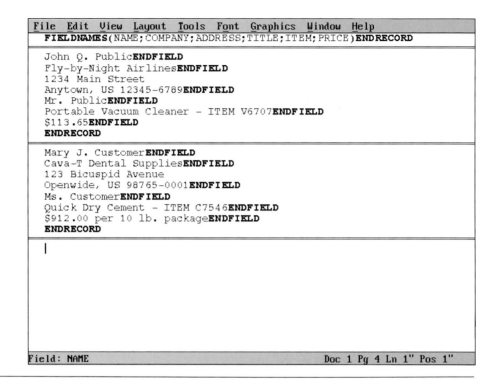

17. Type : (a colon) and press ↵

18. Press ↵ to skip a line

19. Type the rest of the letter as in Figure WP3–13

As you type, enter the fields ITEM, PRICE, and COMPANY when you reach them, and continue with the correct punctuation after each. If you make a mistake, backspace and repeat the procedure.

Saving the File.   Primary files are saved with the standard SAVE command. They can be opened and modified like any other text file.

1.   Save this file as **FORM1**
2.   Clear the screen

Field Names versus Numbers.   WordPerfect lets you either *name* merge fields or number them. For example, the expression *FIELD(NAME)* in FORM1 could have been entered as *FIELD(1); FIELD(COMPANY)* could have read *FIELD(2);* and so forth. Although it is slightly more difficult to use names when creating a secondary merge file, names are easier to understand than numbers. For example, it is easier to see that *FIELD(COMPANY)* refers to a company name than to start guessing what is meant by *FIELD(2)*. The use of field names is highly recommended.

Creating the Secondary File

With the primary file safely on disk, you can now concentrate on the data list to merge with it. In this exercise, you will create two data records, as shown in Figure WP3–15. In real applications, of course, your data list might contain hundreds of entries—but the procedure would be the same.

There are three guidelines to follow when creating a secondary file: (1) All records must have the same number of fields; (2) each field must end with *END-FIELD* and a hard return; (3) each record must end with *ENDRECORD* and a hard *page break*. Fortunately, WordPerfect automates much of this for you.

Although you can create secondary files in any mode, graphics mode lets you see the process more easily. To prepare,

1.   Clear the screen (`F7` `N` `N`)

2.   Switch to graphics mode (select <u>V</u>iew, <u>G</u>raphics)

Naming Fields.   If you used field names in your primary file, you can now name the fields for use. On a clear screen, do the following:

1.   Select <u>T</u>ools, <u>M</u>erge, <u>D</u>efine   [Shift + F9]

☞ **Tip: Be sure to press E for merge. If you press M by mistake, press Esc and repeat.**

Identify the merge document you will create:

2.   Press `D` to select *Data* (Text)

A menu resembling Figure WP3–16a will appear.

You must first indicate the field names that will be used. (If you used field numbers in the primary file, you can skip Steps 3–8.)

3.   Press `N` to select *FIELD NAMES*

You can now enter each field name that will appear in the secondary file. There are six names you will want to enter—NAME, COMPANY, ADDRESS, TITLE, ITEM, and PRICE.

4.   Type **NAME** `↵` in the entry line

The field name is added to the Field Name List as in Figure WP3–16b.

5.   Type **COMPANY** `↵`

6.   Repeat this procedure for the remaining four fields

7.   Press `↵` on the blank entry line

Pressing the Enter key on a blank line tells the program that the list is completed. Your screen will show the field names in the Field Name List (as in Figure WP3–16c). At this point, you could press L to edit the list or accept the list as is.

☞ **Tip: To edit, you would press L, select the desired action, and perform it. When done, press Esc to return to the Field Name entry box.**

8.   Press `↵` (or select "OK") to accept the list

The list of field names now appears across the top row of the screen (as in Figure WP3–15) This list defines the field names and sequence of the data that will follow.

Entering a Record.   You can now fill in data for the first record. The program prompts you for each field at the bottom of the screen. Using the data in Figure WP3–15 as a guide, do the following:

1.   Type **John Q. Public** in answer to "NAME"

2.   Press `F9` to end this field

Figure WP3—16

Naming the Fields

(a) The Merge Codes screen.
(b) Entering field names.
(c) The completed list.

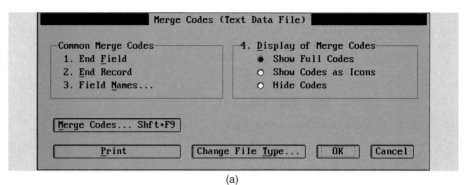

Merge Codes (Text Data File)

```
┌─Common Merge Codes──────┐   4. Display of Merge Codes────┐
│  1. End Field           │    ● Show Full Codes           │
│  2. End Record          │    ○ Show Codes as Icons       │
│  3. Field Names...      │    ○ Hide Codes                │
└─────────────────────────┘                                │

 Merge Codes... Shft+F9

 ┌──── Print ────┐   ┌ Change File Type... ┐  ┌ OK ┐  ┌ Cancel ┐
```

(a)

Field Names

```
        Field Name: [                                        ]

        ┌─Field Name List─────────────────────────────────┐↑
        │ NAME                                            ││
        │                                                 ││
        │                                                 ││
        │                                                 ││
        │                                                 ││
        │                                                 ││
        │                                                 ││
        │                                                 │↓
        └─────────────────────────────────────────────────┘

          Insert Field Name
          Add Field Name at the End
          Edit Field Name
          Delete Field Name
                                        ┌ OK ┐  ┌ Cancel ┐
```

(b)

Field Names

```
     1. Field Name: [                                        ]

        ┌─2. Field Name List──────────────────────────────┐↑
        │ NAME                                            ││
        │ COMPANY                                         ││
        │ ADDRESS                                         ││
        │ TITLE                                           ││
        │ ITEM                                            ││
        │ PRICE                                           ││
        │                                                 ││
        │                                                 │↓
        └─────────────────────────────────────────────────┘

          Insert Field Name
          Add Field Name at the End
          Edit Field Name
          Delete Field Name
                                        ┌ OK ┐  ┌ Cancel ┐
```

(c)

Of course, you could also select Tools, Merge, Define, Endfield, but this is a much longer process. Notice that an "ENDFIELD" marker appears and the insertion point moves to the next line.

3. Type **Fly-By-Night Airlines** in answer to "COMPANY"

4. Press **F9**

Data need not be restricted to one line only. The address line is next. Since it occupies two lines, follow a slightly different procedure:

5. Type **1234 Main Street** in answer to "ADDRESS"

6. Press **↵** to begin a new line

7. Type **Anytown, US 12345–6789** to complete the address

8. Now press **F9** to end this field

9. Continue to enter the data for TITLE, ITEM, and PRICE using Figure WP3–15's list of data

When you reach the end of the first record, you must indicate that all data have been entered. To do this:

10. Select <u>T</u>ools, M<u>e</u>rge, <u>D</u>efine   [Shift + F9]

11. Press **E** to *End record*

An "ENDRECORD" marker appears and a hard page break is added automatically (as seen after the first record in Figure WP3–15). You have completed the first record. (If you are in page mode, the added margins will make this hard to see.) Note that you are now prompted again for NAME. Following the same procedure,

12. Complete the second record, for Mary J. Customer

Remember, you must end each field by pressing the F9 key to create an "END-FIELD" marker, and you must end the complete record by pressing the Shift plus F9 keys (or pull-down menus) and then E to create an "ENDRECORD" marker and hard page break.

   Note that you are now on page 4. Page 1 contains the field names; pages 2 and 3 hold the records. Since there are no more records to enter,

13. Press **Backspace** to clear the last hard return

(If this hard return is left, it will generate a blank form when merge is run.)

14. When you have finished, save the file as **DATA1**
15. Clear the screen

Merge— Combining the Files

Once a primary (form) file and secondary (data) file have been saved, they can be combined to create individual letters. Of course, you can modify either one before merging them together. The following exercise demonstrates the technique for merging. On a blank screen,

1. Select <u>T</u>ools, M<u>e</u>rge, <u>R</u>un   [Ctrl + F9, M]

WP

Figure WP3–17

The Run Merge Screen

A Run Merge screen appears as in Figure WP3–17.

2. Type **FORM1** ↵ in the Form File entry line

3. Type **DATA1** ↵ in the Data File entry line

4. Press ↵ (or select "Merge") to begin

A "Please Wait" message briefly appears on your screen. The time it takes to merge depends on the length of the files. Yours are short, so the merge will be almost immediate. When the merge has finished, the insertion point will be positioned at the end of the newly created file.

5. Press **Home** **Home** **↑** to move to the start

Your screen should resemble Figure WP3–18. Note that the complete letter for John Q. Public has been generated. The status line shows "Pg 1," indicating that this is the first letter.

6. Press **Pg Dn**

Your screen should now resemble Figure WP3–18b, with a complete letter for Mary J. Customer. The status line shows "Pg 2," indicating that this is the second letter. There will be a new page for each record in your secondary file. Notice also that wordwrap has adjusted lines to compensate for variations in the length of the data in some fields, such as ITEM and PRICE.

This document can now be treated as any other that you open or type. You can edit it to change a date, make minor corrections, or remove unwanted pages. Ultimately, you will want to print it.

7. Print this file

You may also want to save the file with a new name, even though it can be created again easily with the MERGE command. For practice,

8. Save the document as **MERGE1**

9. Clear the screen

| File | Edit | View | Layout | Tools | Font | Graphics | Window | Help |

```
                        We Sell Anything, Inc.
                           1001 Knights Road
                        Mobius Strip, NM 12345

November 1, 199X

John Q. Public
Fly-by-Night Airlines
1234 Main Street
Anytown, US 12345-6789

Dear Mr. Public:

Thank you for your letter inquiring about our product, Portable
Vacuum Cleaner - ITEM V6707.  The current price is $113.65, plus
appropriate tax.  We would be happy to fill your order upon
receipt of a Fly-by-Night Airlines purchase order or check.

Sincerely,


Martin Parker
Sales Manager
```

(a)

| File | Edit | View | Layout | Tools | Font | Graphics | Window | Help |

```
                        We Sell Anything, Inc.
                           1001 Knights Road
                        Mobius Strip, NM 12345

November 1, 199X

Mary J. Customer
Cava-T Dental Supplies
123 Bicuspid Avenue
Openwide, US 98765-0001

Dear Ms. Customer:

Thank you for your letter inquiring about our product, Quick Dry
Cement - ITEM C7546.  The current price is $912.00 per 10 lb.
package, plus appropriate tax.  We would be happy to fill your
order upon receipt of a Cava-T Dental Supplies purchase order or
check.

Sincerely,


Martin Parker
Sales Manager
```

(b)

Figure WP3—18
File Merge

Merging files produces customized letters for each record in the secondary file: (a) The first letter displays the data for record 1. (b) The second letter displays the data for record 2.

Checkpoint

☐ Create a primary file with a paragraph that has reserved fields for NAME and PHONE. Save it as WPCHECK3.

☐ Create a secondary file with two records containing a name and phone number each. Save it as WPCHECK4.

☐ Merge WPCHECK4 into WPCHECK3 and print the results.

Module 4: Automating Commands with Macros

After using WordPerfect for a while, you may identify several tasks that you perform on a regular basis. Perhaps you type a company heading each time you start a letter, or you copy and print each file you use. Instead of repeating a complicated set of keystrokes each time you need to perform these tasks, you can create a macro to do it for you. A **macro** is a list of computer instructions that can be activated with one (or more) preset keystrokes. The macro feature in WordPerfect records all the keystrokes you would use to accomplish a task and then stores them in a separate file that can be invoked with a few simple keystrokes, much like the memory dialing feature on many modern telephones. Anything you can do on the keyboard, and more, can be saved in a macro.

There are two steps to using basic macros: creating the macro (defining and saving it), and then running the macro (invoking it for use). The following exercise creates a macro that will type a company heading and date.

Creating a Macro

When designing a macro, you may want to first perform the task step-by-step in WordPerfect, listing each keystroke in proper sequence on paper. Creating the actual macro is then simply a matter of retyping the keystrokes back into the program.

You should also give some thought to the name you select for a macro. This is important, for a macro's name determines how it can be invoked from the keyboard. There are two types of macro names: *one-letter* names—those entered by holding the Alt key while typing one letter—and *multiletter* names—those entered without the Alt key.

One-letter "Alt" macro names can be invoked simply by pressing the Alt key and the letter. These are easy to use but hard to remember, since their names do not provide much of a clue to their use. It helps if the letter in the name reminds you of the macro's purpose—for example, the Alt plus S keys for a "save" macro, the Alt plus P keys for "print," and so forth. However, you can create a maximum of only 26 one-letter macro names (one for each alphabetic key).

Multiletter macro names, consisting of one to eight characters, are invoked by first pressing the MACRO command and then typing the full name of the macro (as you will see). You can create an unlimited supply of these macros. They are easier to remember, since their longer names can better indicate their use, although they take a few more keystrokes to invoke.

Before you begin the macro, you should make sure that it will be saved on your data disk. To do this,

1. Select File, Setup   [Shift + F1]

2. Press **L** for *Location of Files*

Now look at item 2—*Macros/Keyboards/Button Bar*, as shown in Figure WP3–19. If the proper drive appears, then continue with Step 6.

3. If the drive is incorrect, press **M** **P** for *Personal Path*

4. Type the correct drive (**A:** or **B:**) and press ↵

5. Press ↵ to exit the menu

6. If the Setup box appears, press ↵ again to close it

Creating a One-Letter Macro. This exercise creates a one-letter macro that types the heading shown in Figure WP3–20.

Figure WP3—19

Verifying Macro Destinations

The Location of Files screen lets you verify that macros will be saved on (and retrieved from) your data disk.

```
╔═══════════════ Location of Files ═══════════════╗

     1. Backup Files:              [                    ]
     2. Macros/Keyboards/Button Bar...  [C:\WP60\MACROS      ]
     3. Writing Tools...           [C:\WPC60DOS         ]
     4. Printer Files...           [C:\WPC60DOS         ]
     5. Style Files...             [C:\WP60             ]

     6. Graphics Files...          [C:\WP60\GRAPHICS    ]
     7. Documents:                 [C:\WPDOCS           ]
     8. Spreadsheet Files...       [                    ]
     9. QuickFinder Files...       [                    ]

     R. WP.DRS File and *.WFW Files:  [C:\WPC60DOS         ]
     F. Graphics Fonts Data Files...

     ⊠ Update QuickList

  [Directory Tree... F8]  [QuickList... F6]      [ OK ]  [Cancel]
```

Figure WP3—20

The ALTH Macro Will Produce This Heading

```
                    The XYZ Company
                   1234 Fifth Avenue
                New York, New York 10001

     November 1, 199X
```

To access RECORD MACRO:

1. Select <u>T</u>ools, <u>M</u>acro, <u>R</u>ecord   [Ctrl + F10]

The screen now waits for a macro name.

2. Press   **Alt** + **H**

(The *H* need not be uppercase—it is shown this way for clarity.) The use of the Alt key defines this macro name as the one-letter variety. In this case, you are naming the macro *ALTH*; the *H* is a reminder that this is a "heading" macro.

3. Press   **↵**

The message "Recording Macro" now appears in the lower left of your screen, indicating that the program will record any keystrokes you now type. Note that the time it takes you to type each command does not affect the recorded macro; only the keystrokes are entered. You may want to refer to Figure WP3–20 and your screen as you create the heading. Be careful! Every keystroke (including mistakes) is recorded.

Figure WP3—21
The "Closing" Macro
Will Produce This Text

```
Sincerely yours,


Martin Parker
```

4. Press **Shift** + **F6** to center

5. Type **The XYZ Company** and press **↵**

6. Press **Shift** + **F6** to center again

7. Type **New York, New York 10001**

8. Press **↵** twice to skip another line

Here's an interesting use of a function command:

9. Press **Shift** + **F5** to invoke the DATE command

(You can also select <u>T</u>ools, <u>D</u>ate.)

10. Press **T** to select *Insert Date*

This action instructs the program to automatically place the system date on the screen in proper form. Although not required by the macro, it is another notable feature of WordPerfect.

11. Press **↵** twice to skip another line

This completes the keystrokes for the macro.

12. Press **Ctrl** + **F10** to end the definition process

The ALTH macro is compiled, saved to the default disk, and now available for use. Each macro you create is saved separately with a file extension of .WPM (WordPerfect Macro) and can be invoked from within any document.

☞ **Tip: The Esc (cancel) key does not cancel a macro definition. In fact, this key can be used as part of a macro itself. To cancel a macro definition, press the Ctrl and F10 keys. Then, enter the macro name again, and press *R* to replace the old macro.**

Creating a Multiletter Macro.   For comparison, create a multiletter macro that types a short closing, as in Figure WP3—21.

1. Select <u>T</u>ools, <u>M</u>acro, <u>R</u>ecord   [Ctrl + F10]

2. Type **closing** and press **↵** in the macro entry line

This time, you are giving the macro the multiletter name CLOSING. There is no need for the initial Alt key.

The message "Recording Macro" appears in the lower left as before.

3. Press ↵ twice to skip two lines

4. Type **Sincerely yours,**

5. Press ↵ three times to skip two more lines

6. Type your name and press ↵

7. Press **Ctrl** + **F10** to end

This new macro is now compiled, saved, and available for use.

8. Clear the screen

The method by which you invoke a macro depends on its name. The following exercises demonstrate invoking both an "Alt" one-letter macro (the quick one) and a multiletter name.

Invoking with the Alt Key.   A one-letter macro is invoked by simply holding the Alt key and tapping the desired letter.

1. Press **Alt** + **H**

The heading is quickly typed by the macro and appears on your screen.

☞ **Tip: If a macro cannot be found, use the SETUP command to make sure the program is looking at your data disk.**

If the macro was recorded correctly, the date should match the system date (the one you entered when you first booted up) and you should be correctly positioned to begin typing a letter.

2. Press ↵ to skip another line

Invoking by Name.   Macros with multiletter names must be invoked with a different procedure—using the "Play Macro" command.

1. Select Tools, Macro, Play Macro   [Alt + F10]

The screen now displays "Macro:" and awaits the macro name.

2. Type **closing** and press ↵

The CLOSING macro will skip two additional lines on the screen and type "Sincerely yours," and your name.

There is no hard-and-fast rule for naming macros. In general, use one-letter "Alt" macro names for often-used tasks, saving the multiletter names for less utilized macros.

3. Clear the screen before continuing.

Invoking a Macro

Macros can be replaced, deleted, or edited to change or expand their function. To replace a macro with a new one, simply create a new macro with the same name, press Y and 1 to replace, and then type the new macro. To erase a macro, highlight its name in the File Manager screen and delete it.

The following exercise demonstrates a simple edit routine to add a line to your heading macro.

Editing a Macro

WP

Figure WP3—22

Editing a Macro

(a) The Edit screen lets you edit the macro directly. (b) New keystrokes have been inserted.

```
 File   Edit   View   Layout   Tools   Font   Graphics   Window   Help
 DISPLAY(Off!)
 Center
 Type("The XYZ Company")
 HardReturn
 Center
 Type("New York, New York 10001")
 HardReturn
 HardReturn
 DateText
 HardReturn
 HardReturn




 Edit Macro:   Press Shft+F3 to Record              Doc 2 Pg 1 Ln 1" Pos 1"
```

(a)

```
 File   Edit   View   Layout   Tools   Font   Graphics   Window   Help
 DISPLAY(Off!)
 Center
 Type("The XYZ Company")
 HardReturn
 Center
 Type("1234 Fifth Avenue")
 HardReturn
 Center
 Type("New York, New York 10001")
 HardReturn
 HardReturn
 DateText
 HardReturn
 HardReturn
```

(b)

1. Select Tools, Macro, Record   [Ctrl + F10]

2. Press Alt + H to identify your heading macro

3. Press ⏎

The message "ALTH.WPM already exists" appears.

4. Press E for *Edit*

You will now see an edit screen that lists the keystrokes contained in your ALTH macro as in Figure WP3—22a.

5. Press ↓ four times to move to the line beneath "HardReturn"

6. Press Shift + F3 to *Record* (as shown in the status line)

7. Press Shift + F6 to add a CENTER command

8. Type **1234 Fifth Avenue**

9. Press ⏎

10. Press **Shift** + **F3** to return to the *Edit* mode

Your screen will resemble Figure WP3–22b. Note that the new keystrokes have been added to center the new address line.

11. Save the modified Macro (select File, Save)   [Ctrl + F12]

The macro has been modified and saved.

12. Clear the screen (**F7** **N** **N**)

13. Invoke the heading macro to verify its result

14. Clear the screen again

Checkpoint

☐ Create a macro named ALTC that prints your name and address on three centered lines.

☐ Create a macro named WPCHECK5 that will underline the next word already typed on the screen. (*Hint:* use BLOCK, then search for a space, then underline.)

☐ Use the ALTS macro to print your name, then position the insertion point before your first name and use WPCHECK5 to underline it. Print the results.

Module 5: Footnotes and Endnotes

Footnotes and **endnotes** are text added to your document to provide references, explanations, or comments. They may be referenced in the text by a footnote or endnote number. Footnotes are usually placed at the bottom of the page on which they are referenced, whereas endnotes are usually listed at the end of a document. Since the procedures for using footnotes and endnotes are virtually identical, only footnotes will be presented here. Endnotes can be accessed by selecting an E (for endnotes) instead of an F (footnotes) in the appropriate menu.

Creating a Footnote

When you create a footnote, WordPerfect numbers and formats it for you. It is a difficult typing task to properly place footnotes on a page. WordPerfect eliminates this problem by automatically adjusting each page so that the footnote will fit correctly. Creating a footnote is a relatively simple matter: position the insertion point in the text where the footnote marker will appear, invoke the FOOTNOTE command, and type the footnote. The following exercise lets you experience this firsthand.

1. Clear the screen, switch to page mode, and open EXWP3–2

☞ **Tip: If the menu bar disappears from the screen, you pressed "P" instead of "A." This is a common mistake. To correct, press ALT + = (equals sign) then VP. Then select page mode correctly.**

You must first position the insertion point where the footnote number is desired. (The footnote format used in the exercise is one of many styles; you may prefer to use some other format in the future.)

Figure WP3—23

Creating Footnotes

(a) The insertion point is positioned in the text where the footnote reference is desired. (b) The footnote is typed in the footnote edit screen.
(c) Position the second footnote. (d) The second footnote is entered.

```
                                                      2

     According to Charles Parker, "word processing is the use of

computer  technology  to  create,  manipulate,  and  print  text

materials."| These materials include such items as letters, memos,

legal contracts, article manuscripts, and other documents.   As

Parker explains it, word processing saves so much time that most

people  stop  using  their  typewriters  once  they  learn  word

processing.
```

— Insertion point
is placed here

(a)

```
     ¹Parker, Charles S., Understanding Computers and Information
Processing: Today & Tomorrow (Third Edition).  Chicago: The Dryden
Press, 1990: 372.|
```

(b)

```
processing.
     The following story, written by Edward Martin, demonstrates

why word processing is so valuable to a typical office.| The story,

reprinted here with permission of the author, begins as follows:

     Andrea sat nervously in front of the microcomputer screen.

She stretched her fingers over the keyboard while Elissa Roberts,

manager of Freddy Johnson's Travel Agency, looked on.   Andrea had
A:\EXWP3-2                                 Doc 1 Pg 2 Ln 4" Pos 6.35"
```

— Position
insertion
point here

(c)

```
     ²Adapted from Martin, Edward G. and Burstein, Jerome S.,
Computer Systems Fundamentals.  Chicago: The Dryden Press, 1990:
149, 182.|
```

(d)

2. Move the insertion point to page 2, after the quotation at the 2″ line of the first paragraph, as in Figure WP3–23a

3. Select Layout   [Ctrl + F7]

4. Press **F** to select *Footnote* from the menu

5. Press **C** to select *Create* from the menu

A footnote entry screen appears. Notice the superscript "1" to the left of the insertion point, indicating this will be footnote #1.

6. Type the footnote as shown in Figure WP3–23b

Do not press the Enter key when you reach the right margin, but type as you normally would. You are free to use the Backspace, Delete, and Insert keys as needed to correct errors.

7. When you are finished, press   **F7**   to exit (as shown in the status line)

Your document will now display a superscript "1" positioned after the quotation mark. Create one more footnote as follows:

8. Position the insertion point after the word "office" in the second paragraph, as shown in Figure WP3–23c

9. Select Layout   [Ctrl + F7]

10. Press   **F**   **C**

An entry screen for footnote #2 appears.

11. Type the second footnote as shown in Figure WP3–23d

12. Press   **F7**   when you are finished

The footnotes are now completed. Like headers and page numbers, footnotes can be seen in page mode or when the document is printed or previewed. To see the footnotes,

13. Press   **Pg Dn**   and then   **↑**

14. Save the document as **EXWP3–4a**

Figure WP3–24 displays the entire page as it will appear when printed. The subscripted references and the horizontal line separating the footnotes from the text are automatically created by WordPerfect. As you will see shortly, these can be changed to suit other footnote styles.

If you were to add a third footnote on this page, an appropriate number of document text lines would be moved to the next page automatically to ensure that the new footnote would end at the bottom margin. Similarly, removing a footnote would cause text lines from the next page to move up to this page.

You may create new footnotes at any time, and in any position in your document. All subsequent footnotes will be renumbered automatically to reflect the new addition.

The Options Screen

WordPerfect's default footnote style is acceptable for most applications, but it can be changed to suit your specific needs through a *Footnote Options* screen. Examine the options screen as follows:

1. Select Layout   [Ctrl + F7]

2. Press   **F**   to select *Footnote*

3. Press   **O**   for *Options*

A Footnote Options screen appears as in Figure WP3–25, from which you can change spacing, remove subscripts, and change how footnotes are numbered. For example, item 4 resets the footnote counter on each page; item 3 adjusts the length of the horizontal line separating the text and footnotes; item 5 can place all footnotes at the document's end. You may want to experiment with this menu in the future, but for now, do not make any alterations.

4. Press   **Esc**   twice to exit

Figure WP3—24
Printed Footnotes

When printed, footnote references appear as superscripts, with the full citation properly positioned at the bottom of the page (shown condensed here).

```
                                                                          2

         According to Charles Parker, "word processing is the use of
    computer technology to create, manipulate, and print text
    materials."1  These materials include such items as letters, memos,
    legal contracts, article manuscripts, and other documents.  As
    Parker explains it, word processing saves so much time that most
    people stop using their typewriters once they learn word
    processing.
         The following story, written by Edward Martin, demonstrates
    why word processing is so valuable to a typical office.2  The
    story, reprinted here with permission of the author, begins as
    follows:
         Andrea sat nervously in front of the microcomputer screen.
    She stretched her fingers over the keyboard while Elissa Roberts,
    manager of Freddy Johnson's Travel Agency, looked on.  Andrea had
    skipped lunch to finish this work stopping only when the stiffness
    in her neck and fingers forced her to take a break.  This was her
    first big assignment since completing the word processing course at
    Oakridge University.  She could have used more practice with the
    word processor--especially on this keyboard, which differed from
    the one she used at school.  Her fingers kept pressing the wrong
    key for SHIFT, forcing her to backspace and retype more often than
    usual.  If only she was better acquainted with the layout, she'd be
    _____

         1Parker, Charles S., Understanding Computers and Information
    Processing:  Today and Tomorrow (Third Edition). Chicago:  The
    Dryden Press, 1990:  372
         2Adapted from Martin, Edward G. and Burstein, Jerome S.,
    Computer Systems Fundamentals.  Chicago:  The Dryden Press,  1990:
    149, 182.
```

Editing a Footnote

Like other text, footnotes (and endnotes) can be edited to correct a reference or modify a comment. The following exercise examines the editing process.

1. Select Layout   [Ctrl + F7]

2. Press **F** for *Footnote*

3. Press **E** to select *Edit*

The screen will now prompt you for a footnote number.

4. Type **2** ↵ to indicate footnote #2

The screen now displays the original entry screen for the footnote, as you've seen in Figure WP3–23d. At this point, you can modify the footnote, using the cursor keys or the Backspace, Del, or Ins keys as needed, and then press the F7 key to accept it. Try this quick change:

5. Delete the words "Adapted from " (also delete the space)

6. Press **F7** to leave the edit screen

7. Save again as **EXWP3—4a**

```
┌─────────────────────────────────────────────────────┐
│           ███ Footnote Options ███                    │
│                                                       │
│   1. Spacing Between Footnotes:        [0.167"]       │
│                                                       │
│   2. Amount of Footnote to Keep Together: [0.5"]      │
│                                                       │
│   3. Footnote Separator Line...                       │
│                                                       │
│   4. ☐ Restart Footnote Numbers each Page             │
│                                                       │
│   5. ☒ Footnotes at Bottom of Page                    │
│                                                       │
│   6. ☐ Print Continued Message                        │
│                                                       │
│                              [  OK  ]  [Cancel]       │
└─────────────────────────────────────────────────────┘
```

Footnotes can also be removed from the text as easily as other hidden text codes. This exercise deletes the first footnote.

**Deleting a
Footnote**

1. Open EXWP3—4a if it is not on your screen
2. Move to the superscript "1" of the first footnote on page 2

The insertion point is placed correctly when it falls immediately to the left of the number (you could use the REVEAL CODES screen if it helps to verify the insertion point's position).

3. Press **Delete**

The "1" disappears from the screen and the second footnote is automatically renumbered. Footnote deletions (like insertions) affect the footnote numbers that follow. If you are using sequential footnote numbers *throughout* your document (the default setting), then all footnotes after the deleted one will be renumbered. If you have opted to start footnotes anew on each page, then only this page will be amended.

☞ **Tip: Footnotes affect text layout throughout the document. You should use page mode or print preview after you create, edit, or delete footnotes to ensure that the final printed layout will be acceptable.**

4. Clear the screen (or exit without saving)

Checkpoint

☐ Copy any paragraph from this book. Add a footnote at the end noting the page where you found it. Save it as WPCHECK6.

☐ Insert a footnote at the end of the first sentence. Type the citation as "New footnote, p. xxx," filling in the appropriate page number. Save again as WPCHECK and print.

☐ Delete the second footnote.

Module 6: Organizing Data with Outlines and Sorts

WordPerfect offers two features to help organize your text. WordPerfect's *Outline* **feature** helps you create properly numbered outlines of up to eight levels of numbering—each level determined by its tab position. WordPerfect's Sort feature allows you to arrange text in alphabetical or numerical order. The following exercise creates and modifies the outline shown in Figure WP3–26.

Preparing an Outline

The first step in preparing an outline is to invoke the Outline feature as follows:

1. Start WordPerfect or clear the screen

To activate the Outline menu,

2. Select <u>T</u>ools, <u>O</u>utline   [Ctrl + F5]

If you used the menu approach, a menu appears as in Figure WP3–27a. The keyboard approach results in the menu shown in Figure WP3–27b.

3. Press **B** to *Begin new outline*

An "Outline Style List" appears, as in Figure WP3–27c, from which you can select the type of outline you desire.

4. Move the highlight to "Outline" and press **↵**

In this case, "I." appears on the screen.

5. Type **Overview** **↵**

As shown in Figure WP3–28a, the next number in sequence ("II.") appears.

6. Type **Multipage Documents** **↵**

As expected, a "III." appears on the next line.

Changing to a Lower Level.   There is no third line at this level, so you must now change to the next outline level. Here's an easy way:

1. Press **Tab**

As in Figure WP3–28b, the "III." has changed to an "A." in the second level. Continue to type as you did before:

2. Type **Soft Page Break** **↵**

Figure WP3—26

The Outline to Be Created with WordPerfect's Outline Feature

```
I.    Overview
II.   Multipage Documents
      A.    Soft Page Break
      B.    Hard Page Break
            1.    Creating
            2.    Removing
      C.    Headers and Footers
```

Notice how the outline stays within the second level. A "B." now appears on the screen.

3. Type **Hard Page Break** ↵

Now move to the next lower level with the same process as before.

4. Press **Tab**

The "C." changes to a "1." as it becomes the third level.

5. Type **Creating** ↵

The outline now stays within the third level as a "2." appears on the screen.

6. Type **Removing** ↵

A "3." appears and awaits your entry.

Returning to a Higher Level. To return to a higher outline level at this point, you simply use the Shift and Tab keys as follows.

1. Press **Shift** + **Tab**

As seen in Figure WP3–28c, the "3." changes to a "C."—the next entry in the higher level of the outline.

2. Type **Headers and Footers** (but do *not* press ↵)

Now turn off the outline feature as follows:

3. Select <u>T</u>ools, <u>O</u>utline [Ctrl + F5]

4. Press **E** to <u>E</u>nd Outline

You can now return to normal typing. Your completed outline should resemble Figure WP3–26.

5. Save this document as **OUTLINE1**

Like any other text, outlines can be easily modified. Adding or deleting lines will automatically adjust the sequence of outline numbers that follow. Inserting or removing tabs will alter the outline level of that particular line. You can change the style and numbering scheme of the entire outline as well.

Editing the Outline

Adding Lines. Inserting new lines into the outline renumbers all subsequent lines.

1. Open OUTLINE1 if it is not on your screen

2. Position the insertion point *after* the "w" in "Overview"

3. Press ↵

As shown in Figure WP3–28d, a new number is added in sequence at the proper level, and all subsequent numbers on that level have been renumbered.

4. Type **Preparing**

Deleting Lines. Deleting existing lines in an outline will renumber all subsequent lines.

1. Position the insertion point after the "w" in "Overview"

2. Press **Delete**

Figure WP3—27

Preparing an Outline

(a) The menu version of the
Outline menu.

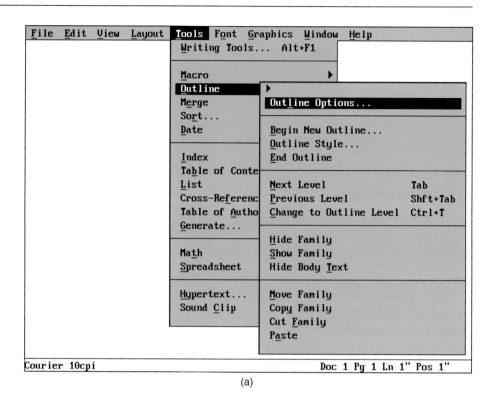

(a)

The "II." has disappeared and the subsequent numbers have been readjusted in sequence.

3.   Delete the rest of the word "Preparing"

Rearranging Outline "Families."   An outline *family* is the block of all subsequent lines contained within a given outline level. You can move or copy these blocks as easily as other text blocks. Unlike normal moving, however, the Outline feature will renumber all subsequent levels to reflect the change.

1.   Open OUTLINE1 if it is not on your screen

2.   Position the insertion point at the beginning of "II. Multipage Documents"

3.   Select Tools, Outline   [Ctrl + F5]

4.   Press **M** for *Move/Copy*

5.   *Press* **M** *to Move Family*

The entire family block is removed from the screen.

6.   Move the insertion point to the beginning of "Overview" (after the "I.")

7.   Press ↵

The block has moved, and all appropriate numbers have been changed to reflect their new position.

8.   Save this document as **OUTLINE2**

```
┌──────────────────────── Outline ────────────────────────┐
│ ┌─Outline Options──────────────┐  ┌─9. Hide/Show────────┐ │
│ │  1. Begin New Outline...     │  │   - Hide Family     │ │
│ │  2. Insert Outline Level (1-8): [1]│ + Show Family    │ │
│ │  3. Outline Style...  [Paragraph]  │ Show Levels      │ │
│ │  4. Set Paragraph Number: [1]      │ Hide Outline     │ │
│ │  5. End Outline                    │ Hide Body Text   │ │
│ │ ┌─6. Adjust Levels──────────────┐  └──────────────────┘ │
│ │ │  Next Level (Tab)            │ ┌─M. Move/Copy──────┐ │
│ │ │  Previous Level (Shft+Tab)   │ │  Move Family      │ │
│ │ │  Change to Body Text (Ctrl+T)│ │  Copy Family      │ │
│ │ │  Change to Outline Level (Ctrl+T)│ Cut Family     │ │
│ │ └──────────────────────────────┘ │  Paste            │ │
│ │                                   └───────────────────┘ │
│ │  7. ☐ Display Outline Bar                               │
│ │  8. ☐ Edit in Outline Mode (Ctrl+O)   [  OK  ] [Cancel]│
│ └─────────────────────────────────────────────────────────┘
└───────────────────────────────────────────────────────────┘
                            (b)
```

```
┌──────────────── Outline Style List ────────────────┐
│ List Styles from: ● Document  ◉ Personal Library  ◉ Shared Library │
│ ┌─Name──────Type──────Description─────────────────┐ ↑ │
│ │ Bullets    •Outline   • ○ - ■ * + · x            │   │
│ │ Headings   •Outline   Document Headings          │   │
│ │ Legal      •Outline   1  1.1  1.1.1  etc.        │   │
│ │ Legal 2    •Outline   1  1.01  1.01.01  etc.     │   │
│ │ Numbers    •Outline   Paragraph Numbers Only (No Level Styles) │
│ │ Outline    •Outline   I. A. 1. a. (1) (a) i) a)  │   │
│ │ Paragraph  •Outline   1. a. i. (1) (a) (i) 1) a) │   │
│ │                                                  │ ↓ │
│ └──────────────────────────────────────────────────┘   │
│  1. Select    3. Edit...   5. Copy...    7. Save...    9. Mark │
│  2. Create... 4. Delete... 6. Options... 8. Retrieve... N. Name Search │
│            • Denotes library style          [Close]    │
└────────────────────────────────────────────────────────┘
                            (c)
```

WP

Figure WP3—27
(continued)

(b) The keystroke version of the Outline menu. (c) The Outline Style List lets you select alternative outline styles.

If the default outline style is not appropriate, you can choose other outline formats or invent your own. To prepare for these exercises,

1. Start WordPerfect or clear your screen
2. Open the OUTLINE1 document

Paragraph Numbering.   Like new page numbers, any outline number can be given any desired value, as follows:

1. Select Tools, Outline   [Ctrl + F5]

2. Press **L** for *Outline Options*

3. Press **S** to *Set Paragraph Number*

Modifying the Outline Format

Figure WP3—28

Continuing the Outline

(a) The next number in sequence ("II.") appears. (b) The "III." has changed to an "A." (c) The "3." changes to a "C." (d) A new number is added in sequence at the proper level, and all subsequent numbers on that level have been renumbered.

```
I.     Overview
II.
```

(a)

```
I.     Overview
II.    Multipage Documents
       A.   |
```

(b)

```
I.   Overview
II.  Multipage Documents
     A.    Soft Page Break
     B.    Hard Page Break
           1.    Creating
           2.    Removing
     C.
```

(c)

```
I.   Overview
II.  |
III. Multipage Documents
     A.    Soft Page Break
     B.    Hard Page Break
           1.    Creating
           2.    Removing
     C.    Headers and Footers
```

(d)

4. Press **3**   **⏎**

The outline has been renumbered starting with your choice—III.

Outline Style.   You can also alter the style used by the outline itself.

1. Select <u>T</u>ools, <u>O</u>utline   [Ctrl + F5]

2. Press **0** to *Define* the outline

Figure WP3—29
*Changing the
Outline Style*

The outline has been changed to
"bullet" style.

```
        •    Overview
        •    Multipage Documents
             o    Soft Page Break
             o    Hard Page Break
                  -    Creating
                  -    Removing
             o    Headers and Footers
```

Figure WP3—30
*Changing the
Outline Style*

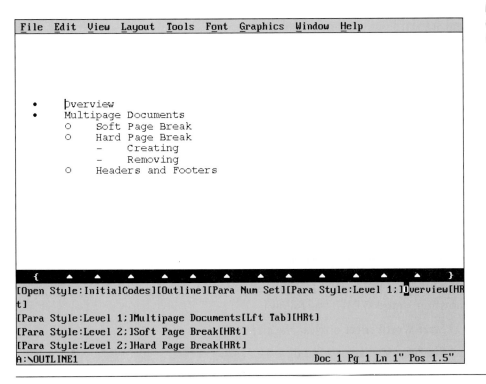

The "Outline Style List" screen appears again as in Figure WP3–27c.

3. Move the highlight to the "Bullets" style

4. Press ⏎ to accept

As shown in Figure WP3–29, the outline now shows bullets (special symbols) instead of numbers.

Canceling Changes. As with other format enhancements, the easiest way to remove changes in an outline format is to locate and remove the change using REVEAL CODES.

1. Select <u>V</u>iew, Reveal <u>C</u>odes   [F11]

2. Move to, and delete, the [Outline] and [Para Num Set] codes as shown in Figure WP3–30.

Figure WP3–31
Sort Document

Text is typed into columns that are separated with tabs.

Customer	City	State
Edwards	New York	NY
Smith	Washington	DC
Parker	Santa Fe	NM
Cottingim	Fort Worth	TX
Hill	Hinsdale	IL
Martin	Rochester	NY
Charles	Albuquerque	NM
Willaims	Boston	MA
Perkins	Chicago	IL

The removal of these enhancements will return the outline to normal numbering and standard outline form.

3. Exit from REVEAL CODES
4. Clear the screen *without* saving this document

Sorting

WordPerfect's **Sort feature** allows you to arrange text in alphabetical or numerical order. You can sort lists, lines of text, paragraphs, or merge records. You can also invoke sort when the cursor is positioned in a table to sort the table rows just as easily. This brief exercise will examine basic sort techniques. Once you have mastered them, feel free to experiment with all the variations.

☞ Tip: It is a good idea to save the original document *before* sorting and to save the sorted results as a new document (with a new filename). This way, not only could you retrieve the document if your sort does not perform as expected, but you will always have the text in its original order if you need to use it again.

Preparing for the Sort.   For this exercise, you will need to create the document shown in Figure WP3–31 as follows:

1. Start WordPerfect or clear the screen
2. Set left tabs at +2″ and +4″ (**Shift** + **F8** , **L** , **T** , **A** , **2** , **↵** , **4** , **↵** , **F7** , **F7** , **F7** ; if you're using the menu, select *Layout* instead of pressing **Shift** + **F8**)
3. Type the data as shown in Figure WP3–31, pressing **Tab** to advance to the next column and **↵** at the end of each line
4. Save this document as **SORT1**

Sorting with One Key.   Basic sorting involves two simple decisions: what portion of the document will be sorted and what key (or keys) will be used. A **key** is a piece of data (such as name or zip code) that provides the basis for the sort. *Any* key can be used. If the key you select uniquely identifies each item (that is, there are no duplicate key values) then you need only one key to completely sort your list. Social security number or driver's license number are examples of unique keys, but last name would work as well if all the last names on your list were different (as in this example). To sort:

1. Indicate the block of text to be sorted, as in Figure WP3–32a.

Figure WP3—32
Sorting with One Key

(a) Identify the text block. (b) The Sort screen. (c) The list is sorted alphabetically by customer name.

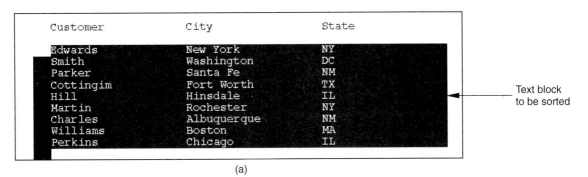

(a)

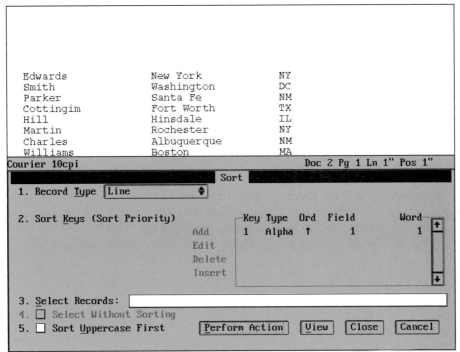

(b)

(c)

(Reminder: Move to the "E" in "Edwards," invoke the BLOCK command, and then move below the last line of the list.)

☞ **Tip: The block to be sorted should include only data, not titles, headings, or summary lines. Otherwise, these lines would be sorted along with the data and appear somewhere in the resulting list.**

2. Select <u>T</u>ools, So<u>r</u>t   [Ctrl + F9]

A "Sort" screen resembling Figure WP3–32b will appear. The commands offered in the lower half of this screen allow you to control such factors as *keys*, *select* (what records will be included), *order* (whether the sort will be ascending or descending), and *type* of sort. You should always review this screen to make sure that the settings are correct for the sort you desire. If they are not, change them appropriately.

At present, the default settings are fine: the leftmost column (shown by Field 1) will be used as the key, and each line in the data block will be sorted in ascending order from A to Z (shown by the up arrow under "Ord").

3. Press **P** to *Perform Action*

The sort appears on your screen as shown in Figure WP3–32c.

4. Save this document as **SORT2**

☞ **Tip: Although it is not evident in this result, WordPerfect sorts special characters (such as @ or ∗) first, followed by numbers, uppercase letters, and lowercase letters. Thus, "Cat" would come before "apple" but after "∗zoo."**

Sorting with Two Keys.   Many times, the key you select does not uniquely identify each item (that is, there are duplicate key values) and you may want to add a second key to differentiate among the duplicates. This exercise, for example, will sort the list of data using "State" as the first (primary) key and "City" as a secondary key.

1. Indicate the block of text to be sorted as in Figure WP3–33a

2. Select <u>T</u>ools, So<u>r</u>t   [Ctrl + F9]

3. Press **K** for *Keys*

You can now identify the first key ("State"), which can be found in the third column of data. WordPerfect uses the tab column to identify the key (the left margin counting as the first column). The current "Key 1" settings of "Alpha ⬆ 1" indicate the default setting—an alphanumeric sort in ascending (⬆) order that uses the first word in the first field as the key.

4. Press **E** to *Edit* this key

An "Edit Sort Key" menu appears as in Figure WP3–33b.

5. Press **F** and then type **3**

to change the first key from the first field column (the default) to the third ("State"). You can leave the type and order as is.

6. Press ↵ to accept

You can now identify a second key.

7. Press **A** to "Add"

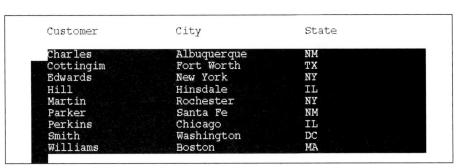

(a)

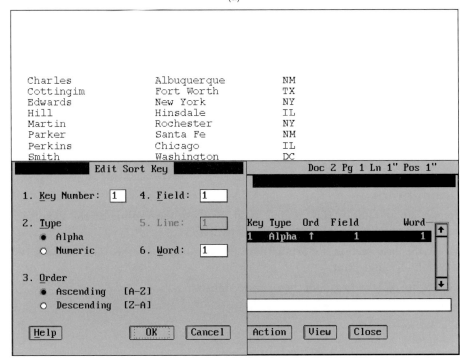

(b)

Customer	City	State
Smith	Washington	DC
Perkins	Chicago	IL
Hill	Hinsdale	IL
Williams	Boston	MA
Charles	Albuquerque	NM
Parker	Santa Fe	NM
Edwards	New York	NY
Martin	Rochester	NY
Cottingim	Fort Worth	TX

(c)

Figure WP3—33

Sorting with Two Keys

(a) Identify the text block.
(b) The "Edit Sort Key" menu.
(c) The list is sorted by state and then city.

WP

The "Edit Sort Key" menu returns.

8. Press `F` to *Set Field*

9. Press **2** and press `↵`

to identify this key as the second column ("City").

10. Press `↵` to accept the key

11. Press `Esc` to return to the menu

12. Press `P` to *Perform Action*

The resultant sort, in state and then city order, appears as shown in Figure WP3–33c.

13. Save this document as **SORT3**
14. Clear the screen

In the future, you may want to experiment with sort order, numerical sorts, and selecting records. Simply invoke the sort menu and follow the command structure.

☞ **Tip: To delete an unneeded key in the sort screen, press K, highlight the unneeded key, and press the Delete key (or D).**

Checkpoint

☐ Prepare an outline of this module (you may use the outline at the chapter's beginning as a reference). Save as WPCHECK7.

☐ Move the last section ("Sorting") to the beginning of the outline. Save as WPCHECK7 and print.

☐ Type a list of 10 words and then sort it alphabetically.

Module 7: Graphics

WordPerfect's **Graphics feature** lets you combine lines or images with text. This capability is useful when you are producing such documents as newsletters and reports, where graphic images, diagrams, company logos, or even pictures are needed.

Simple graphics—lines and boxes—can be drawn directly on the screen. More complicated graphic images can be created with other graphics programs, saved on disk, and brought into the text document.

Drawing Lines and Boxes

Just as an underlined word attracts attention, a simple graphic line or box can add emphasis or make a page more pleasing to the eye. The following exercise creates the graphic boxes and lines shown in Figure WP3–34. First, place the needed text on the screen:

1. Clear the screen and press `↵` twice

2. Space over to position 2.5″ (do not use `Tab`)

3. Type **Computer**

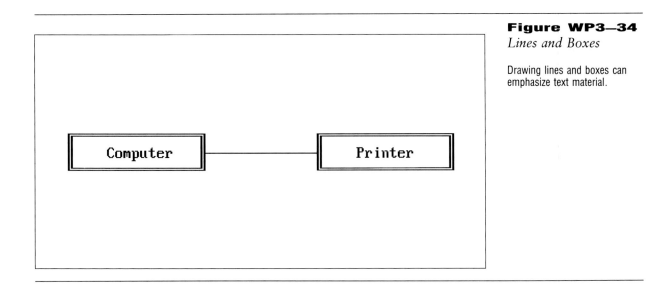

Figure WP3—34
Lines and Boxes

Drawing lines and boxes can emphasize text material.

4. Space over to position 5.5″

5. Type **Printer** and press ↵

You are now ready to draw the boxes around each word.

Drawing and Moving. Drawing screen lines is simply a matter of positioning the insertion point, selecting the appropriate line, and then moving the insertion point (horizontally or vertically) to draw the line. Corners and joined lines are created automatically as you move in various directions.

1. Select Graphics   [Ctrl + F3]

2. Press **L** to select *Line Draw*

A "Line Draw" menu similar to Figure WP3—35a appears beneath the status line. This menu is a "palette" from which you will choose various line options. You can select one of three line types (1, 2, 3), replace one type of graphic symbol with another (4), erase (5), or move (6). This menu will remain onscreen until you exit.

3. Press **M** to select *Move*

The *Move* option turns off the line drawing feature, allowing you to reposition the insertion point without drawing lines as you move. In effect, it lifts the pen off the paper.

4. Move to Ln 1.17″ Pos 2″

5. Press **2** to select double lines

6. Press → 16 times

As the insertion point moves, a horizontal double line is drawn as if you were dragging a pen across the page. Your screen should resemble Figure WP3—35b.

7. Press ↓ twice

The double line has turned downward. Note that a perfect corner was created when you changed direction. Complete the rectangle as follows:

8. Press ← 16 times

9. Press ↑ twice

Figure WP3—35

Creating the Boxes

(a) The Line Draw "palette" appears as a menu beneath the status line. (b) The first horizontal double line is drawn.

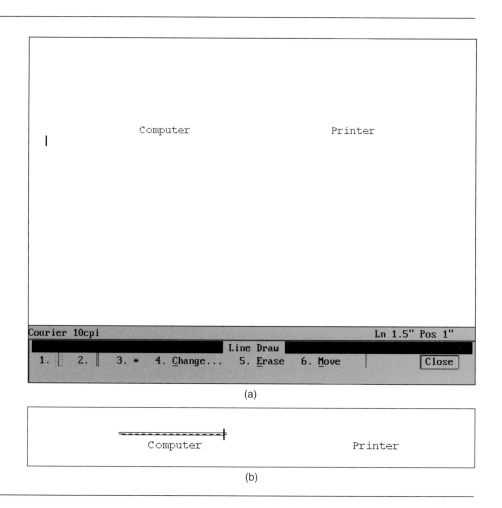

(a)

(b)

You can now move to the word "Printer" and repeat the process:

10. Press **M** or **6** to *Move*

11. Move to Ln 1.17″ Pos 5″

12. Press **2** for double lines

13. Press **→** 16 times

14. Press **↓** twice

15. Press **←** 16 times

16. Press **↑** twice

Now add the single connecting line in a similar fashion.

17. Press **↓** once to position the insertion point

You need not switch to the "move" option because you are drawing the same type of line. (It does not matter if you draw over it again.)

18. Press **1** to select a single line

19. Press **←** 14 times to draw the line

Your screen should now resemble the boxed text in Figure WP3—34.

Figure WP3—36
A WordPerfect Table

This table will be created with
WordPerfect's Table feature.

PHONE LIST		
Last	**First**	**Phone**
Your Last Name	Your First Name	XXX–XXX–XXXX
Martin	Edward	718–555–1234
Parker	Charles	505–555–9876
Kee	Charles	201–555–5678

Erasing.   There will be many times when you draw a line that is too long, or turn in the wrong direction. To erase these mistakes, simply invoke the *Erase* option and move back over the affected position. Try this:

1. Press **E** or **5** for *Erase*

2. Press **→** twice

The line is erased and the double line is returned to its original shape. Redraw the line now:

3. Press **1** for single line

4. Press **←** 2 times to reconnect the line

5. Press **F7** to exit the *Line Draw* screen

6. Save this document as **EXWP3–5a**

☞ **Tip: To experiment with different graphic patterns, you can invoke the Line Draw screen again: press 4, then select a new graphic pattern. Once selected, this pattern will appear as choice 3 and can be used instead of the single or double line.**

The lines and boxes you create with Line Draw can be treated as normal text characters. They can be copied, moved, deleted, and typed over. Like with any other text, however, inserting new text can cause them to shift their position on the screen.

Creating Tables

An extension of simple lines and boxes is WordPerfect's powerful *Table* feature, which can quickly create and edit boxes to present data in columns. The following exercise illustrates the basics of this process by creating the table shown in Figure WP3–36.

The Basic Table Form.   To create the basic table form, do the following:

1. Start WordPerfect or clear the screen

2. Select Layout   [Alt + F7]

3. Press **T** for *Tables*

4. Press **C** for *Create*

A "Create Table" dialog box appears.

5. Type **3** and press **↵** for "Columns"

6. Type **5** and press **↵** for "Rows"

7. Press **↵** (or select "OK") to accept

Figure WP3–37

*Creating a Basic
Table Form*

The basic form (a 3 × 5 table)
has been created.

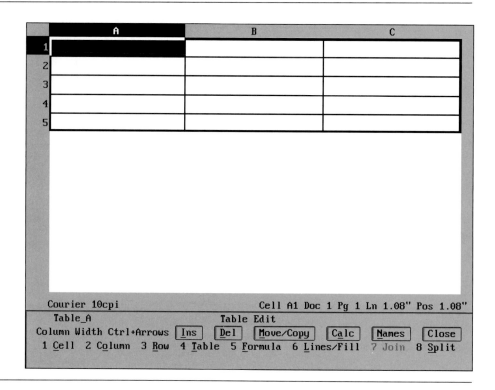

The basic form (set to 3 columns by 5 rows) appears on your screen as in Figure WP3–37.

8. Press   F7   to accept this form

Entering Table Data.   Tables are composed of *cells* formed by the intersection of columns and rows. Each cell is identified by a letter and number, starting with Column A at the left and Row 1 on top. The first cell, therefore, is Cell A1. You can use the arrow keys or the Tab key to move to each cell. Text can be entered into each cell individually as follows:

1. Press   ↓   to move to Cell A2

2. Type **Last** and press   →

3. In Cell B2, type **First** and press   →

4. In Cell B3, type **Phone** and press   →

Your screen should resemble the second row of Figure WP3–38. Complete the rest of the table by filling in the rows for Martin, Parker, and Kee in the three remaining rows of your table (as in Figure WP3–38).

☞ **Tip: If you press the Enter key by mistake, the cell will expand one row. Press the Backspace key to remove the hard return, and then press the right arrow key correctly.**

Table Enhancements.   A table can be enhanced while the form is being created, or after it has been filled with text. As long as the insertion point is within the table, you can access these enhancements by invoking the COLUMNS/TABLE command as follows:

1. Select Layout   [Alt + F7]
2. Select Tables, Edit   [T, E]

Figure WP3—38
*Entering Text
into a Table*

Each cell is entered individually
and then the right arrow key is
pressed to continue.

```
 File  Edit  View  Layout  Tools  Font  Graphics  Window  Help




    ┌─────────────────────┬─────────────────┬──────────────────────┐
    │                     │                 │                      │
    ├─────────────────────┼─────────────────┼──────────────────────┤
    │ Last                │ First           │ Phone                │
    ├─────────────────────┼─────────────────┼──────────────────────┤
    │ Martin              │ Edward          │ 718-555-1234         │
    ├─────────────────────┼─────────────────┼──────────────────────┤
    │ Parker              │ Charles         │ 505-555-9876         │
    ├─────────────────────┼─────────────────┼──────────────────────┤
    │ Kee                 │ Charles         │ 201-555-5678         │
    └─────────────────────┴─────────────────┴──────────────────────┘




  I


 Courier 10cpi                         Doc 1 Pg 1 Ln 3.62" Pos 1"
```

As shown in Figure WP3–39, a menu appears beneath the status line. Note, too, that the current cell's corresponding borders are highlighted. Immediate enhancements include changing column widths, inserting or deleting rows or columns, and moving or copying the table. In addition, you can invoke a multitude of size and format enhancements by pressing the appropriate keystrokes shown in the lower menu.

3. Move to Cell A1

Note: Pull-down menus do not work in this screen.

4. Press   **Alt** + **F4**   to activate the BLOCK command

5. Press   **→**   twice to highlight Row 1

☞ **Tip: The BLOCK command, when used in a table, will affect more than one cell at a time.**

6. Press **J** **Y** for *Join, Yes*

The Row 1 cells have joined to form one long cell. You can join as many cells as you want to form larger boxes, in rows and in columns.

7. Move to Cell A2

8. Press **Alt** + **F4** and **→** twice to highlight the row

9. Press **C** **A** for *Cell, Appearance*

There are nine different options available (as seen on your screen). These are the same options you saw in Chapter 2 when you altered text appearance.

10. Press **B** for *Bold*

11. Press **↵** to accept

Figure WP3—39

Table Enhancements

The table enhancement menu appears at the bottom of the screen.

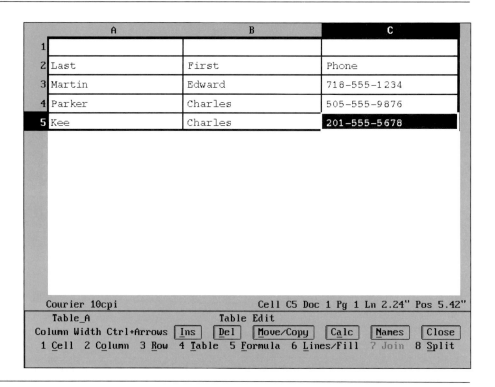

The text now appears in bold type.

12. Move to Cell A2, hold **Ctrl** and press **←** 3 times

(Using the Ctrl key and an arrow key changes the current column width.)

13. Move to Cell B2, hold **Ctrl** and press **←** 5 times

14. Move to Cell C2, hold **Ctrl** and press **←** 6 times

Make a few more changes:

15. Move to Cell A3, press **Insert** to insert a column or row

An "Insert" dialog box appears.

16. Press **R** for *Rows*

17. Press **↵** to insert one row

A new row has been inserted. Rows and columns can be inserted or deleted by moving to the desired location and pressing the Insert or Delete key.

18. In Cell A2, block the cells A2 to C2

19. Press **L** **F** **Y** for *Lines/Fill, Fill, Fill Style*

20. Move the highlight to "10% Shaded Fill" (Of course, you may select any fill percentage.)

21. Press **↵** to acept

22. Press **↵** twice to exit menus

Shading will appear in the blocked cells

23. Press **T** **P** **C** for *Options, Position, Center*

Note that text in tables can be situated at the left, right, center, or any set position as desired.

24. Press ⏎

25. Press **F7** to end the enhancements

Completing the Table. With these enhancements set, you can now fill the empty cells with text.

1. Move to Cell A1 (look at the status line if you're in doubt)

2. Press **Shift** + **F6** to center in the cell

3. Type **PHONE LIST**

4. In Cell A3, type your last name

5. In Cell B3, type your first name

6. In Cell C3, type your phone number

7. Save this document as **TABLE**

Your table should resemble Figure WP3–39. Make sure your printer is ready and then print the table if you want.

When no longer needed, tables can be deleted as any other text formatting. Simply move to the start of the table and press the Delete key. The text contained within the table can then be deleted normally.

Tables can also be used as spreadsheets to perform math. See the Appendix to create formulas.

Adding Graphics Boxes

The Line Draw command lets you draw lines around text for emphasis. With WordPerfect's GRAPHICS command, you can also create separate graphics boxes into which you can retrieve images, graphs, diagrams, charts, or even other documents. Of course, these other items must be available on disk for retrieval. These boxes are like little windows on the screen. Document text automatically wraps around the window, as shown in Figure WP3–40. The following exercise demonstrates the creation and editing of a graphics box.

1. Clear your screen
2. Open the EXWP3–6 document

Note: If you do not have EXWP3–6 on your disk, type in the paragraph text shown in Figure WP3–40 and save it as EXWP3–6. Remember: do not press the Enter key until you reach the end of the paragraph.

Defining a Graphics Box. The first step in incorporating boxed material into your document is defining the type of graphics box you need.

1. Select Graphics   [Alt + F9]

2. Press **B** to select *Boxes*

3. Press **C** to *Create*

A screen resembling Figure WP3–41 appears. Note that some of the parameters have been set by default. Item 8 displays the current position of the proposed box. Item 9 indicates a size. These can be changed, as you will see shortly.

4. Press **F** to select a *Filename*

Figure WP3—40
Positioning the Graphic Figure

The EXWP3—6 text appears to the left of the screen when a graphic figure box is first created.

This is an example of incorporating a graphics box into a WordPerfect document. The box can be positioned anywhere in the document and resized as needed. It can also include a figure number and caption if desired. The box in this example contains a diagram of a 3 1/2" disk that was scanned from another textbook and then saved in a WordPerfect graphics file with the name DISK.WPG. The "WPG" extension indicates that the file is a Word Perfect Graphic. WordPerfect includes a number of graphic images that can be incorporated into your text documents for practice. They are all labelled with the extension "WPG."

This is DISK.WPG

Figure WP3—41
Creating a Figure

The Definition: Figure screen.

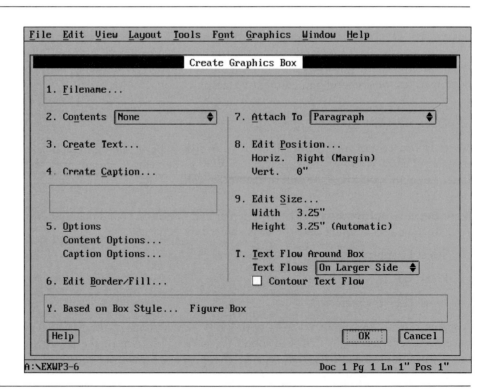

The name that you type here must exactly match the disk filename that will be retrieved into the box. You should have a file named DISK.WPG on your data disk. If not, skip Step 5 and leave the box empty.

5. Type **DISK.WPG** and press ↵

☞ **Tip: You can also press the F5 key to list available files and then select a filename.**

A "File Format" box appears, indicating the format of the graphic (in this case, PCX).

6. Press ↵ to accept the format and continue

The name of the file appears in Item 1. Item 2 indicates that the file is a graphic *image*. You can add a caption now to see the effect on the screen.

7. Press **C** for *Caption*

An entry screen appears. You could leave "Figure 1" as shown, but in this exercise, you'll change it.

8. Press **← Backspace** to erase "Figure 1"

9. Press **Shift** + **F6** to center the caption

10. Type **This is DISK.WPG**

11. Press **F7** to exit this screen (as shown at the bottom)

Note that the caption appears beneath item #4. That's enough change for now. To leave the Figure menu and return to the screen,

12. Press ↵ (or select "OK")

If you are in graphics or page mode, your screen will resemble Figure WP3–40.

13. Save this file as **EXWP3–6A**

Editing a Graphics Box. Graphics box parameters can be adjusted to suit your needs. You can change or delete captions, adjust the box size, shift its position on the page, or change the type of border that surrounds it. You can even adjust the graphic itself. The following exercise adjusts a few of the settings for Figure 1.

1. Select **G**raphics   [Alt + F9]

2. Select Graphic **B**oxes

3. Press **E** for *Edit*

4. Type **1** and press ↵ for *Box number*

To begin the edit,

5. Press ↵ (or select "Edit")

An "Edit Graphics" box appears. You can now adjust any of the parameters that define the figure, or press the F7 key (or select "Cancel") to leave them as they are currently set.

Positioning the Figure. The box containing the figure can be repositioned both vertically (in relation to the paragraph) or horizontally (across the page).

1. Press **P** to edit the *Position*

2. Press **D** to change the *Vertical Distance from Top of Paragraph*

You can now select how far below the top of the paragraph you want the figure box to be placed. It is currently set at zero inches.

3. Type **.5** and press ↵

You can also change the horizontal position of the box.

4. Press **H** to change the *Horizontal* position

You can now select where the box should be positioned across the page: set your own distance, or select left, centered, right, or full (the entire width).

5. Press **L** for *Left*

6. Press ↵ (or select "OK") to accept the changes

The menu should show your changes in item 8.

Sizing the Figure.   The default size of the box can be adjusted as follows:

1. Press **S** for *Size*

A menu appears offering size options. You can: (1) set the width and let the program automatically pick a proportionally correct height; (2) set the height and let the program set the width; (3) set both yourself to any dimensions you please; (4) let the program set both.

2. Press **W** to set *Width*

3. Type **2.3** to set the width at 2.3 inches

4. Press ↵

By leaving item 4 set to automatic, the program selects the appropriate height to maintain the figure's proportions. (You could press H to set the height yourself, or press AU to make both automatic.)

5. Press ↵ to accept

The menu reflects the changes in item 9.

Editing the Image Itself.   You can also "play" with the image to adjust its size, position, and orientation within the box. You can even create a mirror image or a negative image of the figure.

1. Press **E** to access the Image Editor

A screen resembling Figure WP3–42a should appear. The menu at the bottom of the screen lists the options. You can use the arrow keys, and a few others, to adjust the image by set amounts. If you have a mouse, you can use the commands listed in the bar at the top. You may also type in adjustment settings directly using the five numbered options. This exercise is a quick demonstration of some of the arrow techniques. If you make a mistake, press the Ctrl and Home keys (the GO TO command) to reset the image to its original form.

2. Press **N** until the number in the increment box reads "5%"

This action produces a 5 percent change in the image each time you press a key.

☞ Tip: You can also set the adjustment to 25 percent or 10 percent for gross changes, or 1 percent for fine adjustments.

3. Press → once to move the image to the right

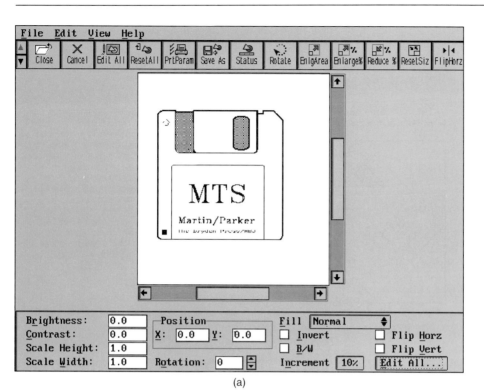

(a)

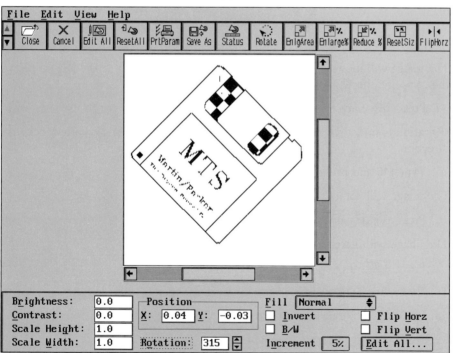

(b)

Figure WP3—42
The Graphics Edit Screen

(a) Helpful menus appear at the bottom of the screen. (b) The image has been moved to the right and rotated clockwise.

Figure WP3—43

The Final Printed Page Displaying the Repositioned and Edited Graphic

```
 File   Edit   View   Layout   Tools   Font   Graphics   Window   Help



         This  is  an  example  of  incorporating  a  graphics  box  into  a
         WordPerfect document.  The box can be positioned anywhere in the
                            document  and  resized  as  needed.   It  can
                            also include a figure number and caption
                            if  desired.   The  box  in  this  example
                            contains a diagram of a 3 1/2" disk that
                            was  scanned  from  another  textbook  and
                            then saved in a WordPerfect graphics file
                            with  the  name  DISK.WPG.   The  "WPG"
                            extension  indicates  that  the  file  is  a
                            Word   Perfect   Graphic.    WordPerfect
                            includes a number of graphic images that
                            can  be  incorporated  into  your  text
                            documents  for  practice.   They  are  all
                            labelled with the extension "WPG."


             This is DISK.WPG




 A:\EXWP3-6B                                      Doc 1 Pg 1 Ln 1" Pos 1"
```

The image will move slightly to the right. (Pressing the Left arrow key will have the opposite effect.)

4. Press **0** once to set rotation

(Rotation is measured in degrees that the image will turn in a counterclockwise direction.)

5. Type **315** and press **↵**

The image will rotate as in Figure WP3—42b.

6. Press **Pg Up** once to enlarge

The image will increase in size. Move it down a little:

7. Press **↓** once

This looks fine. You now need to exit from the menu.

8. Press **F7** to exit the edit screen

9. Press **↵** to return to the work screen

10. Save this document as **EXWP3—6B**

Seeing the Adjusted Document.   Your screen should resemble Figure WP3—43. Notice the graphic box has been moved down three lines, shifted to the left side of the page, and made smaller. The image within the box has been rotated, moved right, made proportionally larger, and moved down.

1. View the document with Print Preview or print it
2. Exit WordPerfect

Checkpoint

☐ Type your name near the center of the page and draw a double-lined box around it. Add designs as you see fit using Line Draw. Save as WPCHECK8.

☐ Create a two-column table that lists each course you are taking this semester and the instructor's name to its right.

☐ Retrieve the DISK.WPG graphic and center it on the page. Add a figure caption that contains your name.

Module 8: Using the Ribbon and Button Bar Features

WordPerfect offers a number of short-cut features—namely, the button bar, ribbon, and outline bar—that can be used with a mouse or other pointing device to provide quick access to many WordPerfect commands. (These features cannot be invoked through the keyboard.) The button bar and ribbon are presented in the examples that follow. *Note:* If you do not have a mouse or trackball, skip this module.

Button Bar

WordPerfect's **button bar** is a set of screen icons (pictures) that lets you quickly access many menu items, features, macros, and other button bars. WordPerfect 6.0 offers seven predefined button bars: WPMain, Fonts, Layout, Macros, Outline, Tables, and Tools. Each bar provides a set of related commands, one command to a "button." You choose the desired command by simply clicking its button with a mouse. You can also create your own buttons and bars to customize access to the commands that you use most often.

Activating the Button Bar. If a button bar is not currently on your screen, it can be activated as follows:

1. Select <u>V</u>iew

(Remember, you can select using the keyboard or clicking the mouse.)

2. Select <u>B</u>utton bar

As shown in Figure WP3–44, a button bar appears on your screen. By default, WordPerfect's main button bar ("WPMain") appears at the top of the screen, just below the menu. (The button bar that appears on your screen, or its position, may differ from the one in the figure.)

3. If your bar does not match Figure WP3–44, press **Alt** + **V** **S** **S** ,

 then highlight "WPMAIN" and press **↵**

 Once activated, a button bar remains on the screen for mouse access. It does not interfere with any other WordPerfect command. If you exit WordPerfect with a button bar still active, it will remain active the next time you use the program.

Invoking a Button Command. Button bar commands are invoked by simply clicking the desired button; that is, pointing to the button and pressing the left mouse button. For example, to invoke the File Manager,

1. Click the "File Mgr" button (the first button)

Figure WP3—44

The WPMain Button Bar

The scroll buttons let you view offscreen buttons.

As expected, the FIle Manager is immediately activated. For now, to exit from the File Manager screen,

2. Press the *right* mouse button (or press **Esc**)

☞ **Tip: Depending on your current WordPerfect activity, some commands may not be appropriate. Those buttons that cannot be selected appear dimmed on the button bar.**

Viewing Offscreen Buttons.   Button bars may contain more command buttons than can be displayed on the screen at one time. However, each button bar includes two scroll buttons at the extreme left (shown as opposite triangles) that allow you to scroll forward or backward to see other available buttons. (Vertical button bars offer scroll buttons at the top.) To view other buttons on the current bar,

1. Click the lower scroll button at the left

Note that additional buttons now appear on the button bar. To return to the first set of command buttons,

2. Click the upper scroll button

Selecting a Different Button Bar.   Figure WP3—45 lists WordPerfect's seven predefined button bars and their commands. (The lines between commands indicate the extent of each screen display.) The WPMain button bar offers a set of general tools, whereas the other six bars offer groups of related commands designed for specific tasks. For example, you may want to have quicker access to font commands. Thus, you might replace the WPMain button bar with the Fonts bar as follows:

1. Select <u>V</u>iew, Button Bar <u>S</u>etup, <u>S</u>elect

2. Highlight the *Fonts* menu bar

3. Press ⏎ (or choose <u>S</u>elect)

To return to the WPMain button bar later, you could repeat the process, highlighting *WPMain* in Step 2. You could also use the button bars themselves as follows:

4. Click the lower scroll button at the left

Note that the next-to-the-last button at the right reads "BBar Sel" (for "Button Bar Select"). As shown in Figure WP3—45, all predefined button bars offer this option as the next-to-the-last button. To activate a different button bar,

5. Click the *BBar Sel* button

Figure WP3—45
WordPerfect's Seven Predefined Button Bars

WPMain	Fonts	Layout	Macros	Outline	Tables	Tools
File Manager	Font	Format Line	Modify Attributes	Outln Edit	Tbl Create	Speller
Save As	Normal	Format Page	Initial Caps	Outln Options	Tbl Edit	Grammatik
Print	Bold	Format Doc.	Pleading	Outln Begin	Insert Row	Thesaurus
Print Preview	Underline	Columns	Space Tabs	Outln End	Delete Row	Macro Play
Font	Dbl Underline	Envelope	Calculate	Outln Style	Col. Wide	Macro Record
Graph Mode	Italics	Format Other	Bullet	Next Level	Col. Narrow	Macro Control
Text Mode	Fine	Margins	Memo	Previous Level	Copy Cell	Merge Define
Envelope	Small	Tab Set	Edit Code	Change Level	Text Format	Merge Run
Speller	Large	Header/Footer	Glossary	Hide Family	Tbl Calculate	Sort
Grammatik	Very Large	Styles	Note Convert	Show Family	Tbl Format	Date Text
Quick Finder	Extra Large	Justify Left	All fonts	Hide Body	Cell Format	Date Code
Table Edit	Normal Size	Justify Center	B-Bar Select	Move Family	Col. Format	Date Format
Search →	Superscript	Justify Right	B-Bar Options	Copy Family	Table Join	Mark Text
B-Bar Select	Subscript	Justify Full		Cut Family	Table Split	Generate
B-Bar Options	Norm. Position	Hard Page		Paste Family	Table Names	Hypertext
	Outline	Indent		B-Bar Select	Calc All	Math On
	Shadow	Dbl Indent		B-Bar Options	Float Cell Create	Math Off
	Small Caps	Back Tab			Float Cell Edit	Math Define
	Redline	Hang Indent			B-Bar Select	Math Calc
	Strikeout	Center			B-Bar Options	Sprdsht Import
	Print Color	Flush Right				Sprdsht Link Create
	WP Characters	Decimal Tab				Sprdsht Link Options
	B-Bar Select	Footnote Create				Sound Play
	B-Bar Options	Footnote Edit				Sound Record
		Footnote Number				Sound Add
		Footnote Options				Sound Set
		Endnote Create				B-Bar Select
		Endnote Edit				B-Bar Options
		Endnote Number				
		Endnote Options				
		Endnote Placement				
		Comment Create				
		Comment Edit				
		Comment Text				
		B-Bar Select				
		B-Bar Options				

A list of available button bars appears.

6.   Double-click the desired bar (in this case, *WPMain*)

The WPMain button bar reappears. Feel free to use the menu or button bar approach as you prefer.

Repositioning the Button Bar.   Although the default position for the button bar is at the top of the screen (just below the menu bar), you may prefer to place it at the bottom of the screen or vertically along either side. To reposition the button bar,

1.   Select View, Button Bar Setup, Options

A "Button Bar Options" menu appears offering Top, Bottom, Left Side, and Right Side options (as shown in Figure WP3–46a).

2.   Select Right and then "OK"

Figure WP3—46

Positioning the Button Bar

As shown in the (a) Button Bar Options screen, the button bar may be placed at the top, (b) side, or (c) bottom of the screen.

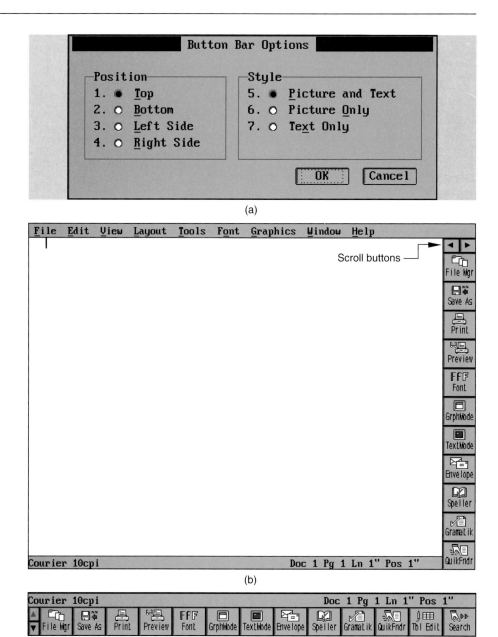

(a)

(b)

(c)

The button bar will be positioned vertically at the right of the screen as in Figure WP3–46b.

As you have seen, you can also use the button bar itself to make the change. For example, place the bar at the screen bottom using this approach:

3. Click the scroll button at the top right

Note that the last button (now at the bottom of the vertical list) reads "BBar Opt" (for "Button Bar Options"). All predefined button bars offer this option as the last button. To adjust position,

4. Click the *BBar Opt* button

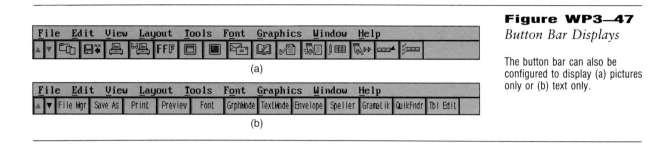

Figure WP3—47
Button Bar Displays

The button bar can also be configured to display (a) pictures only or (b) text only.

The "Button Bar Options" menu returns. Before you complete the position command, examine items 5 through 7 on the menu (as in Figure WP3–46a). Note that you can also adjust the button bar to display pictures and text in each button, or just pictures or text as you prefer (as in Figure WP3–47). For now,

5.   Click the *Bottom* option and then "OK"

The menu has been repositioned at the bottom of the screen.

Deactivating the Button Bar.   If you no longer need the button bar on your screen, it is easily deactivated, allowing more text in your document to be displayed:

1.   Select View
2.   Select Button Bar

The bar is no longer active but can be reactivated whenever needed.

Another useful WordPerfect bar is called the *ribbon*. As shown in Figure WP3–48a, the **ribbon** is a bar, located at the top of the screen, that displays and provides access to features that affect text size and appearance. Specifically, it lets you view and adjust six document settings: display size, outline level, number of columns, text alignment, font style, and point size.

**The
Ribbon**

Activating the Ribbon.   To activate the ribbon (if it is not already on your screen),

1.   Select View
2.   Select Ribbon

The one-line ribbon appears just beneath the menu bar at the top of your screen. Note the current settings in the six separate boxes as displayed in Figure WP3–48a. The following exercise demonstrates how to use the ribbon:

1.   Clear your screen and open **EXWP3-1**

(Any document can be used for this exercise if you do not have EXWP3-1.) You will first change the column setting to two columns from the current single-column setting.

2.   Double-click the box that displays "1 Col"

A pull-down menu appears as in Figure WP3–48b, offering other column choices (equivalent to the menu sequence "Layout, Columns, Number of Columns").

3.   Select *2-cols*

Figure WP3—48

The Ribbon

(a) The ribbon provides access to six text and layout features. (b) Adjusting columns with the ribbon. (c) A two-column layout has been set.

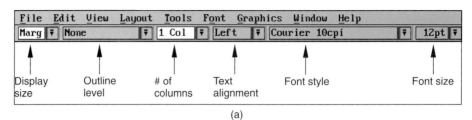

(a)

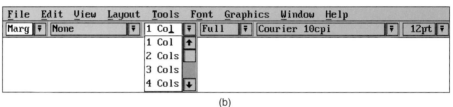

(b)

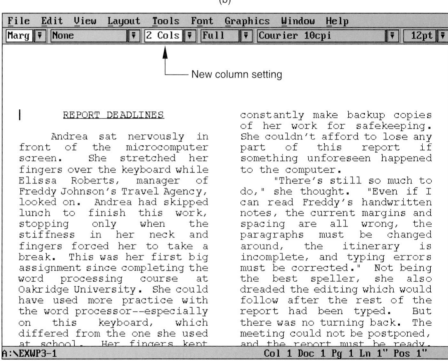

(c)

Note that the document immediately changes to two columns and the bar reflects the new setting, as in Figure WP3—48c. Other changes are made in similar fashion. For example,

4.   Double-click the box that displays "Marg"

This box controls how much text is displayed on the screen (equivalent to the file menu sequence of "View, Zoom"). Currently, it is set to show all text between margins.

5.   Select *150%*

Note that the text becomes larger on the screen—a boon to users who have difficulty seeing small characters.

You can similarly change alignment, font, and type size using the other boxes in the ribbon.

Deactivating the Ribbon.   As with the button bar, you may leave the ribbon on the screen without affecting your work in a document, or remove it if you no longer require the ribbon. To deactivate the ribbon,

1. Select View
2. Select Ribbon

The ribbon is now removed.

Checkpoint

☐ Activate the "Tools" button bar and place it at the bottom of your screen so that it displays only pictures.

☐ Invoke the Speller program from the button bar and then cancel the Speller to return to the document.

☐ Deactivate the button bar.

Module 9: Sharing Files among Applications

There are times when you may want to move data from WordPerfect to another software package, such as a spreadsheet, database, or even another word processing program. Conversely, you may want to move data prepared in another program into WordPerfect. Fortunately, there is a way to translate data into other software formats.

The exercises in this module use two files that were contained on the student data disk included with this book: EMPLOY.WP and EMPLOY.WK1 (a spreadsheet). Figures WP3–49a and WP3–49b present the contents of these files. Both should have been copied to your data disk when you began this chapter and are now available for use. (If they are not, review the "Preparing for This Chapter" material.)

Exporting and Importing

EXPORT and IMPORT commands facilitate data transfer by converting data into formats that can be read by other software packages. **Exporting** *saves* data in another format; **importing** *retrieves* data that has been saved in another format.

Direct Conversion.   The easiest way to share data is to translate them into a form that another program can readily understand. Some slight adjustments may have to be made, but these are usually minimal. Typically, direct conversions are offered for the most popular software packages. You'll try some direct conversions soon.

ASCII—The Common Denominator.   When direct conversion is not available, *ASCII* conversion may still allow data transfer. **ASCII** (pronounced "ask-key") stands for the American Standard Code for Information Interchange. It is one of a few standard formats adopted by the computer industry for representing typed characters. ASCII eliminates the symbols unique to each software package, providing a common style for sharing data.

Figure WP3—49

The Import/Export Files

```
Employee List
                Home            Annual      Date
Sales Staff     Phone           Salary      Hired
----------------------------------------------------------
Burstein, J.    408-555-1010    $23,450     06-Jul-78
Laudon, J.      914-555-9876     33,600     07-Oct-81
Martin, E.      718-555-1234     31,750     01-Nov-79
Parker, C.      505-555-5678     37,500     25-Apr-82
Williams, C.    312-555-0202     38,000     17-Feb-75
----------------------------------------------------------
Total                           $164,300
```

(a) The EMPLOY.WP document.

```
         A              B              C           D

  1  Employee List
  2                 Home            Annual      Date
  3  Sales Staff    Phone           Salary      Hired
  4  ----------------------------------------------------------
  5  Burstein, J.   408-555-1010    $23,450     06-Jul-78
  6  Laudon, J.     914-555-9876     33,600     07-Oct-81
  7  Martin, E.     718-555-1234     31,750     01-Nov-79
  8  Parker, C.     505-555-5678     37,500     25-Apr-82
  9  Williams, D.   312-555-0202     38,000     17-Feb-75
 10  ----------------------------------------------------------
 11  Total                          $164,300
```

(b) The EMPLOY.WK1 spreadsheet.

Exporting Files from Word-Perfect

To prepare for these exercises,

1. Start WordPerfect
2. Set the default drive to A: (or B:)
3. Open the EMPLOY.WP file

Creating an ASCII File.   To save a copy of the EMPLOY.WP document in ASCII format,

1. Select File, Save As   [F10]

The "Save Document 1" menu appears on the screen as usual. You can now change the format as follows:

2. Type **EMWP.TXT** and press ↵

☞ **Tip: The .TXT extension is optional, but it is useful for indicating that the file is saved in text (ASCII) format.**

3. Press ↓ to move to "Format"

4. Press **R** to activate the format list as in Figure WP3–50

5. Move the highlight up to "ASCII Text (Standard)"

```
Rich-Text-Format (RTF)
WordPerfect 4.2
WordPerfect 5.0
WordPerfect 5.1/5.2
*WordPerfect 6.0
```

6. Press ↵ to accept

7. Press ↵ to save

Exporting a WordPerfect 4.2 or 5.0 File.   WordPerfect can also save a file in a format that can be read by earlier versions of WordPerfect. For example, to save a copy of the EMPLOY.WP document in WordPerfect 4.2 format, do the following:

1. Select File, Save As   [F10]
2. Type **EMWP.W42**

The optional extension .W42 reminds you that the file is saved in WordPerfect 4.2 format. (You might use .W50 for WordPerfect 5.0.)

3. Press ↓   R to see other formats

4. Move the highlight to "WordPerfect 4.2" (use **Pg Dn** if needed)

5. Press ↵ twice

Exporting to a Spreadsheet.   Any ASCII file can be read by a spreadsheet program. However, two minor procedural adjustments are needed: (1) Prior to exporting, set the document's left margin to zero so that the text will be placed correctly in the spreadsheet; (2) Use a .PRN extension. ASCII files are called "print files" in spreadsheet programs and identified with the .PRN extension. If a .PRN extension is not used, the document may not be recognized when you try to retrieve it in a spreadsheet.

Exporting to a Database Program.   ASCII files can also be read by database programs. Data can be in column form as in the EMPLOY.WP file (Figure WP3—49a) where each field is a fixed distance from the left margin. Data can also contain fields of variable lengths, as long as they are enclosed in quote marks and separated by commas.

Again, the procedure is identical to creating other ASCII files, except that you must first adjust settings and remove characters that the database may not understand, and then save the file with an appropriate extension.

Data in column form must contain only the lines that represent records, and all numeric data must be free of commas and dollar signs.

1. Clear the screen and open **EMPLOY.WP** if needed

As shown in Figure WP3—51, you must first remove all lines that do not contain record data as follows:

2. Delete the *first* four lines
3. Delete the *last* two lines

Figure WP3–51

Preparing a File for a Database

Only lines representing records can be included, and numeric data must be free of commas and dollar signs.

```
Burstein, J.     408-555-1010     23450    06-Jul-78
Laudon, J.       914-555-9876     33600    07-Oct-81
Martin, E.       718-555-1234     31750    01-Nov-79
Parker, C.       505-555-5678     37500    25-Apr-82
Williams, D.     312-555-0202     38000    17-Feb-75
```

Figure WP3–52

The Delimited File

Data are separated (delimited) by commas.

```
"Burstein, J.","408-555-1010",23450,"07/06/78"
"Laudon, J.","914-555-9876",33600,"10/07/81"
"Martin, E.","718-555-1234",31750,"11/01/79"
"Parker, C.","505-555-5678",37500,"04/25/82"
"Williams, D.","312-555-0202",38000,"02/17/75"
```

You must now remove dollar signs and commas from numeric data, making sure that you do not change the relative position of the values. To do this, use typeover mode or search and replace to change each dollar sign to a space.

☞ **Tip: To remove commas, it is best to insert a space to the left of the number and then delete its comma. This way, all numbers will maintain their decimal position from the left margin.**

4. Remove the $ symbol and commas from the numeric data so that your screen resembles Figure WP3–51. You can now save the adjusted file in ASCII format as before.

5. Select File, Save As

6. Type **EMWP.SDF**

The .SDF extension identifies this file format as "System Data Format"—a format that is readable by most database programs.

7. Press ↓ R

8. Highlight "ASCII Text (Standard)"

9. Press ↵ twice

Data can also be prepared in WordPerfect in a variable-length format, as in Figure WP3–52. Character fields are enclosed in quotes, and fields are separated by commas (one record on each line). This is a standard mail merge format used in some word processing programs.

Figure WP3–53
Importing ASCII Text

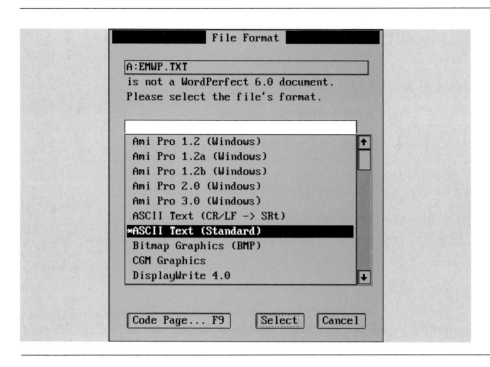

10. Clear your screen and open **EMWP.SDF**
11. Edit the document to make it look like Figure WP3–52 by removing spaces and inserting commas or quotes and changing dates where appropriate.
12. Export the document as an ASCII file named **EMWP.DEL**

In this case, the .DEL extension identifies this file as a standard "delimited" file ("delimited" means "separated with commas").

Importing Files into Word-Perfect

ASCII text files (or files saved in earlier WordPerfect formats) can be read directly with WordPerfect's normal open commands (the keys Shift plus F10, then the F5 key, or the menu sequence File, Open). Once opened, they can be modified and saved with normal WordPerfect commands. Here are a few examples:

1. Clear your screen

2. Select <u>F</u>ile, <u>O</u>pen   [Shift + F10]

3. Type **EMWP.TXT** and press ↵

(You could also use File Manager to select the file you want to open.) WordPerfect recognizes the file as ASCII format and offers to read it, as in Figure WP3–53.

4. Press ↵ to accept

   The ASCII file is read into WordPerfect and appears on your screen.

☞ **Tip: If you want to save this file in WP6.0 format, you must use the File, Save As procedure and then select WP6.0 format.**

5. Clear your screen with `F7` `N` `N`

6. Select <u>F</u>ile, <u>O</u>pen   [Shift + F10]

7. Type **EMWP.W42** and press ↵

Again, the file is automatically recognized.

8. Press ⏎ to accept

The WordPerfect 4.2 document has been opened.

9. Clear your screen

Importing from a Spreadsheet.   There are a few ways to import spreadsheet data into WordPerfect. Print files created by a spreadsheet can be opened as any other ASCII file. There is no need to repeat the process here.

WordPerfect can also open a worksheet directly into text or table format— a technique that is highly recommended; it can also place a spreadsheet graph directly into a graphics box. Here are a few examples:

1. Start WordPerfect or clear the screen

The normal open command will import a spreadsheet directly into a table.

2. Open **EMPLOY.WK1**

3. Press ⏎ to accept the noted format

☞ **Tip: The .WK1 extension indicates a worksheet created in a standard Lotus 1-2-3 format. WordPerfect will also import other spreadsheet formats, such as Excel, Plan Perfect, and Quattro Pro.**

In a few moments, the entire spreadsheet is translated into a WordPerfect table as shown in Figure WP3–54. This table can now be modified and saved as a "normal" WordPerfect table.

4. Clear the screen

You can also use the Spreadsheet Import command to retrieve a worksheet. This command gives you the flexibility to adjust the range that is imported, or open the worksheet as text.

5. Select Tools   [Alt + F7]

6. Press **S** for *Spreadsheet*

7. Press **I** for *Import*

All you need do now is specify the worksheet, indicate a range, and perform the import as follows:

8. Type **EMPLOY.WK1** ⏎

The entire range appears in Item 2 on your screen. This range, which reflects the entire worksheet, is often too big for use in WordPerfect. You can simply retype the range with the one you desire.

9. Press **R** for *Range*

10. Type **A1.D11** and press ⏎ to set this new range

You now can select whether you want to import this file as text or directly into a WordPerfect table. For now, leave the setting as "Import as Table."

11. Press **I** to *Import*

The table appears as expected.
Spreadsheets can be imported as *text* as well. To see this,

12. Clear the screen and select Tools   [Alt + F7]

13. Press **S** **I** for *Spreadsheet—Import*

Table may extend beyond margin

Figure WP3—54
Importing a Worksheet as a Table

Employee List				
	Home	Annual	Date	
Sales Staff	Phone	Salary	Hired	
---------------	---------------	---------	-----------	
Burstein, J.	408-555-1010	$23,450	06-Jul-78	
Laudon, J.	914-555-9876	33,600	07-Oct-81	
Martin, E.	718-555-1234	31,750	01-Nov-79	
Parker, C.	505-555-5678	37,500	25-Apr-82	
Williams, D.	312-555-0202	38,000	17-Feb-75	
---------------	---------------	---------	-----------	
Total		$164,300		

WP

The spreadsheet import screen appears again. Notice that all the settings remain. Now, change the "Table" setting to "Text,"

14. Press **Esc** twice to activate choices

15. Press **T** for *Type*

16. Press **X** for *Text*

17. Press **I** to *Import*

A text version of the file appears on the screen at the current insertion point.

18. Clear the screen

Importing a Spreadsheet Graphic.   You can also import graphics files (with .PIC extensions) directly into WordPerfect graphic boxes. To accomplish this, use the same procedure as outlined in the section in Module 7 titled "Adding Graphic Boxes" presented earlier in this chapter, being sure to use the .PIC extension as part of the filename.

Importing Files from a Database.   ASCII files created by a database program (whether saved delimited or in system data format) can also be read directly with normal open commands. The following exercises demonstrate opening some database files into WordPerfect.

1. Open EMWP.SDF

2. Press **↵** to accept "ASCII text"

Figure WP3—55

*The Delimited File with
Quotes Removed*

```
Burstein, J.,408-555-1010, 23450, 07/06/78
Laudon, J., 914-555-9876, 33600, 10/07/81
Martin, E., 718-555-1234, 31750, 11/01/79
Parker, C., 505-555-5678, 37500, 04/25/82
Williams, D.,312-555-0202, 38000, 02/17/75
```

The document appears on your screen (resembling Figure WP3–51).

3. Clear the screen

A delimited file can also be retrieved directly into WordPerfect and then modified, or it can be translated directly into a secondary merge file (as you will see shortly). The first method is accomplished in the normal manner:

4. Open EMWP.DEL

5. Press ↵ to accept "ASCII text"

The file appears on your screen (resembling Figure WP3–52). These data are not that useful in this form but can be adjusted easily. For example, you might use search and replace to remove the quotation marks and replace the delimiting commas with tabs. Do this as follows:

6. Press **Alt** + **F2** for *Search and Replace*

7. Press **"** to search for quotes

8. Press ↵ to replace with nothing

9. Press **F2** to replace the quotes

10. Press ↵ to accept the changes

(in effect, removing the quotes from the file).

Your screen should resemble Figure WP3–55—all quotes have been removed. You can now replace the delimiting commas with tabs. This is not as easy as it first appears, for you do not want *all* commas removed—the comma after the last name should remain. Of course, you could delete the commas individually, or use search and replace with confirm, but this would be tedious in a long file. Here's a "trick" that works because, in this document, only the comma after the last name is followed by a space (all other commas *are not* followed by spaces). Therefore, you can replace the last name commas with a different character, then replace all the other commas with tabs, and finally replace the original commas where they belong. It may seem like a long process, but these three replace commands save time and effort in a long document. Try it:

11. Move to the beginning of the document.

12. Press `Alt` + `F2` for *Search and Replace*

13. Press `,` `Space` to search for a comma and a space

Note: Including the space *as part of the search condition* eliminates all the other commas from this replace command.

14. Press `↵` to continue

15. Press `*` `Space` to replace with an asterisk and a space

16. Press `↵` and then `F2`

17. Press `↵` to accept

The commas after the last name have been replaced with asterisks; only the delimiting commas remain. Now replace all three commas with tabs:

18. Move to the beginning of the document

19. Press `Alt` + `F2`

20. Press `,` `↵`

21. Press `F5` to see codes

22. Move the highlight to "Lft Tab"

23. Press `↵` to select

24. Press `↵` `F2` to replace

25. Press `↵` to accept

Now, replace the original commas in their proper positions:

26. Move to the beginning of the document

27. Press `Alt` + `F2`

28. Press `*` `↵`

29. Press `,` `↵`

30. Press `F2` and then `↵`

Your screen should resemble Figure WP3–51.

☞ **Tip: If you are going to use delimited files often, you may want to save all these key-strokes in a macro for future use.**

You could now add dollar signs and commas to the salary column and then use the document normally in WordPerfect.

31. Save this file as **EMWP.W60**
32. Clear the screen

Translating Delimited Files into Merge Files. Delimited files can also be opened directly into WordPerfect secondary merge files for use with WordPerfect primary files.

1. Clear the screen

2. Switch to graphics mode

3. Select <u>F</u>ile, <u>O</u>pen   [Shift + F10]

4. Type **EMWP.DEL** `↵`

Figure WP3—56

The Delimited Text Options Dialog Box

```
┌──────────────────── Delimited Text Options ────────────────────┐
│                                                                 │
│   1. Field Delimiter:                    [,            ]        │
│                                                                 │
│   2. Record Delimiter:                   [CR][LF]               │
│                                                                 │
│   3. Field Encapsulate Character:        ["]                    │
│                                                                 │
│   4. Strip Characters:                   [            ]         │
│                                                                 │
│   5. □ Save Setup Options                                       │
│                                                                 │
│        [Codes... F5]              [  OK  ]   [Cancel]           │
└─────────────────────────────────────────────────────────────────┘
```

Figure WP3—57

The Converted File in Merge Format

File Edit View Layout   Tools Font Graphics Window Help
Burstein, J.**ENDFIELD**
408-555-1010**ENDFIELD**
23450**ENDFIELD**
07/06/78**ENDFIELD**
ENDRECORD
Laudon, J.**ENDFIELD**
914-555-9876**ENDFIELD**
33600**ENDFIELD**
10/07/81**ENDFIELD**
ENDRECORD
Martin, E.**ENDFIELD**
718-555-1234**ENDFIELD**
31750**ENDFIELD**
11/01/79**ENDFIELD**
ENDRECORD
Parker, C.**ENDFIELD**
505-555-5678**ENDFIELD**
37500**ENDFIELD**
04/25/82**ENDFIELD**
ENDRECORD
Williams, D.**ENDFIELD**
312-555-0202**ENDFIELD**
38000**ENDFIELD**
02/17/75**ENDFIELD**
ENDRECORD
A:\EMWP.DEL   Doc 1 Pg 1 Ln 1" Pos 1"

When WordPerfect identifies the file as "ASCII Text,"

5. Move the highlight to *DOS Delimited Text*

6. Press ↵ to accept

A "Delimited Text Options" dialog box appears as in Figure WP3–56. These settings reflect the default standard configuration, in which each field is separated by a comma, each record ends with a hard return [CR] and a line feed [LF], and fields are placed within quotes. Because you want to remove the quotes, you must now indicate which characters should be "stripped" (removed) from the file when it is converted.

7. Press **S** to *Strip Characters*

8. Press **"** **↵**

9. Press **↵** again to accept

The delimited file should now appear on your screen in merge format, as in Figure WP3–57.

10. Save this file in WP6.0 format as **EMWP.MRG**

(Remember to use "File, Save As" and then change the format to WP6.0.)

If you used field *numbers* in the primary merge file, this secondary file is now ready for use as is. However, if you used field *names* (the recommended approach), you would now add the field names to the secondary file by going to the start of the document and then following the steps normally used to name the fields. These are listed in Module 3 (Merging Files), in the "Naming Fields" section, Steps 1 through 3.

Checkpoint

Using WordPerfect and the correct file extensions:

☐ Export the EMPLOY.WP document into a file named EMWP.W50 in Word-Perfect 5.0 format. Clear your screen.

☐ Import the EMWP.W50 document into a fresh screen. Place two blank lines at the end of the text. After these lines, import the range A5.D9 of the EMPLOY.WK1 spreadsheet as a table. Save the file as EMCHECK. Clear the screen.

Summary

- Document pages can be divided by soft page breaks, inserted automatically by WordPerfect, or hard page breaks, created by the user. Soft page breaks change their location as the document is modified; hard page breaks remain fixed unless removed by the user.

- Headers and footers are lines of descriptive text that can appear on every printed page of a multipage document. Headers are placed at the top of the document page; footers at the bottom. Headers and footers can be created, edited, or deleted.

- WordPerfect's page number feature allows numbers to be placed at the top or bottom of each printed page, positioned at the left, center, or right. Each page will be consecutively numbered unless changed by the user.

- The GO TO command allows the user to reposition the cursor on any page of a multipage document.

- WordPerfect allows the user to work with two documents at one time. Each document is placed in its own screen, labeled as Doc 1 or Doc 2. The user can then press the Shift and F3 keys to switch between them to read text or copy text from one to the other. Documents can be put in frames and tiled or cascaded to allow documents to appear on the screen at the same time.

- Merge is a process by which information from two sources is combined to produce a third document. Merge usually combines a primary file (which contains text and instructions for merging) with a secondary file (which contains the specific data to be merged). Both files must be created through the Merge Codes process, and then combined with MERGE.

- A macro is a list of computer instructions that can be activated with one (or more) preset keystroke. Macros must first be defined and saved before they can be invoked for use. Macro names can be up to eight characters in length. A macro named with "Alt" and one letter can be invoked quickly by simply pressing the Alt key and that letter. Macros with longer names must be invoked through the Macro process.

- Footnotes and endnotes are text added to your document to provide source references, more detailed explanations, or comments. Footnotes are usually placed at the bottom of the page where they are referenced. Endnotes are usually listed at the end of the document. These notes can be inserted, edited, deleted, and renumbered as needed.
- WordPerfect's Outline feature eases the task of creating and editing outlines using a number of standard formats. WordPerfect's Sort feature can arrange text in alphabetic or numeric order.
- WordPerfect's Graphics feature allows lines and images to be combined with text in the same document. Lines and boxes can be drawn by positioning the insertion point, invoking the LINE DRAW command, selecting a line form, and then moving the insertion point. Tables allow text to be professionally displayed in columns and rows. Separate graphics boxes can also be created into which graphic images can be retrieved. These boxes are like little windows on the screen around which document text will automatically wrap. Graphics boxes can be repositioned and resized as needed.
- The button bar and ribbon allow the mouse to quickly access many commands.
- ASCII file format is a standard for data transfer. It excludes all special symbols, providing a common data style.
- Files can be exported (saved in another format) or imported (retrieved from a compatible format).
- Data in fixed-length columns can be saved in ASCII files for use with spreadsheets or database programs. Data in variable-length fields can be saved in a delimited format. Delimited files separate data with commas and surround character data with quotation marks.
- WordPerfect's normal OPEN command will read most files into WordPerfect.

Key Terms

Shown in parentheses are the page numbers on which key terms are boldfaced.

ASCII (WP169)	Importing (WP169)
Button bar (WP163)	Key (WP146)
Cascade (WP119)	Macro (WP130)
Endnote (WP135)	Merge (WP122)
Exporting (WP169)	Outline feature
Footer (WP107)	(WP140)
Footnote (WP135)	Primary file (WP122)
GO TO (WP113)	Ribbon (WP167)
Graphics feature	Secondary file (WP122)
(WP150)	Soft page break
Hard page break	(WP103)
(WP106)	Sort feature (WP146)
Header (WP107)	Tile (WP119)

Quiz

True/False

1. The location of a soft page return within the text will change if text is inserted or deleted before it.
2. Headers do not usually appear on a document's first page.
3. Page numbers and headers are displayed on the work screen for easy editing.

4. The GO TO command is used to switch to another document file.

5. WordPerfect can display more than one document on one screen at the same time.

6. In a merge operation, the data to be merged are kept in a primary file.

7. Merge field *names* are easier to create but harder to use than field *numbers*.

8. Anything that can be typed on a keyboard can be saved in a macro.

9. Footnote reference numbers appear within work screen text, but the footnote itself does not.

10. The WordPerfect Graphics feature allows pictures to be drawn on the screen by the user.

Multiple Choice

11. A _____ is displayed as a single line across the work screen.
    a. soft page break
    b. hard page break
    c. merged document
    d. table cell

12. Which of these is *not* an option for page number placement?
    a. top right of each page
    b. bottom left of each page
    c. top inside corner of alternating pages
    d. bottom outside corner of alternating pages

13. The most important reason for using two documents at one time is for
    a. referencing footnotes.
    b. comparing files.
    c. numbering pages.
    d. copying text.

14. How does WordPerfect indicate the active document when two documents are displayed in separate frames at the same time?
    a. The document's name is cascaded.
    b. The title bar is highlighted in color.
    c. A pop-up screen lists the active document's number.
    d. A box is drawn around the active document area.

15. Which of these is *not* a requirement for secondary merge files?
    a. All records must contain the same number of fields.
    b. Each field must end with an END FIELD marker.
    c. Each record must end with an END RECORD marker.
    d. Each record must be separated by a soft page break.

16. Which one of these macro names can be invoked by pressing just the Alt key and the letter H?
    a. ALTH
    b. H
    c. HALT
    d. MACRO-H

17. Which WordPerfect feature cannot be removed from the text with the Delete key?
    a. headers
    b. footnotes
    c. hard page breaks
    d. soft page breaks

18. Which LINE DRAW command allows the user to reposition the insertion point without drawing a line?

    a. Options

    b. Move

    c. Erase

    d. Single line

19. Which of these screens can display the graphic images that are contained in figure boxes?

    a. work screen

    b. split document screen

    c. REVEAL CODES screen

    d. Print preview screen

20. The Graphics edit screen includes all but which one of these commands?

    a. enlarge an image

    b. move an image

    c. rotate an image

    d. combine two images

Matching

Select the term that best matches each phrase below:

a.	Figure	g.	Endnote
b.	Footnote	h.	Hard page break
c.	GO TO	i.	Macro
d.	Merge	j.	Header
e.	Graphics feature	k.	Secondary file
f.	Primary file	l.	Soft page break

21. Text containing descriptive information that appears at the top of each page in a multipage document

22. A list of computer instructions or keystrokes that can be activated with one or more preset keystrokes

23. A WordPerfect feature that allows the user to combine lines and images with text in the same document

24. A document used in a merge process that contains specific data to be merged into another document

25. A page divider created by the user that remains fixed at a specific text location unless removed by the user

26. A page divider automatically created, or relocated, by a word processor when text reaches the end of a page

27. Text added to a document, usually appearing at the bottom of each page and identified by number, to provide source references, more detailed explanations, or comments

28. A document used in a merge process that contains text and instructions for the merge

29. A process by which information from two sources is combined to form a third document

30. A word processing command that relocates the insertion point on any named page of a multipage document

Answers

True/False: 1. T; 2. T; 3. F; 4. F; 5. T; 6. F; 7. F; 8. T; 9. T; 10. F

Multiple Choice: 11. a; 12. c; 13. d; 14. b; 15. d; 16. a; 17. d; 18. b; 19. d; 20. d

Matching: 21. j; 22. i; 23. e; 24. k; 25. h; 26. l; 27. b; 28. f; 29. d; 30. c

Exercises

I. Operations

Provide the WordPerfect sequence of keystrokes and actions required to do each of the operations shown below. For each operation, assume a system with a hard disk and a diskette in Drive A. A 10-page document called LETTER1 has been retrieved onto the work screen. Further assume that the default drive has been set to Drive A, and that the following files are contained on the data disk: LETTER1, LETTER2, ROSTER, ALTS.WPM, ZAP.WPM, COMPUTE.WPG.

1. Create a hard page break after the first paragraph.
2. Create a header that states "Reference Letter 1."
3. Number all pages beginning with page 2, positioning the number at the bottom center of each page.
4. Renumber page 2 to show a page number of 1.
5. Open LETTER2 into Doc 2 and create two frames on the screen.
6. Copy the first paragraph of Doc 2 at the end of Doc 1.
7. Clear Doc 2 and return to a full-screen display.
8. Merge the data contained in the ROSTER file with the LETTER2 form letter.
9. Invoke the ALTS macro and then the ZAP macro.
10. Create a macro named BYE that will save the current document back onto disk and then clear the screen.
11. Delete the third footnote in the LETTER1 file.
12. Draw a box with single lines that is eight characters across and four lines down.
13. Create a figure box to display the image contained in the COMPUTE file.

II. Commands

Describe fully, using as few words as possible in each case, what command is initiated, or what is accomplished, in WordPerfect by pressing each series of keystrokes given below. Assume that each exercise part is independent of any previous parts.

Function Key Commands

1. `Ctrl` + `↵`
2. `Shift` + `F8` , `H` , `H` , `A`
3. `Shift` + `F8` , `P` , `N` , `P` , `I` , `F7`
4. `Ctrl` + `Home` , `4` , `↵`
5. `Shift` + `F3`
6. `Ctrl` + `F3` , `W` , `A`
7. `Ctrl` + `F9` , `M` , ABC, `↵` , DEF, `↵`
8. `Alt` + `S`
9. `Alt` + `F10` , START, `↵`
10. `Ctrl` + `F10` , `Alt` + `D` , `↵`
11. `Ctrl` + `F7` , `F` , `C`
12. `Ctrl` + `F3` , `L` , `1`
13. `Alt` + `F7` , `T` , `C`
14. `Ctrl` + `F5` , `B`

Pull-Down Menus

1. Layout, Alignment, Hard Page
2. Layout, Header, H, A
3. Layout, Page, N, P, I, F7
4. Edit, Go to, 4, Enter
5. Window, Switch Document
6. Window, Maximize
7. Tools, Merge, Run, ABC, Enter, DEF, Enter
8. Alt+S
9. Tools, Macro, Play Macro, START, Enter
10. Tools, Macro, Record
11. Layout, Footnote, Create
12. Graphics, Line Draw, 1
13. Layout, Tables, Create
14. Tools, Outline, Begin

III. Applications

Perform the following operations using your computer system. You will need a hard drive or network with WordPerfect on it, or a DOS disk and WordPerfect program disks. You will also need your data disk to store the results of this exercise and to retrieve the DISK.WPG graphic. In a few words, describe how you accomplished each operation, and its result. Save the document as RESEARCH after each operation is completed so that you can continue this exercise later.

Application 1: Advanced Tasks

1. To prepare for this exercise, select an article that contains at least 600 words from a recent magazine or newspaper. Bring a copy of it (or the original article) to your computer's location. Start WordPerfect.

2. Type the headline of the article centered on the first page of your document. Skip two lines. Center your name, class, and date on three separate lines beneath the heading.

3. Create a hard page break on the line after the date, and set line spacing to double-spaced text at the beginning of page 2. Save your document as RESEARCH often as you work. You can always stop and continue this assignment later.

4. Type the article heading once again, centered and underlined at the top of the page. Skip a line. Type the article exactly as it appears. End paragraphs where they end in the article and indent as needed. Copy as much of the article as you need to fill *two* full pages of your document. (The insertion point should be positioned somewhere on page 4 when you stop—approximately 600 words.)

5. Create a header that displays your full name to start on the page after the title page, and continue on all other pages.

6. Add page numbering at the bottom center of the page starting after the title page. Renumber this page to be counted as page 1.

7. Place a footnote at the end of the heading on the first full page of typing. In the footnote reference (which will appear at the bottom of the page), indicate the author (if known), source, date, and page numbers of the article you selected.

8. Edit the header you created earlier to display your class designation in parentheses after your name.

9. Copy the first paragraph of the document into the empty Doc 2 screen. Switch to Doc 2, skip a line, and type your name after the paragraph. Save this new document as RESEAR-A. Clear the screen; return to Doc 1.

10. Move to the title page of the RESEARCH document. Draw a single-lined box around your name, class, and date.

11. Move to the second paragraph of the typed article. Create a figure box that will be positioned two lines below the top of this paragraph, positioned on the right side of the page. Add a caption to read "Figure 1. A Sample." Set the width of the box to 2″ (20 characters wide), allowing the program to calculate the corresponding height. If your disk contains the DISK.WPG graphic, import it into the figure box. If it does not, leave the box empty. Save the RESEARCH document with these changes.

12. Create a table at the end of the article to summarize any numerical or text data that may be of interest.

13. Print out copies of RESEARCH and RESEAR-A. Attach a copy of the original article to your work.

14. Create an outline of at least two levels that summarizes the key points made in the article. Save this outline as RESEAR-B.

15. Recall RESEAR-B and change the outline to legal style. Then move one family block of text to the end of the outline. Save this document as RESEAR-C.

Application 2: Tables, Fonts, and Sorts

1. Boot your computer and start WordPerfect. Type your name, class, and date at the upper left of a new document. Skip two lines.

2. Prepare a short phone list by creating a table with three columns and ten rows. Label the top cells in the table "Last," "First," and "Phone," respectively. In the remaining rows, type information for nine friends (or just make up the data). Save the document as PHONE1.

3. Change the base font to a proportional font (if available) or another font of your choice.

4. Boldface the labels in the title row of the table. Save the document as PHONE2.

5. Sort the table by last name and save the file as PHONE3.

6. Sort the table by phone number and save the file as PHONE4.

7. Print out copies of all four PHONE files.

8. Exit WordPerfect.

Application 3: Merge Exercise

1. To prepare for these exercises, start WordPerfect and open the FORM1 primary file into the work screen. Refer to Figure WP3–13 for a copy of this file.

2. Add a period (.) after the word "letter" in the first sentence. Delete the remainder of the sentence, and the one that follows. The letter should now read "Thank you for your recent letter. We would be happy to fill your order upon receipt of a (Field) COMPANY purchase order or check." Type your name in place of "Martin Parker." Save this file as FORM2.

3. Create a secondary file called DATA2. Create fields for NAME, COMPANY, ADDRESS, and TITLE. Type three separate records into the file.

4. Merge FORM2 and DATA2. Upon completion, print out only the first two letters of the file.

5. Print out the DATA2 file and attach it to your letters.

6. Exit WordPerfect.

WordPerfect 6.0
Feature and
Operation Reference

WordPerfect Keys

Special keys used by WordPerfect are described below. For the specific location of these keys, check your particular keyboard.

Alt `Alt`
Used only in combination with other keys, the Alt key is held down when striking another key. When this is done, a WordPerfect command is invoked.

Arrow Keys `→` `←` `↑` `↓`
Used to move the cursor, one character at a time, in the direction indicated by the arrow. Also can be used in combination with other keys to move the cursor faster — say, to the beginning of a page or the end of a document. Additionally, the arrow keys can be used to advance the pointer on a menu, in a dialog box, or through a Help session.

Backspace `← Backspace`
Erases characters to the left of the screen cursor position.

Caps Lock `Caps Lock`
Used to keep the Shift key active automatically so that all characters being typed are uppercase.

Ctrl `Ctrl`
Used only in combination with other keys, the Ctrl key is held down when striking another key. When this is done, a WordPerfect command is invoked.

Del (Delete) `Del` or `Delete`
Erases characters at the cursor position.

Enter `↵` or `Enter ↵`
Serves two principal functions: (1) Used to enter a hard return into a document. (2) Used to complete a WordPerfect command, after typing in text or keystroke sequences or after making a choice on a menu or in a dialog box.

Note: In Graphics and page modes, the screen cursor appears as a vertical line and is often referred to as the *insertion point.*

Esc (Escape)   `Esc`
Commonly used to backtrack from WordPerfect menus to the document screen and to cancel commands.

Function Keys   `F1`   `F2`   `F3`   . . .
Numbered F1 through F12, the function keys are used alone — or in combination with the Alt, Ctrl, and Shift keys — to invoke WordPerfect commands. A ready-to-cut-out (or copy) keyboard template showing function-key combinations is provided at the very end of this module.

Home   `Home`
Used with arrow keys to move the cursor in various ways.

Ins (Insert)   `Ins`   or   `Insert`
Used to toggle between the insert mode and the typeover mode. When in the insert mode (the default mode), characters being typed in are inserted at the cursor, and any text to the right of the cursor moves farther right. When in the typeover mode, characters being typed replace characters already on the screen.

NumLock   `NumLock`
Used to activate the numeric keypad, on the right side of most keyboards. NumLock works as a toggle key; hitting it once activates the keypad, whereas hitting it again deactivates the keypad.

Pg Up and Pg Dn (Page Up and Page Down)   `Pg Up`   and   `Pg Dn`
Used to scroll a document or Help screen one page backward (up) or forward (down).

Shift   `↑`   or   `Shift`
Serves two principal functions: (1) Works like the Shift key on a typewriter; when it is held down and a letter or number key is struck, an uppercase letter or the symbol assigned to the number key is produced. (2) Used in combination with the function keys; when the Shift key is held down and a function key is struck, a WordPerfect command is invoked.

Spacebar   `Space`
Used to provide one or more blank spaces in a document and to select and deselect choices in some dialog boxes.

Tab   `↤→`   or   `Tab`
Used to reach a preset Tab stop and to advance the pointer on a menu or in a dialog box.

Cursor Movement Keystrokes

The Cursor Moves. . . .	When You Press. . . .
One character right	→
One character left	←
One line up	↑
One line down	↓

(continued)

The Cursor Moves. . . .	When You Press. . . .
One word right	`Ctrl` + `→`
One word left	`Ctrl` + `←`
To the beginning of the current line	`Home` `←`
To the end of the current line	`Home` `→`
To the top of the document	`Home` `Home` `↑`
To the bottom of the document	`Home` `Home` `↓`
To page *n*	`Ctrl` + `Home` `n` `↵`
One screen back (up)	`−` (from numeric keypad)
One screen forward (down)	`+` (from numeric keypad)
One page back (up)	`Pg Up`
One page forward (down)	`Pg Dn`
One column right	`Ctrl` + `Home` `→`
One column left	`Ctrl` + `Home` `←`

Note: The arrow keys can also be used to navigate through menus, dialog boxes, and Help screens. Where the arrow keys cannot access choices in a dialog box, try the Tab key instead. To navigate quickly through Help screens, use the Pg Up and Pg Dn keys.

Mouse Operations

To	Do the Following with Your Mouse . . . .
Move the screen cursor	Click* at the place in the document where you wish to move
Select (block) text	Click at the start of the block, hold down the mouse button and drag to the end of the block, and release the mouse button
Select (block) a word	Double-click anywhere on the word
Select (block) a sentence	Triple-click anywhere in the sentence
Select (block) a paragraph	Quadruple-click anywhere in the paragraph
Select a button from the Button Bar	Click on the button
Deselect a block	Click the mouse button
Move a block	Point to (select) the block, drag it to the desired location, and release the mouse button

*Unless specified otherwise, use the left mouse button to click.

To	Do the Following with Your Mouse . . . .
Move a graphic	Click on the graphic to select it, drag it to the desired location, and release the mouse button
Resize a graphic	Click on the graphic, drag a box handle in or out, and release the mouse button
Activate/cancel menus	Click the right mouse button
Navigate menus	Click on the menu title and/or command
Navigate dialog boxes	Click on the appropriate icon or command button (double-click items in list, or drop-down, boxes)
Arrange windows	Position the mouse pointer on the title bar of the window, drag to the appropriate place, and release the mouse button
Resize windows	Position the mouse pointer on the border of the window, drag in or out, and release the mouse button
Use scroll bars	See "Menu and Box Navigation" in section entitled "Summary of Common WordPerfect Operations"

WP

Summary of Common WordPerfect Operations

Following is a brief, step-by-step summary showing how to perform common WordPerfect tasks.

Use the procedure below to assign special formats; to delete, move, or copy text; and to save blocks of text such as frequently used paragraphs.

Blocking (Selecting) Text

Using a Mouse

1. Move the mouse pointer to the beginning of the text to be blocked
2. Select the text to be blocked

Note that the blocked text is highlighted on the screen.

3. Perform desired procedures on block
4. Click the left mouse button to turn blocking off, if necessary

Using a Keyboard

1. Move the cursor to the beginning of the text to be blocked
2. Select Edit, Block [**Alt** + **F4**]
3. Use the arrow keys or any other cursor movement tools to block the text

Note that the blocked text is highlighted on the screen.

4. Perform desired procedures on block
5. Press **Esc** to turn blocking off, if necessary.

Boldfacing Text

Boldfacing enables you to output text with thicker strokes than normal text.

Before Typing the Text	**After Typing the Text**
1. Press **F6** to turn on the boldfacing feature ·	1. Block the text to be boldfaced
2. Type the text to be boldfaced	2. Press **F6**
3. Press **F6** again, to turn off the boldfacing feature	

Button Bars

The Button Bar feature lets you tailor WordPerfect to your own needs. There are seven principal button bars included in WordPerfect 6.0 — Fonts, Layout, Macros, Outline, Tables, Tools, and WPMain — as well as a few auxiliary ones. You can also create your own bars and buttons. To use button bars you should have a mouse, trackball, or some other such pointing device. You can use the Button Bar feature text, graphics, or page modes.

Activating the Button Bar Display and Invoking a Button

1. Select View
2. Select the mode: Text Mode, Graphics Mode, or Page Mode

If a button bar is displayed, skip Step 3.

3. Select View, Button Bar

To invoke a button on the bar,

4. Select the desired button

Viewing Offscreen Buttons. Many button bars contain more buttons than can fit in a single display. To the left of a bar is usually a pair of scroll buttons that lets you scroll the listing of available buttons forward (▼) or backward (▲). To see other buttons on the bar,

Select an appropriate scroll button

(Note that in the graphics and page modes, inappropriate buttons are dimmed.)

Switching Button Bars. To change from one bar to another,

1. Select View, Button Bar Setup
2. Choose Select
3. Select the button bar you wish to now use

Repositioning Button Bars

1. Select View, Button Bar Setup, Options

The "Button Bar Options" dialog box will appear. To relocate the bar to another place on the screen,

2. Select one of the following options:
   Top: Places the bar at the top of the screen (default)
   Bottom: Places the bar at the bottom of the screen
   Left Side: Places the bar at the left side of the screen
   Right Side: Places the bar at the right side of the screen
3. Select "OK" to exit the dialog box

Restyling Button Bars

1. Select Vıew, Button Bar Setup, Options

The "Button Bar Options" dialog box will appear. To restyle the buttons on the bar to contain either text or pictures or both text and pictures,

2. Select one of the following options:
   Picture and Text: Provides both text and pictures (default)
   Picture Only: Provides pictures and no text
   Text Only: Provides text and no pictures
3. Select "OK" to exit the dialog box

Creating a Button Bar. To first create a name for the bar,

1. Select Vıew, Button Bar Setup, Select
2. Select Create
3. Type and enter a name for the bar, without an extension

The "Edit Button Bar" dialog box will appear. At this point you are ready to create buttons for the bar.

4. You can create a button through any one of the following procedures:
   Add Menu Item: Use this if your button will consist of a sequence of menu commands; use the mouse to choose the commands in the sequence
   Add Feature: Choosing this option will produce a list (drop-down) box of dozens of WordPerfect features and operations, any of which can be made into a button
   Add Macro: This enables you to choose a supplied or custom macro as a button; supply the macro name
   Add Button Bar: Lets you switch automatically to another button bar; supply the name of the other bar
5. Repeat Step 4 to create other buttons and/or select "OK" to close the dialog box when you are finished

Note: You can also edit or delete any button bar you create by performing Step 1 again, highlighting the bar, and selecting Edit or Delete from the "Select Button Bar" dialog box.

Moving Buttons

1. Select Vıew, Button Bar Setup, Edit

The "Edit Button Bar" dialog box will appear.

2. Select from the list in the box the name of the button you wish to move
3. Select Move Button
4. Reposition the box highlight on the name of the button that is to appear immediately after the button to be moved
5. Select Paste Button
6. Select "OK" to return to document

Deleting Buttons

1. Select Vıew, Button Bar Setup, Edit

The "Edit Button Bar" dialog box will appear.

2. Select from the list in the box the name of the button you wish to delete

3. Press **Del**

4. Select Yes to confirm

5. Select "OK" to return to document

Deactivating the Button Bar Display

1. Select View

Note that there is a check mark or asterisk by the Button Bar command on the pull-down menu, indicating the button bar display is active.

2. Select Button Bar

This removes the check mark or asterisk on the command menu and deactivates the button bar display.

Canceling a Command

Canceling a command enables you to abort a partially completed menu or prompt.

1. Press Esc

2. If you are not fully back to the document, continue pressing Esc until you return there

Centering Text

The centering command enables text to be centered on a line, either before or after you type the text.

Before Typing the Text	After Typing the Text
1. Select Layout, Alignment, Center	1. Move the cursor to beginning of text to be centered
2. Type the text to be centered	2. Select Layout, Alignment, Center [Shift + F6]

Changing the Default Drive

The default drive usually must be changed when you enter WordPerfect so files are saved to and retrieved from a data diskette. To change the default drive,

1. Select File, File Manager   [F5]

The default directory is highlighted. To default to another directory,

2. Press

3. Select Change Default Directory

When the "Change Default Directory" dialog box appears,

4. Type and enter the name of the directory you wish to switch to

Note: If you are taken back to an earlier dialog box, press the Esc key once or twice to return to your document.

Clearing the Screen

Clearing the screen allows you to start fresh, in the current document window.

1. Press F7

A "Save" box appears.

2. Select one of the following:

   Save As . . . : Use this option when the current document is untitled and you want to save it; type and enter a filename to which to save

   Yes: Use this option when the current document already has a title and you wish to save and replace

   No: Use this option when you do not wish to save the current document

3. Select No to the "Exit WordPerfect?" prompt or the "Exit Document?" prompt (whichever you get) to clear the screen

Note: You can also use the File Close command to clear the screen; see "Closing Document Windows."

The CLOSE command causes an open document file to become temporarily inactive—leaving you with a clear screen in its associated window.

Closing Document Windows

Closing the Current Document Window

1. Select File, Close

A "Save" box appears.

2. Select one of the following:

   Save As . . . : Use this option when the current document is untitled and you want to save it; type and enter a filename to which to save

   Yes: Use this option when the current document already has a title and you wish to save and replace

   No: Use this option when you do not wish to save the current document

At this point you will be placed in the last active document window and the screen will be cleared in the closed window.

Closing a Noncurrent Document Window

1. Select Window, Switch to . . .   [**F3**]
2. Select the number of the window you wish to close

The window will be made current.

3. Close the window as per the procedure described in the last sequence of steps

Note: See also "Clearing the Screen."

Copying allows a block of text or a graphic to be replicated elsewhere. There are two principal ways to copy:

Copying

- *Copy-and-paste:* The "copy and paste" operation is used to make an immediate copy in a single location.
- *Copy-now-paste-later:* A separate "copy" operation is used to temporarily save the text or graphic to a special buffer. Anytime later, the text or graphic can be fetched and pasted (with the "paste" operation) in one or more places.

Copying and Pasting

Using a Mouse

1. Select (block) the text or graphic that is to be copied
2. Drag the selected text or graphic to the new location; press `Ctrl` while releasing the mouse button

Using a Keyboard

1. Select (block) the text or graphic that is to be copied

2. Select Edit, Copy and

   Paste   [`Ctrl` + `Ins`]

If the copying is to take place in the same document, go immediately to Step 3; otherwise, first open or switch to the other document.

3. Place the cursor where the text or graphic is to go

4. Press `↵`

Copying

1. Select (block) the text or graphic that is to be copied

2. Select Edit, Copy   [`Ctrl` + `C`]

Note: The previous contents of the copy buffer are erased.

Pasting

1. Place the cursor where the text or graphic is to go

2. Select Edit, Paste   [`Ctrl` + `V`]

Cutting and Pasting

See the section entitled "Moving."

Deleting Text and Codes

Deleting physically removes text from a document.

Deleting a Character or a Word at a Time, or Deleting to the End of a Line or Page.   Follow the instructions below:

To Delete . . .	Press . . .
The current character	`Del`
The character to the left	`← Backspace`
The current word	`Ctrl` + `← Backspace`
To the end of a line	`Ctrl` + `End`
To the end of a page	`Ctrl` + `Pg Dn`

Deleting a Block of Text

1. Block the text to be deleted

2. Press `Del` or `Backspace`

Deleting Codes

1. Press **Alt** + **F3** or **F11** to view the REVEAL CODES screen
2. Move the cursor to the code you want to delete
3. Press **Del** to delete the code
4. Press **Alt** + **F3** or **F11** again to return to the document

---

Exiting Word-Perfect

To exit WordPerfect for DOS,

1. Select File, Exit WP . . .

A dialog box will appear asking you which opened documents you wish to save before exiting.

2. If necessary, move to the "Save" column and press **Space** to place check marks to the left of the documents you wish to save and erase any check marks on documents you do not wish to save; you can use the arrow keys to navigate among the choices

3. Select the Save and Exit (or Exit, if there is nothing to save) button

---

Extended Characters

WP

There are over 1,500 characters available with WordPerfect. Depending on your printer, you will be able to print all or some of these.

Most people using WordPerfect will be working with the ASCII character set (Character Set 0 in WordPerfect). There are, however, 14 other built-in character sets available, as well as a provision for users to define their own characters. Here, we will explain how to access these other character sets, such as the typographic and iconic symbol sets shown in the figure on page WP196.

Viewing Available Characters.   To see onscreen any of the sets of available characters,

1. Get into the graphic mode (View, Graphics)

Note: Many of the characters do not display well in text mode.

2. Select Font, WP Characters   [**Ctrl** + **W**]
3. Choose Set to see a menu of the sets of available characters

Hint: Use the Tab key to highlight "Set" and then select it.

4. Select a set that may interest you, to see what it looks like
5. Repeat Step 3 and 4, as necessary, to inspect other sets
6. When you are through, select the Cancel button to get back to your document

Selecting Characters (Long Method).   Use this approach for selecting characters when you aren't sure of the character you want or its special number:

1. Place the cursor where you wish to put an extended character
2. Follow the steps given earlier for viewing a particular character set

With the set of characters you wish to choose from onscreen,

3. Use the Tab key to move into the array of characters

Extended Characters

Shown here are characters from WordPerfect's Typographic and Iconic symbol sets.

Character Set 4 (Typographic Symbols)

	0	1	2	3	4	5	6	7	8	9
	●	○	■	•	⋆	¶	§	¡	¿	«
10	»	£	¥	Pt	ƒ	ª	º	½	¼	¢
20	²	ⁿ	®	©	¤	¾	³	‛	’	‘
30	"	"	"	–	—	‹	›	○	□	†
40	‡	™	SM	℞	●	○	■	▪	□	▫
50	–	ff	ffi	ffl	fi	fl	…	$	₣	₡
60	₠	£	‚	„	⅓	⅔	⅛	⅜	⅝	⅞
70	ⓦ	ⓟ	ⓤ	℅	℀	‰	№	–	¹	Hₜ
80	Fₑ	₢	Lₑ	Nₗ	Vₜ	⊛	₩	₦	₨	MD
90	MC	▶	■	⏸	⏮	⏭	⏺	⏪	⏩	⏏
100	𝄞	,								

Character Set 5 (Iconic Symbols)

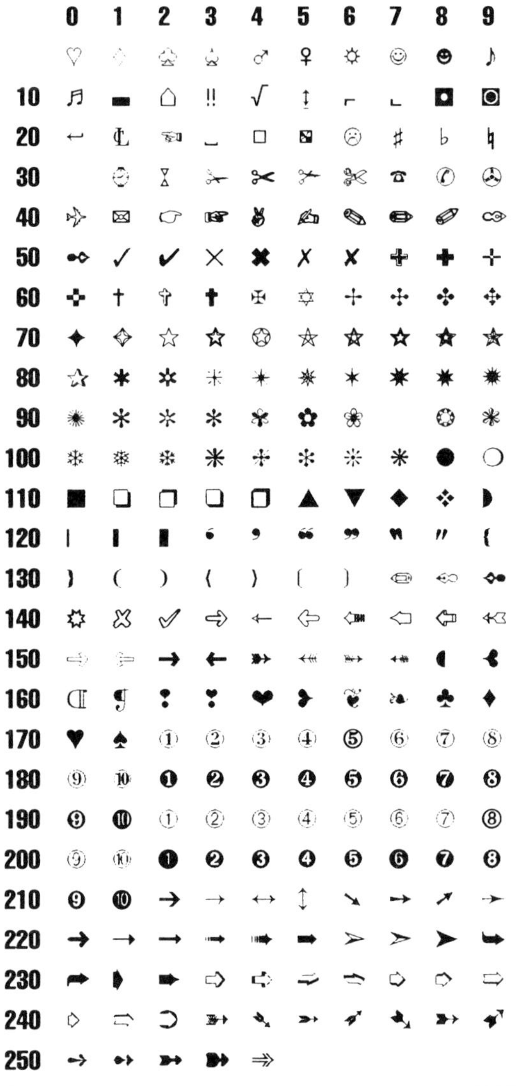

	0	1	2	3	4	5	6	7	8	9
10										
20										
30										
40										
50										
60										
70										
80										
90										
100										
110										
120										
130										
140										
150										
160										
170										
180										
190										
200										
210										
220										
230										
240										
250										

4. Once you are in the array, use the arrow keys to navigate through the characters and highlight the one you want

5. Press ⏎

Note: In text mode the character displayed might not look like the one you requested. It will, however, be in your document when it is previewed or printed out.

Selecting Characters (Short Method). If you know the special number assigned to a character, you can enter it much faster. For instance, to get the copyright symbol "©" (see, in the figure, symbol 23 in character set 4, typographic symbols), you would

1. Place the cursor where you wish to put the copyright symbol

2. Press `Ctrl` + `2` followed by `4` , `23` `↵`

Erasing Characters.   Use the Delete or Backspace key in the normal manner.

Different fonts can be used to print text in a special way. Depending on the printer you have, you may or may not be able to fully take advantage of the features in WordPerfect's FONT command.

Fonts

Setting a Font for the Entire Document.   With the cursor at the beginning of the document,

1. Select L̲ayout, D̲ocument   [`Shift` + `F8` `4`]

2. Select Initial F̲ont   [`3`]

3. From the "Initial Font" dialog box, make typeface and point size selections:
    F̲ont: Use the list (drop-down) box to select the font that you

    want   [`1`]

    S̲ize: Use the list (drop-down) box to select the point size that you

    want   [`2`]

4. Also in the "Initial Font" dialog box, select either of these choices:
    C̲urrent Document Only: Use this if typeface and point sizes apply only to

    the current document   [`3`]

    All N̲ew Documents: Use this if typeface and point size apply to this

    document and all new ones   [`4`]

5. Select "OK" or press `↵` until you return to your document screen.

Changing Styling within a Document.   To style a block of text or a head in a particular way,

1. Select (block) the text that's to receive special treatment

2. Select F̲ont, F̲ont to get the Font menu   [`Ctrl` + `F8`]

3. Make any of the following choices:
    F̲ont: Use the list (drop-down) box to select the font that you

    want   [`1`]

    S̲ize: Use the list (drop-down) box to select the point size that you

    want   [`2`]

    A̲ppearance: Check off one or more choices to style the text in a certain

    way — for instance, bold, italic, or both   [`3`]

    R̲elative Size: Use this option to pick a size for the selected text, relative to

    the body copy   [`4`]

    P̲osition: Use this for superscripting and subscripting   [`5`]

    U̲nderline: Use this for special treatment of tabs and spaces   [`6`]

When you are finished making selections,

4. Select "OK" or press `↵`

Note: If you later change your mind on any of the styling attributes, delete its code from the REVEAL CODES screen.

Footnotes and Endnotes

Footnotes provide supplemental information at the bottom of each appropriate page; endnotes place all such information at the end of the document. WordPerfect enables you to create, edit, and delete footnotes and endnotes.

Creating a Footnote or Endnote

1. Select Layout, Footnote   (for footnotes)   [**Ctrl** + **F7** **1**]

    or Layout, Endnote   (for endnotes)   [**Ctrl** + **F7** **3**]

2. Select Create   [**1**]

3. Create the note

4. Select File, Exit to return to your document   [**F7**]

Note: If the created note is one that's being inserted into a list of existing notes, WordPerfect automatically renumbers subsequent notes for you.

Editing a Footnote or Endnote

1. Select Layout, Footnote   (for footnotes)   [**Ctrl** + **F7** **1**]

    or Layout, Endnote   (for endnotes)   [**Ctrl** + **F7** **3**]

2. Select Edit   [**2**]

3. Type the number of the note you wish to edit

4. Select "OK" or press ⏎

5. Edit the note

6. Select File, Exit to return to your document   [**F7**]

Deleting a Footnote or Endnote.   Use standard deleting procedures; that is, either delete the note number on the document screen or delect the code on the REVEAL CODES screen. When you delete a note, WordPerfect automatically renumbers subsequent notes.

Graphics Boxes

Graphics boxes are used to insert such graphics as drawings, clip art, charts, text, tables, sidebars, and equations into a document. You should be in the graphics or page modes when creating, resizing, or editing graphics boxes.

Creating a Graphics Box

1. Place the cursor where you want the graphics box to go

2. Select Graphics, Graphics Boxes   [**Alt** + **F9** **1**]

3. Select Create   [**1**]

4. Select Based on Box Style

5. Highlight and select the type of box style you want; the choices are as follows:
    Figure Box: Use for clip-art images, charts, logos, and drawings
    Table Box: Use for spreadsheets, tables, statisical data
    Text Box: Use for quotes and sidebars

User Box: Use clip-art images, charts, drawings, equations, and tables, where you want an invisible border

Button Box: Use to represent a keystroke or icon

Note: You can also choose among the following, although special procedures are required to set up the box:

Equation Box: Use for equations and formulas

Watermark Image Box: Use to represent a faint background image on page—say, a clip-art image, drawing, logo, and the like

Inline Equation Box: Use for equations and formulas that go within a text line

6. Select Filename [**1**]

7. Type and enter a filename or press **F5** and then **↵** to select from a list of WordPerfect graphics files; if you are choosing from the list of WordPerfect graphics files, select from a file from the list

8. If you want to create a caption, select Create Caption; when the Caption Editor is displayed, type and enter the caption and press **F7** when through

9. Select "OK" or press **↵** to return to your document

Moving a Graphics Box (Using a Mouse)

1. Select the image

When the dotted box with handles with it appears around the image,

2. Drag the image to the desired location
3. Release the mouse button

Resizing a Graphics Box (Using a Mouse)

1. Select the image

When the dotted box with handles on it appears around the image,

2. Drag any handle in or out to resize
3. Release the mouse button

Editing a Graphics Box

1. Select Graphics, Graphics Boxes [**Alt** + **F9** **1**]
2. Select Edit [**2**]
3. Identify the image to be edited
4. Select Edit Box

The "Edit Graphics Box" dialog box is displayed.

5. Perform the appropriate editing option; the Edit Graphics Box enables you to do such things as edit the image, create and edit captions, resize the image, change border and fill styles, remove the border in order to contour text around the image, and the like

When you are finished,

6. Select "OK" to return to your document

Deleting a Graphics Box

- In text mode, delete the reveal code.
- In graphics mode or page mode, click on the box, press **Del** , and select "Yes" to confirm.

Graphics Mode

In graphics mode, WordPerfect attempts to display as closely as possible what your final document will look like in print, as you work on it. Graphics mode enables you to see such things as fonts, font attributes, and extended characters. While it does not display headers, footers, footnotes, and endnotes, as page mode does, graphic mode lets you see more of your document onscreen.

To work on your document in graphics mode,

Select View, Graphics Mode   [**Ctrl** + **F3** **3**]

To return to text mode,

Select View, Text Mode   [**Ctrl** + **F3** **2**]

Headers and Footers

Headers and footers contain brief information that identifies a page. You can create headers and/or footers for odd pages, even pages, or all pages.

Creating Headers and Footers

1. Move the cursor to the place on the page where you want the header or footer to begin

2. Select Layout, Header/Footer/Watermark

3. Select Headers   [**1**]

    or Footers   [**2**]

4. Select Header (Footer) A or Header (Footer) B

Note: You are allowed a maximum of two headers and two footers. "A" refers to the first header/footer; "B" refers to the second (optional) header/footer.

5. Select one of the following:

    All Pages: Use to place header/footer on every page   [**1**]

    Even Pages: Use to place header/footer on even-numbered

    pages only   [**2**]

    Odd Pages: Use to place header/footer on odd-numbered

    pages only   [**3**]

6. Select Create

7. Type the header or footer

Note: If you want to have additional space between the body text and the header or footer, use the Enter key *after* the header or *before* the footer to insert the necessary blank lines.

8. Select File, Exit when finished   [**F7**]

Note: Repeat Steps 4 through 7 for additional headers or footers.

9. Select "OK" or press ↵ when through

Editing Headers and Footers

1. Select Layout, Header/Footer/Watermark

2. Select the specific header or footer to be edited

3. Select Edit

4. Edit the header or footer

5. Select File, Exit when finished   [**F7**]

Deleting Headers and Footers.   Delete the code from the REVEAL CODES
screen.

The HELP feature lets you learn more about a particular feature in WordPerfect
without having to turn to the printed reference material.

**HELP
Feature**

Requesting Help

1. Press **F1**

The Help menu now appears.

2. Select a topic from the Help menu and follow any instructions given

3. Select the Cancel button or press **Esc** to return to your document

Searching for a Specific Topic

1. Select Help, Index

The Help menu now appears.

2. Select Name Search

3. At the cursor position in the "Name Search" box, begin typing in the letters
    of the topic in which you are interested

Note that as you type in each letter, the index changes in response.

4. Either finish typing in the topic on which you need help or use the arrow
    keys or mouse to highlight it

As soon as the topic you want help on is highlighted,

5. Select the Look button

6. When the first screen for the topic appears, perform whatever operations are
    necessary to get further help—for instance, scrolling to see subsequent screens

7. Select the Cancel button or press **Esc** to return to your document

Normally, WordPerfect does not hyphenate words. That is, when a word extends
beyond the right margin, WordPerfect will move it to the next line or page.

**Hyphen-
ation**

Turning Hyphenation On and Off

1. Place the cursor where hyphenation is to be turned on or off

2. Select Layout, Line   [**Shift** + **F8** **1**]

The "Line Format" dialog box appears. If hyphenation is checked, the feature is on; if not, it's off.

3. Select Hyphenation to turn hyphenation on or off   [ ]

Note that the check mark appears or disappears.

4. Select "OK" or press ↵

Note: If you used Shift + F8, you must press the Enter key a second time.

Indenting Para-graphs

Indenting is appropriate both for a numbered list of sentences or paragraphs and for sentences or paragraphs that are not numbered.

1. Place the cursor at the beginning of the paragraph to be indented

2. Select Layout, Alignment

3. Select one of the following:

    Indent →: Indents from the left margin only   [ ]

    Indent →←: Indents from both the right and left

      margins   []

    Hanging Indent: Indents from the left margin only, except for the first line

Note the following:

- A hard return (hitting the Enter key) stops an indent.
- To indent farther than the standard five spaces, repeat the command as necessary. For instance, pressing the F4 key twice produces an indent of ten spaces from the left.
- You can indent before or after you type text.
- To indent a nonstandard number of spaces, see "Margin Adjustment."

Index Prepara-tion

Indexes can be prepared in two ways: (1) by marking words or phrases in the document or (2) by creating a list of words that you want indexed and storing the list in a file (called a *concordance file*). You can identify words for an index by using either one of the two ways or by combining them. Once you've identified the words and phrases for the index, a separate procedure is required to create the index itself.

Marking Words or Phrases for an Index.   Repeat the steps below for each index entry:

1. In your document, select (block) the word or phrase that's to go into the index

2. Select Tools, Index, Mark   [   ]

A "Mark Index" box appears with the selected index entry.

3. If necessary, edit the entry

4. Do one of the following:
    To mark the entry as a heading only: Select "OK"
    To mark the entry as a heading and to include a subheading: Move
      to the Subheading box, enter the subheading, and select "OK"

To mark the entry as a subheading: Enter a heading in the Heading box, press
↵ . The original selection will be automatically moved to the Subheading
box; finally, select "OK" or press ↵ to close the "Mark Index" box

Creating a Concordance File

1. Select File, New to open a fresh document window

2. Type (or copy and paste from your document) each word or phrase you want
   in the index, pressing ↵ after each one

3. Use the Sort command to alphabetize the list (see the section entitled "Sorting"); WordPerfect generates the index faster if the concordance file is al-
   phabetized first

4. Save the file

Defining the Index

1. Assuming the index is to appear at the end of the document, move the cursor
   there

2. To start the index on a fresh page, press **Ctrl** + ↵

3. Type in a title for the index, pressing ↵ as many times as you need to
   after this to add extra spacing

4. Select Tools, Index, Define   [**Alt** + **F5** **2** **4**]

5. Select a Numbering Mode; the choices are as follows:

   None: No page numbers   [**1**]

   # Follows Entry: Page numbers after heads   [**2**]

   (#) Follows Entry: Page numbers in parentheses after heads   [**3**]

   # Flush Right: Page numbers flush right   [**4**]

   . . . # Flush Right: Page numbers flush right with dot leaders   [**5**]

6. Select Combine Sequential Page Numbers   [**7**]

7. If you have a concordance file, select Concordance File and enter the name
   of the file in the text box

8. Select "OK" or press ↵

Generating the Index

1. Select Tools, Generate   [**Alt** + **F5** **4**]

2. Select "OK" or press ↵

Note: If you later edit your document, you may need to regenerate your index.

Inserting allows text to be added at the cursor position, pushing existing text
over to the right. To insert text:

1. Make sure the insert mode is active

Inserting
Text

WP

Note: The insert mode is the default mode; if the word "Typeover" appears at the bottom left of your screen, you are not in the insert mode and must press the Ins key to get there.

2. Move the cursor to the place where you want to insert text
3. Type the text to be inserted

Note: The text of your document will be reformatted automatically as soon as you press one of the cursor movement keys.

Justification

WordPerfect automatically defaults to left justification. You can change justification for an entire document, a block, or a line.

Setting Justification

1. Position the cursor where you want the justification to be set in a certain way

2. Select Layout, Justification   [**Shift** + **F8** **1** **2**]

3. Choose one of the following options:
    Left: Left-justifies text (right edge stays ragged)
    Center: Centers text between left and right margins
    Right: Right-justifies text (left edge stays ragged)
    Full: Provides smooth edge on both left and right; spacing between words is changed to make edges smooth
    Full, All Lines: Used principally to format titles and headings; letters in lines are evenly spaced between margins

Setting Justification for Selected Text

1. Select (block) the text

2. Follow Steps 2 and 3 under "Setting Justification"

Line Drawing

The Line Draw feature is used to draw lines, boxes, graphs, borders, and certain other types of illustrations.

Drawing Lines.   To draw lines in a document,

1. Place the cursor where you want to begin drawing lines

2. Select Graphics, Line Draw   [**Ctrl** + **F3** **5**]

A "Line Draw" menu will appear at the bottom of the screen.

3. Choose one of the following options:

    Single Line: Press **1** or select the appropriate icon

    Double Line: Press **2** or select the appropriate icon

    Line of Asterisks: Press **3** or select the appropriate icon

    Other: More exotic lines are possible by selecting Change and then User-defined. For instance, when the cursor is at the asterisk, type **Ctrl** + **2** to access any of the WordPerfect characters (see the "Short Method" in the section on "Extended Characters")

You will now be placed back in your document, with the "Line Draw" menu still at the bottom of the screen.

4. Use the appropriate arrow keys to draw the line

Note: By holding down the Home key and hitting one of the arrow keys, you will be able to extend the line clear to the margin, in the direction of the arrow key that you hit.

5. Select the Close button or press [**F7**] when you are finished

Erasing Lines.   To erase lines, use any of the following procedures:

- Erase with the Delete or Backspace keys in the normal way.
- Select (block) any part of the lines and press the Delete key.
- Invoke the Erase button in the "Line Draw" menu and retrace the lines with the arrow keys.

The line spacing option allows text to be single-spaced, double-spaced, triple-spaced, and so on. Fractional spacing, to tenths of an inch, is also allowed. The default is single-spaced text.

1. Move the cursor to the place in the document where line spacing is to be changed

2. Select Layout, Line, Line Spacing   [**Shift** + **F8** **1** **3**]

3. Type a number that corresponds to the line spacing you would like (e.g., 2 for double-spacing)

4. Press [↵]

5. Select "OK" or press [↵]

Line Spacing

A macro is a set of keystrokes that is automatically invoked when summoned. Macros are handy for storing (recording) programs and blocks of text that are used over and over.

Macros

Recording a Macro

1. Select Tools, Macro, Record   [**Ctrl** + **F10**]

2. Type the name of the macro

3. Press [↵]

The message "Recording Macro" now appears at the bottom of the screen.

4. Type in the program or text that will serve as the macro

5. When you are through, select Tools, Macro, Stop

The macro will now be saved in the macro library.

"Playing" (Retrieving) a Macro

1. Position the cursor where you want the macro to play

2. Select Tools, Macro, Play   [**Alt** + **F10**]

3. Type the name of the macro

4. Press [↵]

WP

Editing a Macro

1. Select Tools, Macro, Record   [**Ctrl** + **F10**]

2. Select the "Edit Macro" check box

3. Type the name of the macro and press ↵

The macro should appear on the screen. If you forgot the name of the macro, press the F5 key to access the macro library.

4. Edit the macro

5. When finished, select Tools, Macro, Stop

6. To save the macro, press **Ctrl** + **F12**

Margin Adjustment

WordPerfect lets you adjust the left, right, top, and bottom margins of a document and the left and right margins of a paragraph. The default margins are one inch on all sides of the paper.

Setting Document Margins

1. Place the cursor where you would like to change the margins

2. Select Layout, Margins   [**Shift** + **F8** **2**]

3. In the "Margin Format" box, select in the Document Margins area a margin you wish to change. The choices are as follows:

Left   [**1**]

Right   [**2**]

Top   [**3**]

Bottom   [**4**]

4. Type the new margin setting and press ↵

5. Repeat Steps 3 and 4 for other margins you wish to set

6. Choose "OK" or press ↵ once or twice, to return to your document

Setting Paragraph Margins

1. Select (block) the paragraph that is to have special margins

2. Select Layout, Margins   [**Shift** + **F8** **2**]

3. In the "Margin Format" box, select in the Paragraph Margins area any of the following:
   Left Margin Adjustment: Enter a positive number to indent

   or a negative number to "outdent"   [**5**]

   Right Margin Adjustment: Enter a positive number to indent

   or a negative number to "outdent"   [**6**]

   First Line Indent: Enter a number to indent the first line

   of a paragraph by the same amount   [**7**]

   Paragraph Spacing: Enter the number of blank lines to

   automatically insert between paragraphs   [**8**]

4. Choose "OK" or press ↵ once or twice, to return to your document

Resetting Margins

- To reset margins to normal, delete the code in the REVEAL CODES screen.
- To reset margins in a special way, follow procedures for setting margins.

Many choices in WordPerfect can be made with either a mouse or a keyboard.

Menu and Box Navigation

Making Menu Selections

Using a Mouse

1. Move the mouse pointer to the name of the choice on the menu bar whose pull-down menu you want
2. Click the left mouse button to select it
3. Continue selecting subsequent menu choices by moving the mouse pointer to them and clicking

Note: Dimmed choices cannot be selected.

Using a Keyboard

1. Hold down **Alt** while pressing the colored (highlighted) letter of the command in the menu bar whose pull-down menu you want (or press **Alt** + **=** to activate the menu bar, move to the choice, and press **↵**)
2. Make subsequent menu choices by pressing the colored (highlighted) letters (or move to the choice with the arrow keys and press **↵**)

Note: Dimmed choices cannot be selected.

Moving between Menus and Document Windows.   To move the cursor from the menu bar to the document (or vice versa),

Using a Mouse

Position the cursor and press the left mouse button

Using a Keyboard

Press **Alt** + **=**

Making Box Selections

Using a Mouse

1. Move the mouse pointer to the choice you wish to select
2. Click the left mouse button to select it; list (drop-down) box items require a double click

Note: Dimmed choices cannot be selected.

Using a Keyboard

Use the arrow keys to highlight the choice and press **↵** . In cases where the arrow keys are ineffective, try **↤→** instead.

Note: Dimmed choices cannot be selected.

Canceling Selections from Menus or Boxes

Press **Esc** as many times as necessary, to backtrack

Using Scroll Bars.   If the scroll bar you need is already onscreen, go to Step 3; otherwise, perform Step 1 and/or Step 2 as necessary.

1. Select View, Horizontal Scroll Bar

A horizontal scroll bar should appear.

2. Select <u>V</u>iew, <u>V</u>ertical Scroll Bar

A vertical scroll bar should appear.

3. Scroll by doing one of the following:

Using a Mouse	**Using a Keyboard**
• Clicking one of the vertical scroll arrows will move the text up or down by one line. • For long or wide documents, dragging the scroll box along the bar will move the cursor to the relative place in the file. • Clicking above or below a scroll box will move a screen at a time.	Use the arrow keys or the PgUp and PgDn keys to navigate.

Note: Many drop-down lists contain scroll bars that work by the principles in Step 3.

4. You can turn off either of the scroll bars by invoking Steps 1 or 2 again, whichever is appropriate

Merging Files

Merging files enables you to create customized form letters. Assuming you have followed the procedures described in the text to create a form file (the boilerplate letter itself) and data file (the customized information to place in the letter), follow the steps below to merge the two into a third document.

1. Select <u>T</u>ools, <u>M</u>erge, <u>R</u>un   [**Ctrl** + **F9** **1**]
2. Type the name of the <u>F</u>orm File and press ↵
3. Type the name of the <u>D</u>ata File and press ↵
4. Select one of the following <u>O</u>utput options:
    <u>C</u>urrent Document: Displays the merged file in the current document window
    <u>U</u>nused Document: Displays the merged file in a new document window
    <u>P</u>rinter: The merged file is printed
    <u>F</u>ile: The merged file is saved on disk; type filename and press ↵
5. If doing anything other than a straightforward merge, select the Data File Option and perform the required steps; options are available that enable you to create envelope form files, merge only selected records, and so forth
6. Select the Merge button

Moving

Moving allows a block of text or a graphic to be relocated elsewhere. There are two principal ways to move.

• *Cut-and-paste:* The "cut and paste" operation is used to make an immediate relocation into a single location.
• *Cut-now-paste-later:* A separate "cut" operation is used to temporarily save the text or graphic to a special buffer. Anytime later, it can be fetched and pasted (with the "paste" operation) in one place or more.

Cutting and Pasting

Using a Mouse

1. Select (block) the text or graphic that is to be moved
2. Drag the selected text or graphic to the new location
3. Release the mouse button

Using a Keyboard

1. Select (block) the text or graphic that is to be moved
2. Select Edit, Cut and

   Paste   [**Ctrl** + **Del**]

   If the move is to take place in the same document, go immediately to Step 3; otherwise, first open or switch to the other document.

3. Place the cursor where the text or graphic is to go
4. Press

Cutting

1. Select (block) the text or graphic that is to be moved
2. Select Edit, Cut   [**Ctrl** + **X**]

Note: The previous contents of the buffer are erased.

Pasting

1. Place the cursor where the text or grapic is to go
2. Select Edit, Paste   [**Ctrl** + **V**]

WordPerfect enables you to create multicolumn text, similar to that which you see in a newspaper.

Multi-column Text

Defining Columns before Typing Text

1. Select Layout, Columns   [**Alt** + **F7** **1**]

At this point, many users will choose to accept the default of double-column newspaper text shown in the "Text Columns" box. If you are one of these users, proceed to Step 6. Otherwise, to choose the type of columns you would like,

2. Select Column Type

3. Select one of the following:
   Newspaper: Text completely fills one column before going

   into another   [**1**]

   Balanced Newspaper: Text flows into columns so the columns

   are of equal length   [**2**]

   Parallel: For specific text allocated to columns and when one

   column can wind up ending on another page   [**3**]

   Parallel with Block Protect: For specific text allocated to columns
   and when text in a column spills to another page (as will corresponding

   text in other columns)   [**4**]

To choose the number of columns you would like,

4.   Select Number of Columns   2

5.   Type in the number of columns and press   ↵

At this point, you can select D, S, and/or B to respectively change the distance between columns, change the spacing between rows, and/or choose a column border style. If, on the other hand, you wish to accept the defaults, proceed to Step 6.

6.   Select "OK" to accept all of the settings in the "Text Columns" box

Note: To move from column to column as you fill each one with text, insert a hard page break by pressing   Ctrl   +   ↵

Turning Off the Columns Feature

1.   Select Layout, Columns   [Alt + F7]

2.   Select Off

Converting a Noncolumn File or Block to Multicolumn

- Converting an entire file: Place the cursor where you want multicolumns to begin and follow the procedures for defining columns before typing text.
- Converting a block: Block the text, and, with the "Block On" message still showing, follow the procedures for defining columns before typing text.

Moving between Columns

Using a Mouse

Click anywhere in another column

Using a Keyboard

1.   Press   Ctrl   +   Home

When the "Goto" dialog box appears

2.   Press   →   to move to the right column or   ←   to move to the column to the left

Opening Document Windows

WordPerfect lets you open a maximum of nine document windows concurrently. You can open a new window from the active window in any of several different ways. Two of these are discussed below; for others, see "Windows."

Opening a Fresh Screen.   From the active window,
    Select File New
WordPerfect will automatically open up a new window for you—with a fresh screen—and move you to it. (To open a specific window, use the F3 key.)

Bringing an Existing Document into a New Window.   From the active window,

1.   Select File, Open   [Shift + F10]

2.   Type the name of the file and press   ↵

Note: WordPerfect will automatically open a new window for you, place the file in it, and move you to it. You can also use File Manager (the F5 key) to find the filename and enter it.

For eliminating orphans and widows, see "Page Breaks."

WordPerfect's outlining feature is useful for organizing ideas that are to go into a paper or lecture. It enables you to create "outline text" and to combine it with "body text"—text that is not part of the outline.

Creating an Outline

1. Place the cursor where the outline is to begin

2. Select Tools, Outline   [**Ctrl** + **F5**]

3. Select Begin New Outline   [**1**]

A list box will appear.

4. Highlight the outline style that you want and pick Select   [**1**]

The first number, letter, or bullet will appear onscreen.

5. Type the first outline entry and press ↵

6. For all subsequent outline entries, if, relative to the previous entry, they are at
    The same level: Type the entry and press ↵

    A lower level: Press ↤⇥ to indent. type the entry, and press ↵

    A higher level: Press **Shift** + ↤⇥ to "outdent," type the entry, and

    press ↵

When finished with the outline,

7. Select Tools, Outline, End Outline   [**Ctrl** + **F5** **5**]

Moving, Copying, and Cutting Outline Families. An outline family consists of an outline item and all items subordinate to it. To move, copy, or cut,

1. Place the cursor on the topmost item in the family

2. Select Tools, Outline

3. Do one of the following
    To move the family: Select Move Family; then, move cursor to new location

    and press ↵

    To copy the family: Select Copy Family; then, move cursor to new location

    and press ↵

    To cut the family (for subsequent moving or copying): Select Cut Family

Collapsing and Expanding the Outline. To display fewer or more outline levels,

1. Select Tools, Outline, Outline Options to get the

    "Outline" dialog box   [**Ctrl** + **F5**]

2. Select Hide/Show to perform any of the following operations to collapse or

    expand the outline   [**9**]

    − (minus sign): Hides all sublevels of current level (also called Hide

    Family)   [**1**]

+ (plus sign): Displays all sublevels of current level (also called Show Family)   [**2**]

Show Levels: Collapses or expands the outline to the level you specify; select a level from the list box (note that All restores all levels)   [**3**]

Hide Outline: Hides the entire outline   [**4**]

Hide Body Text: Switches between hiding and showing body text   [**5**]

Changing an Outline Item to Normal Text

1. Place the cursor on the item

2. Select Tools, Outline, Change to Body Text   [**Ctrl** + **T**]

Outline Bar.   To turn the Outline Bar on and off,

Select View, Outline Bar   [**Ctrl** + **F5** **7**]

Page Breaks

WordPerfect has features that enable you to force page breaks when you want them, to keep certain blocks of text (such as tables) from being split between two pages, and to eliminate orphans and widows in a document.

Hard Page Breaks.   To produce a hard break,

1. Place the cursor where you want to begin a new page

2. Press **Ctrl** + **↵**

Conditional Page Breaks.   To keep a specified number of lines from being split by a soft page break,

1. Place the cursor on the line above the block of text that is to remain intact

2. Select Layout, Other   [**Shift** + **F8** + **7**]

3. Select Conditional End of Page   [**2**]

A dialog box will now appear.

4. Type the number of lines that should remain intact

5. Press **↵**

6. Select "OK" and/or press **↵** once or twice

Eliminating Orphans and Widows.   Orphans and widows are aesthetically undesirable line breaks. The first line of a paragraph is called an orphan when it is separated from the rest of the paragraph by a page or column break. The last line of a paragraph is called a widow when it is separated from the rest of the paragraph by being forced onto a new page or column. To eliminate orphans and widows,

1. Place the cursor at the beginning of the place where you want to eliminate orphans and widows (say, at the beginning of your document)

2. Select Layout, Other   [**Shift** + **F8** **7**]

3. Select Widow/Orphan Protect   [**3**]

4. Select "OK" and/or press **↵** once or twice

In page mode, WordPerfect attempts to display as closely as possible what your final document will look like in print, as you work on it. Page mode enables you to see such things as fonts, font attributes, and extended characters, as well as a few items you won't find in graphics mode—such as headers, footers, footnotes, and endnotes.

Page Mode

To work on your document in the page mode,

Select <u>V</u>iew, <u>P</u>age Mode   [**Ctrl** + **F3** **4**]

To return to text mode,

Select <u>V</u>iew, <u>T</u>ext Mode   [**Ctrl** + **F3** **2**]

The WordPerfect default is no page numbers. To number pages of a WordPerfect document and to choose a page-numbering style,

Page Numbering

1. Place the cursor on the page where the page numbers will start

2. Select <u>L</u>ayout, <u>P</u>age   [**Shift** + **F8** **3**]

3. Select Page <u>N</u>umbering   [**1**]

4. Select Page Number <u>P</u>osition   [**1**]

5. Type a number from 1 to 8, corresponding to the page number position

6. If you wish to change the appearance of the page numbers, select Font/Attributes/Color and make any appropriate adjustments in the "Font" dialog box that appears

7. Select "OK" or press ↵ as many times as necessary to return to your document

The Print Preview feature enables you to inspect, on the screen, a fully formatted document before it is printed. Headers, footers, page numbers, footnotes, text of all sizes and appearances, special characters, and graphics are all displayed as close in appearance as possible to what you will see on the printed page. To preview a document,

Previewing Documents

1. Select <u>F</u>ile, <u>P</u>rint/Fax   [**Shift** + **F7**]

2. Select Print Pre<u>v</u>iew   [**7**]

You will now get a WYSIWYG preview screen. To see more of the document,

Using a Mouse

3. Either use the scroll bars or select another previewing option from the button bar

You will now get another WYSIWYG preview screen. Perform Step 3 as many times as is necessary, or,

4. Click on the Close button to leave the Print Preview feature

Using a Keyboard

3. Either use the cursor movement keys or, to choose another previewing option, select <u>V</u>iew from the menu bar and make the appropriate selection from the pull-down menu

You will now get another WYSIWYG preview screen. Perform Step 3 as many times as is necessary, or,

4. To leave the Print Preview feature, select <u>F</u>ile, <u>C</u>lose   [**F7**]

Printing Documents

WordPerfect allows several printing options, including printing an entire document, a single page, or a range of pages.

Printing Any or All of a Document

1. Select File, Print/Fax   [**Shift** + **F7**]

2. Select one of the following options:

    Full Document: Use this to print the entire document   [**1**]

    Page: Use this to print the current page only   [**2**]

    Document on Disk: Use this to print a document that's currently on disk;
    when the dialog box appears, enter the name of the document file and

    (possibly) its path   [**3**]

    Multiple Pages: Select this option if you wish a range of pages; then, select

    Page/Label Range and enter the range; some examples of valid ranges are

    as follows: [**4**]

    *   11, 17 (means pages 11 and 17 only)
    *   11-17 (means pages 11 through 17)
    *   10, 12-14 (means pages 10, 12, 13, and 14)
    *   11- (means from page 11 on)
    *   -11 (means up to page 11)

    Blocked Text: Use this to print any currently selected block of text   [**5**]

3. Select the Print button or press [**↵**]

Printing Pages in Reverse Order.   Many printers will eject finished pages face up, causing you to have to manually put them in reverse order. To get the pages to automatically print in reverse order,

1. Select File, Print/Fax   [**Shift** + **F7**]

2. Select Multiple Pages   [**4**]

In the "Print Multiple Pages" dialog box, leave the default of having all the pages print, but

3. Select Descending Order (Last Page First)

Printing Multiple Copics of a Document

1. Select File, Print/Fax   [**Shift** + **F7**]

2. Choose what you want to print—for instance, the full document, a single page, a text block, etc.

3. Select Number of Copies

4. Type in the number of copies and press [**↵**]

5. Select the Print button or press [**↵**]

Canceling a Print Job

1. Select File, Print/Fax   [**Shift** + **F7**]

2. Select Control Printer   [**6**]

A box now appears onscreen.

3.   Highlight the job you want to cance!

4.   Select Cancel Job   [**1**]

5.   Select Yes

6.   Select the Close button

Previewing a Document before Printing.   See the section called "Previewing Documents."

Renaming allows you to change filenames. To rename a document,

1.   Select File, File Manager to access the File Manager   [**F5**]

2.   If the file you wish to rename is in the default directory, press ↵ ; otherwise, type the name of the appropriate directory and press ↵

3.   Using the mouse or arrow keys, move to the name of the file you wish to rename

4.   Select Move/Rename   [**5**]

5.   Type the new name of the file

6.   Press ↵

Renaming Files

Replacement requires you to identify both the text string you want to search for in the document as well as the text string you want to replace it with. To search for a text string and replace it with another,

1.   Place the cursor where you want to begin the replacement

2.   Select Edit, Replace   [**Alt** + **F2**]

3.   Type the word or text string you wish to replace

4.   Press ↵

5.   Enter the word or text string you wish to replace with

6.   If necessary, select any options as follows:

Confirm Replacement: Lets you confirm each replacement occurrence; choose Yes to make the replacement, No to not make it, and Replace All to replace without further confirmation   [**3**]

Backward Search: Searches backward from cursor   [**4**]

Case Sensitive Search: Only exact matches are replaced—in other words, upper and lowercase letters are full respected   [**5**]

Find Whole Words Only: Only exact matches that are whole words are replaced   [**6**]

Extended Search: Search is extended to footnotes and endnotes, headers and footers, etc.   [**7**]

Limit Number of Matches: Places a limit on the number of matches that can be made   [**8**]

Replacing Text in Documents

WP

Note: If no options are chosen, the default is forward replacement and all matches are replaced.

7.   Select the Replace button   [**F2**]

When the dialog box appears,

8.   Choose "OK" or press   **↵**

Restoring Deleted Text

WordPerfect allows you to see and restore the three most recent deletions.

Undoing the Effects of the Most Recent Edit

Select Edit, Undo   [**Ctrl** + **Z**]

Note: Undo restores an item to its original location. To restore an item elsewhere, choose Undelete, which follows.

Recovering Deleted Text or Graphics

1.   Place the cursor where you want the previously deleted item restored

2.   Select Edit, Undelete   [**Esc**]

3.   Choose one of the following:

To restore the last deletion: Select Restore   [**1**]

To restore the next-to-last deletion: Select Previous Deletion,

Restore   [**2** **1**]

To restore the second-to-last deletion: Select Previous Deletion twice, then

Restore   [**2** **2** **1**]

Retrieving Documents

Retrieving is the act of fetching a document from disk and loading it into an existing open document. To retrieve a document, you can either type in its name or select it off the File Manager listings.

Typing in the Document Name.   With the cursor positioned where you want the retrieved document placed,

1.   Select File, Retrieve

2.   Type the name of the file to retrieve

3.   Press   **↵**

Selecting the Document off the File Manager Listings.   With the cursor positioned where you want the retrieved document placed,

1.   Press   **F5**   to get the "Specify File Manager List" dialog box

The default directory is highlighted.

2.   If the default directory contains the file to be retrieved, press   **↵**   ; otherwise,

type the name of the directory that contains the file and press   **↵**

3.   Using the mouse or arrow keys, move the name of the file you wish to retrieve and select Retrieve into Current Doc

REVEAL CODES

Use the REVEAL CODES command to see all formats, tabs, indents, and other formatting codes. You may edit and delete formats from the REVEAL CODES screen as well as add text.

Enabling/Disabling the REVEAL CODES Screen

1. Select V̲iew, Reveal C̲odes to enable (or view) the reveal codes

   screen   [**Alt** + **F3** or **F11**]

2. Select V̲iew, Reveal C̲odes again to disable the reveal codes screen (make it

   disappear)   [**Alt** + **F3** or **F11**]

Deleting Codes from the REVEAL CODES Screen

1. Enable the REVEAL CODES screen

2. Position the pointer on the code you wish to delete

3. Press **Del**

4. Disable the REVEAL CODES screen

Follow the procedures below to save documents or blocks of text.

Saving Documents

Naming and Saving Documents.   To name a new document before you save it, or to provide a different name to an existing document that you have just finished editing,

Using the F10 Key	**Using the F7 Key**
1. Select F̲ile, Save A̲s [**F10**]	1. Press **F7**
Note: A "Save Document" box will now appear. By typing over an existing filename, you will save to the new name.	2. Select S̲ave As
	Note: A "Save Document" box will now appear. By typing over an existing filename, you will save to the new name.
2. Type a filename	3. Type a filename
3. Press **↵**	4. Press **↵**
4. Select "OK" or press **↵**	5. Select one of the following:
	Y̲es to exit
	N̲o to clear the screen
	Cancel to return to your
	document

Resaving Documents

Using the F10 Key	**Using the F7 Key**
1. Press **F10**	1. Press **F7**
2. Select "OK"	2. Select the Yes button
WordPerfect will now ask if you wish to save and replace.	Your document is automatically resaved and you will next be asked if you wish to exit WordPerfect.
3. Select Y̲es	3. Select one of the following:
	Y̲es to exit
	N̲o to clear the screen
	Cancel to return to your
	document

WP

Note: You can also resave using the File Command. To do this,

Select <u>F</u>ile, <u>S</u>ave   [**Ctrl** + **F12**]

Resaving this way, you will get no prompts; the save is made and you are returned to your document.

Saving and Resaving Blocks of Text

1. Select (block) the text to be saved

2. Press **F10**

3. Follow the usual procedures for saving and resaving documents

Searching for Directories and Files

Often, disks are so capacious that it's cumbersome to search entry by entry for specific files and directories. It's easier to do a name search, as described below.

1. Press **F5** to get the "Specify File Manager List" dialog box

The default directory is highlighted. If the default directory contains the directory or file you are looking for, proceed to Step 3; otherwise,

2. Type the name of a directory superior to the directory or file you want

3. Press **↵**

A directory window will now appear, showing subordinate directories and files.

4. Select <u>N</u>ame Search

Note that a "Name Search" box appears at the bottom of the screen.

5. Start typing the name of the file or directory

Note that as you keystroke, the directory window will change in correspondence to what you are typing. When you see a familiar directory name or file appear in the window,

6. Use the arrow keys to move into the list and highlight it or, if it is already highlighted, press **Esc**

Note that the "Name Search" box disappears and the list of options at the right of the screen is activated.

7. Press the appropriate keystroke from the list of options

Another directory window may appear. At this point you may see the name of the directory or file you are looking for or you may decide to repeat Steps 4 through 7 to narrow the search.

Searching Documents for Text and Codes

Searching requires you to identify the string of characters you want to find. There are separate commands for searching and replacing (see "Replacing Text in Documents").

Searching for Text

1. Place the cursor where you want to begin the search

2. Select <u>E</u>dit, <u>S</u>earch   [**F2**]

3. Type the word or text string you are searching for

4. If necessary, select options

Note: Options are listed in Step 6 of the section entitled "Replacing Text in Documents." If no options are chosen, the default is forward search, and the cursor will be placed at the end of the first occurrence of the string.

5. Select the Search button   [**F2**]

Either the string will not be found (press the Enter key to get back to your document) or, as mentioned, the cursor is placed after the first occurrence in the document (if you are using the default search). To search for the next occurrence with the default,

6. Press **F2** twice

Perform Step 6 as necessary to look for further occurrences.

Searching for Reveal Codes

1. Place the cursor where you want to begin the search

2. Select <u>E</u>dit, Searc<u>h</u>   [**F2**]

3. Choose the Codes button or press **F5**

A drop-down (list) box of codes now appears.

4. Select the code you want

The code will now be placed in the "Search For" text box.

5. Follow Steps 4 through 6 listed earlier, under "Searching for Text"

To sort a contiguous list of items alphabetically,   ***Sorting***

1. Select (block) the list

2. Select <u>T</u>ools, So<u>r</u>t   [**Ctrl** + **F9**]

3. Select <u>P</u>erform Action

WordPerfect's spelling checker is used to check a document for allegedly mis-   ***Speller***
spelled words. In standard installations, the checker will also flag numbers in words, double words, and irregular capitalization. To spell check a document,

1. Place the cursor anywhere in the document

2. Select <u>T</u>ools, <u>W</u>riting Tools   [**Alt** + **F1**]

3. Select <u>S</u>peller   [**1**]

4. Select one of the following options:

    <u>W</u>ord: Checks the current word only   [**1**]

    <u>P</u>age: Checks all words on the current page only   [**2**]

    <u>D</u>ocument: Checks the entire document   [**3**]

    <u>F</u>rom Cursor: Checks from the cursor forward   [**4**]

The first word that WordPerfect doesn't recognize is now highlighted and replacement suggestions are given.

5. To make a replacement from the suggestions, double-click it (using the mouse) or highlight it and select <u>R</u>eplace Word (keyboard); other options you may wish to choose include the following:

Skip <u>O</u>nce: Leaves word as is   [**1**]

<u>S</u>kip in this Document: Leaves word as is and ignores it for the remainder of the document   [**2**]

Edit <u>W</u>ord: Returns to document; edit word and press **F7** to continue spell-check session   [**4**]

6. When the message "Spell Check Completed" appears, select "OK" or press ↵

Note: You can also block certain parts of the document off from the speller in the following way: For each block to be disabled, (1) select the block, (2) select <u>T</u>ools, <u>W</u>riting Tools, <u>D</u>isable Speller/Grammatik. To enable a disabled block, perform the steps again.

Tables

A table is a rectangular block of columns and rows into which you can add column or row titles, numbers, formulas, and functions.

Creating Tables

1. Select <u>L</u>ayout, <u>T</u>ables, <u>C</u>reate   [**Alt** + **F7** **2** **1**]

A box will appear.

2. Separately enter the number of columns and rows
3. Select "OK"

You are now in the table edit mode. In this mode you will be able to change the structure of the table but you cannot enter data into it.

4. Change the structure of the table, if necessary (see list of common table operations that follows)

5. Press **F7** to exit

Reentering the Table Edit Mode

Select <u>L</u>ayout, <u>T</u>ables, <u>E</u>dit   [**Alt** + **F11**]

Exiting the Table Edit Mode

Press **F7**

Entering and Editing Table Data.   Enter and edit the data directly in your document; use the arrow keys to move from column to column.

Common Operations in Table Edit Mode

- Joining cells for titles: Press **Alt** + **F4** to begin blocking cells and use the arrow keys to select the cells to join; then, select <u>J</u>oin, <u>Y</u>es

- Moving from cell to cell: Use the mouse to click on the cell or, if at a keyboard, use the arrows keys; **Tab** and **Shift** + **Tab** can also be used to move left and right

- Changing cell width: Move to the cell; press **Ctrl** + **→** to make the cells wider; **Ctrl** + **←** to make the cells narrower

- Changing justification within cells: Move to the correct cell or block the appropriate cells; select Cell, Justification to perform such operations as centering titles, justifying numbers right, etc.

- Changing the appearance of data within cells: Move to the correct cell or block the appropriate cells; select Cell, Appearance to boldface, italicize, etc.

- Placing commas in large numbers: Make sure the cell width is large enough; then, with the pointer in the correct column, select Cell, Number Type, Options and check off "Use Commas"

- Defining formulas: Move to the correct cell; select Formula and enter the formula in the box supplied

- Copying formulas: Select Move/Copy, Copy; next, select the direction of the copy (e.g., up or down); finally, enter the number of cells to copy to

- Changing border thickness: Select Lines/Fill, Border/Fill, Border Style, and then select a style from the dialog box

- Shading tables: Select Lines/Fill, Border/Fill, Fill Style, and then select a fill style from the dialog box

Table of Contents

Preparing a table of contents is done in three steps. First, headings and subheadings to appear in the table must be marked in the document. Second, the table is defined. Third, the table is generated.

Marking Headings and Subheadings. To mark headings and subheadings (or "heads"), perform the following steps for each head:

1. Select (block) the text that is to become a head

2. Select Tools, Table of Contents, Mark   [**Alt** + **F5** **1**]

3. Type the level of the head

4. Select "OK" or press ↵

Note: You are allowed up to five levels of heads, with "1" corresponding to the highest level and "5" the lowest level.

Defining the Table of Contents

1. Assuming the table of contents is to be at the beginning of the document, move the cursor there

2. If you want the table generated on a page of its own, press **Ctrl** + ↵

   followed by ↑

3. Type the title of the table

4. Press ↵ as many times as you need to after this to add extra spacing

5. Select Tools, Table of Contents, Define   [**Alt** + **F5** **2** **1**]

6. Select Number of Levels   [**1**]

7. Enter the number of levels you've established by marking and press ↵

8. Select a Numbering Mode; the choices are as follows:

   None: No page numbers   [**1**]

   # Follows Entry: Page numbers after heads   [**2**]

(#) Follows Entry: Page numbers in parentheses after heads   [**3**]

Flush Right: Page numbers flush right   [**4**]

. . . # Flush Right: Page numbers flush right with dot leaders   [**5**]

9. If you want the last-level heads placed on the same line instead of separated by line breaks (the default), select Wrap the Last Level

10. If you want a page-numbering format different than the document, select Page Number Format and then Different from Document; then, press **F5** to select Choose Number Codes, and, finally, select a code

11. Select "OK" or press **↵** as necessary to return to document

Generating the Table of Contents

1. Select Tools, Generate   [**Alt** + **F5** **4**]

2. Select "OK" or press **↵**

Note: If you later edit your document, you may need to regenerate the table of contents.

Tab Settings

WordPerfect, like most word processors, has default tab settings. However, you can change any of these by following the procedures described below.

Setting Tabs

1. Place the cursor where you want to begin the new tab(s)

2. Select Layout, Tab Set   [**Shift** + **F8** **1** **1**]

A "Tab Set" box will next appear.

3. Select either Absolute or Relative tabs

4. Select either Left, Right, Center, or Decimal

For the first new tab,

5. Select Set Tab, type the location of the tab, and press **↵**

Note that the new tab stop appears on the ruler line. If you want other tabs that are not at regular intervals, repeat Step 5.

6. If you want to repeat the tab established in Step 5 at regular intervals, select Repeat Every, type the interval, and press **↵**

7. If you want a dot leader, select Dot Leader

8. Select "OK" to return to document   [**F7**]

Deleting Tabs

1. Place the cursor where you want to begin deleting tabs

2. Select Layout, Tab Set   [**Shift** + **F8** **1** **1**]

A "Tab Set" box will next appear.

3. Choose one of the following:

To delete a single tab: Move the cursor over it and select Clear
One [**Del**]

To delete all tabs: Select Clear All [**Ctrl** + **End**]

4. Select "OK" to return to document [**F7**]

Thesaurus

The thesaurus is used to find synonyms and antonyms for words. To use the thesaurus,

1. Place the cursor on the word you wish to look up

2. Select Tools, Writing Tools [**Alt** + **F1**]

3. Select Thesaurus [**2**]

Replacement suggestions are provided.

4. If you see a replacement you like, highlight it and select Replace; otherwise,
press **F7** to return to document

Underlining Text

Underlining enables you to output text that is underlined.

Before Typing the Text	**After Typing the Text**
1. Press **F8** , for UNDERLINE, to turn on the underlining feature	1. Block the text to be underlined
2. Type the text to be underlined	2. Press **F8**
3. Press **F8** again, to turn off the underlining feature	

Windows

WordPerfect 6.0 allows a maximum of nine document windows open at any one time; the one you are currently working on is called the "active" window. You can display a window full-screen-sized (maximized) or frame windows and resize them—making it possible to tile or cascade several windows onscreen simultaneously.

Opening Windows. A document window is automatically opened when you enter WordPerfect. To create other document windows,

- Select File New to start at a fresh screen in a new window.
- Select File, Open to bring an existing disk file into a new window.

Switching among Windows. To switch from one open document window to another, thereby making the second window "active," do any of the following:

- To toggle between the two most recently used windows:
  Select Window, Switch [**Shift** + **F3**]

- To make a selection from among all windows:
  Select Window, Switch To and make a choice from the list [**F3**]

WP

- To make the next open window in the sequence active:
  Select Window, Next   [Ctrl + F3 1 6]

- To make the previous open window in the sequence active:
  Select Window, Previous   [Ctrl + F3 1 7]

- To make a noncurrent window displayed onscreen active:
  Click on it

Framing a Window. To place a frame (border) around a maximized window,

Select Window, Frame   [Ctrl + F3 1 2]

A frame will appear around the window. Once a window is framed, you can size
or move it.

Sizing Windows. To change the size of a window, follow any of the procedures
below:

Using a Mouse

- To change window to a specific
  size: Place the mouse pointer on
  an appropriate border and drag
  in or out, to make the window
  smaller or larger. Alternatively,
  you can place the mouse pointer
  on an appropriate corner and
  drag in or out, to make the
  window proportionally smaller or
  larger.
- To minimize the window to a
  small rectangle: First click on
  Window, then click on Minimize.
- To make the window full-screen-
  sized: First click on Window,
  then click on Maximize.

Using a Keyboard

- To change window to a specific
  size: Press Ctrl + F3 1
  S to select size; next, use any
  of the arrow keys to move a
  corresponding border in or out;
  finally, press ↵ .
- To minimize the window to a
  small rectangle: Select Window,
  Minimize.
- To make the window full-screen-
  sized: Select Window, Maximize.

Arranging Windows. To arrange windows, choose any of the following
methods:

Using a Mouse

- To move a framed window
  anywhere, click on the title bar
  and drag it where you want.
- To tile windows, first click on
  Window, then click on Tile.
- To cascade windows, first click
  on Window, then click on
  Cascade.

Using a Keyboard

- To move the active window
  anywhere, press Ctrl + F3
  1 5 to select Move; next,
  use any of the arrow keys to
  move in any direction; finally,
  press ↵ .
- To tile windows, select Window,
  Tile.
- To cascade windows, select
  Window, Cascade.

Closing Windows.   Closing a window erases its contents and requires it to be reopened for further use. To close a window, do either of the following:

- Select File, Close.
- Click the "Close" box of the window.

Comprehensive Quick Reference to Features

Feature	Keystrokes
Appearance of text	`Ctrl` + `F8` `3`
Backspace	`Backspace`
Backup	`Shift` + `F1` `3` `1`
Block protect (with block on)	`Shift` + `F8` `7` `1`
Block text	`Alt` + `F4` *or* `F12`
Boldface text	`F6`
Bookmark	`Shift` + `F12`
Borders	`Alt` + `F9` `3`
Cancel	`Esc`
Center	`Shift` + `F6`
Clipboard	`Ctrl` + `F1`
Columns	`Alt` + `F7` `1`
Comment	`Ctrl` + `F7` `2`
Conditional end of page	`Shift` + `F8` `7` `2`
Convert case (with block on)	`Shift` + `F3`
Copy and paste text (with block on)	`Ctrl` + `Ins` *or* `Ctrl` + `F4` `2`
Copy file	`F5` `↵` {highlight filename} `4`
Copy text (with block on)	`Ctrl` + `C`
Create directory	`F5` {select *OK*} `H` {type directory name} {select *OK*} {select *OK*}
Cursor (insertion point) speed control	`Shift` + `F1` `3` `3`
Cut and paste text (with block on)	`Ctrl` + `Del` *or* `Ctrl` + `F4` `1`
Cut text (with block on)	`Ctrl` + `X`

(continued)

Feature	Keystrokes
Date	**Shift** + **F5**
Decimal/align character	**Shift** + **F8** **6** **1**
Decimal tab	**Ctrl** + **F6**
Delete	
Character at cursor	**Del**
Character to left	**Backspace**
Directory	**F5** {select *OK*} {highlight directory} **6** {select *Yes*}
File	**F5** {select *OK*} {highlight filename} **6** {select *Yes*}
To end of line	**Ctrl** + **End**
To end of page	**Ctrl** + **Pg Dn**
Word	**Ctrl** + **Del** *or* **Ctrl** + **Backspace**
Directory listing	**F5**
Directory tree	**F5** **F8**
Display setup	**Shift** + **F1** **2**
DOS prompt	**Ctrl** + **F1** **D**
Dot leader	**Shift** + **F8** **6** **3**
Double underline	**Ctrl** + **F8** **3** **3**
End field	**F9**
Endnote	**Ctrl** + **F7** **3**
Exit document	**F7**
Exit WordPerfect	**Home** **F7**
Extended characters	**Shift** + **F11** *or* **Ctrl** + **W**
Fill styles	**Alt** + **F9** **4**
Flush right	**Alt** + **F6**
Font	**Ctrl** + **F8**
Appearance	**Ctrl** + **F8** **3**
Base font	**Ctrl** + **F8** **1**
Position	**Ctrl** + **F8** **5**
Relative size	**Ctrl** + **F8** **4**
Size	**Ctrl** + **F8** **2**
Underline	**Ctrl** + **F8** **6**
Footers	**Shift** + **F8** **5** **2**

Feature	Keystrokes
Footnote	`Ctrl` + `F7` `1`
Format document	`Shift` + `F8` `4`
Generate indexes, tables, etc.	`Alt` + `F5` `4`
Go to page	`Ctrl` + `Home`
Grammatik	`Alt` + `F1` `3`
Graphics	`Alt` + `F9`
Box	`Alt` + `F9` `1`
Line	`Alt` + `F9` `2`
Graphics mode	`Ctrl` + `F3` `3`
Hard page break	`Ctrl` + `↵`
Hard return	`↵`
Hard space	`Home` + `Space`
Headers	`Shift` + `F8` `5` `1`
Help	`F1`
Hidden text	`Alt` + `F5` `7`
Hyphenation	`Shift` + `F8` `1` `6`
Indent	
Left	`F4`
Left and right	`Shift` + `F4`
Index	`Alt` + `F5`
Italics	`Ctrl` + `I` *or* `Ctrl` + `F8` `3` `4`
Justification	`Shift` + `F8` `1` `2`
Leading adjustment	`Shift` + `F8` `7` `9` `4`
Line	
Draw	`Ctrl` + `F3` `5`
Format	`Shift` + `F8` `1`
Height	`Shift` + `F8` `1` `8`
Justification	`Shift` + `F8` `1` `2`
Numbering	`Shift` + `F8` `1` `4`
Spacing	`Shift` + `F8` `1` `3`
Macros	
Play	`Alt` + `F10`

(continued)

WP

Feature	Keystrokes
Record	Ctrl + F10
Margins	Shift + F8
Math feature	Alt + F7 3
Merge files	Ctrl + F9 1
Merge codes	Shift + F9
Mouse control	Shift + F1 1
Move text	Ctrl + F4
Normal text (turn attributes off)	Ctrl + N
Number of copies	Shift + F7 N
Open document	Shift + F10
Outline	Ctrl + F5
Overstrike	Shift + F8 6
Page borders	Shift + F8 3 B
Page format	Shift + F8 3
Page mode	Ctrl + F3 4
Page numbering	Shift + F8 3 1
Paragraph borders	Shift + F8 1 5
Password	F10 F8
Paste text	Ctrl + V
Print	Shift + F7
Current page only	Shift + F7 2
Document on disk	Shift + F7 3 {Type filename} ↵
Full document	Shift + F7 1
Multiple copies	Shift + F7 4 {Type number of copies} ↵
Preview document	Shift + F7 7
Range of pages	Shift + F7 4 {Type page numbers} ↵
Stop printing	Shift + F7 6 S
QuickFinder	F5 F4
QuickList	F5 F6
Quickmark	
Find	Ctrl + F
Set	Ctrl + Q

Feature	Keystrokes
Redline	`Ctrl` + `F8` `3` `8`
Replace text	`Alt` + `F2`
Retrieve text	`Shift` + `F10`
Reveal codes	`Alt` + `F3` *or* `F11`
Save	`Ctrl` + `F12`
Save as	`F10`
Save block (with block on)	`F10`
Search	
And replace	`Alt` + `F2`
Backward	`Shift` + `F2`
Forward	`F2`
Setup	`Shift` + `F1`
Shadow	`Ctrl` + `F8` `3` `6`
Shell	`Ctrl` + `F1`
Small caps	`Ctrl` + `F8` `3` `7`
Sort	`Ctrl` + `F9` `2`
Spell check	`Ctrl` + `F2` *or* `Alt` + `F1` `1`
Spreadsheet	`Alt` + `F7` `5`
Strikeout	`Ctrl` + `F8` `3` `9`
Style	`Alt` + `F8`
Subscript	`Ctrl` + `F8` `5` `3`
Superscript	`Ctrl` + `F8` `5` `2`
Switch	`Shift` + `F3`
Tab	
Backward	`Shift` + `⟻⟶`
Forward	`⟻⟶`
Table of contents	`Alt` + `F5`
Tables	`Alt` + `F7` `2`
Tab settings	`Shift` + `F8` `1` `1` *or* `Ctrl` + `F11`
Text mode	`Ctrl` + `F3` `2`
Thesaurus	`Alt` + `F1` `2`
Typeover mode	`Ins`

(continued)

WP

Feature	Keystrokes
Undelete	`Esc`
Underline	
Double	`Ctrl` + `F8` `3` `3`
Single	`F8`
Undo	`Ctrl` + `Z`
Widow/orphan protection	`Shift` + `F8` `7` `3`
Windows	`Ctrl` + `F3` `1`
Cascade	`Ctrl` + `F3` `1` `5`
Tile	`Ctrl` + `F3` `1` `4`

Codes

The list below contains WordPerfect codes that may appear in the REVEAL CODES screen.

Code	Description
—	Hard hyphen (character)
[— Hyphen]	Hyphen
[— Soft Hyphen]	Soft hyphen
[— Soft Hyphen EOL]	Soft hyphen at end of line
[Auto Hyphen EOL]	Automatic hyphen at end of line
[Back Tab]	Back tab (margin release)
[Bar Code]	Bar code
[Begin Gen Txt]	Beginning of generated text
[Binding Width]	Binding width
[Block]	Block
[Block Pro]*	Block protect
[Bold]*	Bold
[Bookmark]	Bookmark
[Bot Mar]	Bottom margin
[Box Num Dec]	Box number decrement
[Box Num Disp]	Box number display
[Box Num Inc]	Box number increment

Code	Description
[Box Num Meth]	Box numbering method
[Box Num Set]	Box number set
[Calc Col]	Calculation column (math)
[Cancel Hyph]	Cancel hyphenation of word
[Cell]	Table cell
[Change BOL Char]	Change beginning of line character
[Change EOL Char]	Change end of line character
[Chap Num Dec]	Chapter number decrement
[Chap Num Disp]	Chapter number display
[Chap Num Inc]	Chapter number increment
[Chap Num Meth]	Chapter numbering method
[Chap Num Set]	Chapter number set
[Char Box]	Character box
[Char Shade Change]	Character shade change
[Char Style]*	Character style
[Cntr Cur Pg]	Center current page (top to bottom)
[Cntr on Cur Pos]	Center on cursor position
[Cntr on Mar]	Center on margins
[Cntr on Mar (Dot)]	Center on margins with dot leader
[Cntr Pgs]	Center pages (top to bottom)
[CNTR TAB]	Hard centered tab
[Cntr Tab]	Centered tab
[CNTR TAB (DOT)]	Hard centered tab with dot leader
[Cntr Tab (Dot)]	Centered tab with dot leader
[Col Border]	Column border
[Col Def]	Column definition
[Color]	Text color
[Comment]	Document comment
[Condl EOP]	Conditional end of page
[Count Dec]	Counter decrement
[Count Disp]	Counter display
[Count Inc]	Counter increment

(continued)

WP

Code	Description
[Count Meth]	Counter method
[Count Set]	Counter set
[Date]	Date/time function
[Date Fmt]	Date/time format
[Dbl Und]*	Double underline
[Dbl-Sided Print]	Double-sided printing
[Dec/Align Char]	Decimal/alignment character
[DEC TAB]	Hard decimal-aligned tab
[Dec Tab]	Decimal-aligned tab
[DEC TAB (DOT)]	Hard decimal-aligned tab with dot leader
[Dec Tab (Dot)]	Decimal-aligned tab with dot leader
[Def Mark]	Definition marker for index, list, table of authorities, or table of contents
[Delay]*	Delay
[Do Grand Tot]	Calculate grand total (math)
[Do Subtot]	Calculate subtotal (math)
[Do Total]	Calculate total (math)
[Dorm HRt]	Dormant hard return
[Dot Lead Char]	Dot leader character
[End Cntr/Align]	End of centering/alignment
[End Gen Txt]	End of generated text
[Endnote]	Endnote
[Endnote Min]	Endnote minimum amount
[Endnote Num Dec]	Endnote number decrement
[Endnote Num Disp]	Endnote number display
[Endnote Num Inc]	Endnote number increment
[Endnote Num Meth]	Endnote numbering method
[Endnote Num Set]	Endnote number set
[Endnote Placement]	Endnote placement
[Endnote Space]	Endnote spacing
[Ext Large]*	Extra large font size
[Filename]	Filename
[Fine]*	Fine font size

Code	Description
[First Ln Ind]	First line indent
[Flsh Rgt]	Flush right
[Flsh Rgt (Dot)]	Flush right with dot leader
[Flt Cell Begin]	Floating cell begin
[Flt Cell End]	Floating cell end
[Font]	Font
[Font Size]	Font size
[Footer A]	Footer A
[Footer B]	Footer B
[Footer Sep]	Footer separator space
[Footnote]	Footnote
[Footnote Cont Msg]	Footnote continued message
[Footnote Min]	Footnote minimum amount
[Footnote Num Dec]	Footnote number decrement
[Footnote Num Disp]	Footnote number display
[Footnote Num Each Pg]	Restart footnote numbers each document page
[Footnote Num Inc]	Footnote number increment
[Footnote Num Meth]	Footnote numbering method
[Footnote Num Set]	Footnote number set
[Footnote Sep Ln]	Footnote separator line
[Footnote Space]	Footnote spacing
[Footnote Txt Pos]	Footnote text position
[Force]	Force odd/even page
[Formatted Pg Num]	Formatted page number
[Graph Line]	Graphics line
[HAdv]	Horizontal advance
[HCol]	Hard column break
[HCol-SPg]	Hard column break-soft page break
[Header A]	Header A
[Header B]	Header B
[Header Sep]	Header separator space

WP

(continued)

Code	Description
[Hidden]*	Hidden text
[Hidden Txt]	Hidden body text (outline)
[HPg]	Hard page break
[HRow-HCol]	Hard table row-hard column break
[HRow-HCol-SPg]	Hard table row-hard column break-soft page break
[HRow-HPg]	Hard table row-hard page break
[HRt]	Hard return
[HRt-SCol]	Hard return-soft column break
[HRt-SPg]	Hard return-soft page break
[HSpace]	Hard space
[Hypertext Begin]	Hypertext begin
[Hypertext End]	Hypertext end
[Hyph]	Hyphenation state
[Hyph SRt]	Hyphenation soft return
[Index]	Index entry
[Italc]*	Italics
[Just]	Justification
[Just Lim]	Word spacing justification limits
[Kern]	Kerning
[Labels Form]	Labels form
[Lang]	Language
[Large]*	Large font size
[Leading Adj]	Leading adjustment
[Lft HZone]	Left edge of hyphenation zone
[Lft Indent]	Left indent
[Lft Mar]	Left margin
[Lft Mar Adj]	Left margin adjustment
[LFT TAB]	Hard left-aligned tab
[Lft Tab]	Left-aligned tab
[LFT TAB (DOT)]	Hard left-aligned tab with dot leader
[Lft Tab (Dot)	Left-aligned tab with dot leader
[Lft/Rgt Indent]	Left and right (double) indent

Code	Description
[Link]	Spreadsheet link
[Link End]	Spreadsheet link end
[Ln Height]	Line height
[Ln Num]	Line numbering
[Ln Num Meth]	Line numbering method
[Ln Num Set]	Line number set
[Ln Spacing]	Line spacing
[Macro Func]	Macro function
[Math]	Math state
[Math Def]	Definition of math columns
[Math Neg]	Math negate
[MRG:*command*]	Merge programming command
[Mrk Txt List Begin]	Beginning of list entry
[Mrk Txt List End]	End of list entry
[Mrk Txt ToC Begin]	Beginning of table of contents entry
[Mrk Txt ToC End]	End of table of contents entry
[Open Style]	Open style
[Outline]	Outline
[Outln]*	Outline (font attribute)
[Ovrstk]	Overstrike
[Paper Sz/Typ]	Paper size and type
[Para Border]	Paragraph border
[Para Box]	Paragraph box
[Para Num]	Paragraph number
[Para Num Set]	Paragraph number set
[Para Spacing]	Paragraph spacing
[Para Style]	Paragraph style
[Para Style End]	Paragraph style end
[Pause Ptr]	Pause printer
[Pg Border]	Page border
[Pg Box]	Page box
[Pg Num Dec]	Page number decrement

WP

(continued)

Code	Description
[Pg Num Disp]	Page number display
[Pg Num Fmt]	Page number format
[Pg Num Inc]	Page number increment
[Pg Num Meth]	Page numbering method
[Pg Num Pos]	Page number position
[Pg Num Set]	Page number set
[Ptr Cmnd]	Printer command
[Redln]*	Redline
[Ref Box]	Reference to graphics box
[Ref Chap]	Reference to chapter
[Ref Count]	Reference to counter
[Ref Endnote]	Reference to endnote
[Ref Footnote]	Reference to footnote
[Ref Para]	Reference to paragraph
[Ref Pg]	Reference to page
[Ref Sec Pg]	Reference to secondary page
[Ref Vol]	Reference to volume
[Rgt HZone]	Right edge of hyphenation zone
[Rgt Mar]	Right margin
[Rgt Mar Adj]	Right margin adjustment
[RGT TAB]	Hard right-aligned tab
[Rgt Tab]	Right-aligned tab
[RGT TAB (DOT)]	Hard right-aligned tab with dot leader
[Rgt Tab (Dot)]	Right-aligned tab with dot leader
[Row]	Table row
[Row-SCol]	Table row-soft column break
[Row-SPg]	Table row-soft page break
[Sec Pg Num Dec]	Secondary page number decrement
[Sec Pg Num Disp]	Secondary page number display
[Sec Pg Num Inc]	Secondary page number increment
[Sec Pg Num Meth]	Secondary page numbering method
[Sec Pg Num Set]	Secondary page number set

Code	Description
[Shadw]*	Shadow
[Small]*	Small font size
[Sm Cap]*	Small caps
[Sound]	Sound clip
[Speller/Grammatik]	Speller/Grammatik state
[SRt]	Soft return
[SRt-SCol]	Soft return-soft column break
[SRt-SPg]	Soft return-soft page break
[StkOut]*	Strikeout
[Subdivided Pg]	Subdivided page
[Subdoc]	Subdocument (master document)
[Subdoc Begin]	Beginning of subdocument
[Subdoc End]	End of subdocument
[Subscpt]*	Subscript
[Subtot Entry]	Subtotal entry (math)
[Suppress]	Suppress header, footer, watermark, or page number
[Suprscpt]*	Superscript
[Tab Set]	Tab set
[Target]	Target (cross-reference)
[Tbl Dec Tab]	Table decimal tab
[Tbl Def]	Table definition
[Tbl Off]	Table off
[Tbl Off-SCol]	Table off-soft column break
[Tbl Off-SPg]	Table off-soft page break
[Tbl Tab]	Table tab
[THCol]	Temporary hard column break
[THCol-SPg]	Temporary hard column break-soft page break
[Third Party]	Third party (non-WordPerfect Corporation) code
[Thousands Char]	Thousands character

(continued)

WP

Code	Description
[THPg]	Temporary hard page break
[THRt]	Temporary hard return
[THRt-SCol]	Temporary hard return-soft column break
[THRt-SPg]	Temporary hard return-soft page break
[ToA]	Table of authorities entry
[Top Mar]	Top margin
[Total Entry]	Total entry (math)
[TSRt]	Temporary soft return
[TSRt-SCol]	Temporary soft return-soft column break
[TSRt-SPg]	Temporary soft return-soft page break
[Und]*	Underline
[Undrln Space]	Underline spaces
[Undrln Tab]	Underline tabs
[Unknown]	Unknown code
[VAdv]	Vertical advance
[Very Large]*	Very large font size
[Vol Num Dec]	Volume number decrement
[Vol Num Disp]	Volume number display
[Vol Num Inc]	Volume number increment
[Vol Num Meth]	Volume numbering method
[Vol Num Set]	Volume number set
[Watermark A]	Watermark A
[Watermark B]	Watermark B
[Wid/Orph]	Widow/orphan protect state
[Wrd/Ltr Spacing]	Word spacing and letterspacing

*Code is inserted by WordPerfect with the words "ON" or "OFF," respectively indicating whether the feature is being activated or deactivated—for instance, [Block Pro On] and [Block Pro Off]

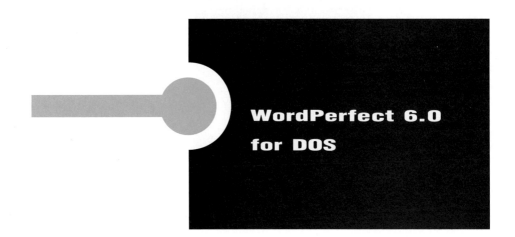

WordPerfect 6.0
for DOS

Glossary
Index

WP

Glossary

Absolute tab. A tab setting measured from the left edge of the page. (WP74)

ASCII (American Standard Code for Information Interchange). A standard format for transferring data among software programs. (WP169)

Background printing. A WordPerfect feature that sends a copy of the document to the printer, freeing the program for continued work. (WP48)

Backspace key. A key that removes the character to the immediate left of the cursor. (WP28)

Base font. The typestyle used by WordPerfect to display normal text. (WP78)

Block. A segment of contiguous text. (WP57)

BLOCK commands. A WordPerfect feature that allows you to edit or format complete words, sentences, paragraphs, or entire documents at one time. (WP57)

Block enhancement. A process by which a formatting change is made to a block of text that is already on the screen. (WP62)

Bold. A text enhancement in which printed text appears darker (F6 key). (WP31)

Button bar. A set of screen icons that provides quick access to many WordPerfect menu items, features, macros, and other button bars. (WP163)

CANCEL command. A WordPerfect feature that allows you to back out of a WordPerfect menu without saving changes, or retrieve previously deleted text (F1 key). (WP9)

Cascade. A command that overlaps document windows so that only their title bars appear. (WP119)

Center feature. Aligning text so that it is equally spaced from the right and left margins (Shift plus F6 keys). (WP29)

Delete key. A key that removes the character at the cursor position. (WP27)

Document number. A status line message that indicates which one of two possible documents is currently on the screen. (WP6)

Endnote. Text added to the end of a document to provide source references, more detailed explanations, or comments. (WP135)

Exporting. The process of saving a file in a format other than the software's default format so that it can be read by other programs. (WP169)

File manager. A WordPerfect feature that provides a file directory and menu from which file manager commands may be selected. (WP44)

Footer. Text containing descriptive information that appears at the bottom of each page in a multipage document. (WP107)

Footnote. Text added to a document, usually appearing at the bottom of each page and identified by number, to provide source references, more detailed explanations, or comments. (WP135)

Full justification. The alignment of text at both the right and left margins. (WP70)

GO TO. A word processing command that relocates the cursor on any named page of a multipage document. (WP113)

Grammar Checker. A WordPerfect auxiliary program that checks for grammatical errors in your writing. (WP92)

Graphics feature. A WordPerfect feature that allows you to combine lines and images with text in the same document. (WP150)

Hard page break. A page divider created by the user that remains fixed at a specific text location unless removed by the user. (WP106)

Hard return. A line break inserted into the text by the user (Enter key). (WP21)

Header. Text containing descriptive information that appears at the top of each page in a multipage document. (WP107)

Help feature. An onscreen reference that provides an alphabetical listing of WordPerfect features, keystrokes, and menu options (F3 key). (WP9)

Importing. The process of retrieving a file that was saved in a format other than the default format for the current program. (WP169)

INDENT. A word processing feature that indents an entire paragraph without changing margins elsewhere in the document. (WP73)

Insert mode. The default WordPerfect setting in which existing text is pushed forward as new text is typed. (WP22)

Insertion point. (Cursor) A placeholder showing where the next keystroke you type will appear. (WP6)

Justification. Alignment of text so that it falls exactly at a margin. (WP70)

Key. A piece of data (text or number) that provides the basis for a sort. (WP146)

Layout. The arrangement of text and white space on a page. (WP66)

Ln message. A status line message, expressed in inches or lines, that indicates the cursor's vertical position on the page. (WP7)

Look. A WordPerfect function, invoked from LIST FILES, that allows a file to be viewed without retrieving it into the work screen. (WP47)

Macro. A list of computer instructions or keystrokes that can be activated with one or more preset keystrokes. (WP130)

Menu bar. The initial selection menu that appears at the top of the screen when using pull-down menus. (WP6)

Merge. A process by which information from two sources is combined to form a third document. (WP122)

Open. A WordPerfect command that retrieves a document from disk and places it into a new document window. (WP17)

Outline feature. A WordPerfect feature that allows you to create outlines of up to eight levels. (WP140)

Pg message. A status line message, expressed as a number, that indicates the document page on which the cursor is currently positioned. (WP7)

Point. A measure of type size equal to about 1/72nd of an inch. (WP81)

Pos message. A status line message, expressed in inches or columns, that indicates the cursor's horizontal position on the line. (WP7)

Primary file. A document used in a merge process that contains text and instructions for the merge. (WP122)

Pull-down menus. An alternate menu system in WordPerfect that can be operated by keystrokes or a mouse. (WP10)

Relative tab. A tab setting measured in relation to the left margin setting. (WP74)

REPLACE. A word processing feature that locates each occurrence of a specified text string in the current document and replaces it with another. (WP85)

REVEAL CODES. A WordPerfect feature that allows the user to see on screen the hidden formatting codes in the current document. (WP54)

Ribbon. A bar at the top of a screen that displays and provides access to features that affect text size and appearance. (WP167)

SEARCH. A word processing feature that locates each occurrence of a specified text string in the current document. (WP84)

Secondary file. A document used in a merge process that contains specific data to be merged into another document. (WP122)

Soft page break. A page divider automatically created, or relocated, by a word processor when text reaches the end of a page. (WP103)

Soft return. A line break inserted into the text automatically by WordPerfect's wordwrap feature so that text will not go beyond the right margin setting. (WP21)

Sort feature. A WordPerfect feature that allows you to arrange text, tables, or merge records in alphabetical or numerical order. (WP146)

Speller. A WordPerfect auxiliary program that checks each word in a document for correct spelling. (WP87)

Status line. An indicator line, located near the bottom of the WordPerfect screen, that displays information about the document, the current cursor position, and text enhancement settings. (WP6)

Tab. A formatting feature that allows text to be placed in specific positions on a line. (WP74)

Text string. A collection of contiguous characters or words. (WP84)

Thesaurus. A word processing feature that suggests synonyms for selected words. (WP90)

Tile. A WordPerfect command that places documents side-by-side with no overlapping. (WP119)

Typeover mode. A WordPerfect setting, invoked by the Ins key, in which existing text is replaced by new text that is typed. (WP25)

Underline. A text enhancement, invoked by the F8 key, in which text is underscored for emphasis. (WP30)

View Document. A WordPerfect option that allows the user to see a screen representation of a document as it will appear when printed. (WP71)

Word processing. The use of computer technology to create, manipulate, save, and print text materials. (WP4)

Wordwrap. A word processing feature in which text that does not fit at the right margin is automatically moved to the next line by the insertion of a soft return. (WP21)

WP

Index

WP